MOUNT MARY COLLEGE LIBRARY
Milwaukee,

S0-BYQ-154

# TWAYNE'S WORLD LEADERS SERIES

EDITOR OF THIS VOLUME

Hans L. Trefousse

*Brooklyn College of*
*The City University of New York*

Robert Marion La Follette

*Photo by John A. Glarder, Manitowoc, Wis., 1922*
*Courtesy of the State Historical Society of Wisconsin*

# Robert Marion La Follette

MOUNT MARY COLLEGE LIBRARY
Milwaukee, Wisconsin 53222

# Robert Marion La Follette

## FRED GREENBAUM

*Queensborough Community College
of the City University of New York*

## TWAYNE PUBLISHERS
### A DIVISION OF G. K. HALL & CO., BOSTON

75-2085

*Copyright © 1975 by G. K. Hall & Co.*

All Rights Reserved

**Library of Congress Cataloging in Publication Data**
Greenbaum, Fred, 1930—
    Robert Marion La Follette.

    (Twayne's world leaders series)
    Bibliography: p. 257-66.
    Includes index.
    1. La Follette, Robert Marion, 1855-1925.
E664.L16G73            973.91'092'4 [B]            74-26675
ISBN 0-8057-3057-5

MANUFACTURED IN THE UNITED STATES OF AMERICA

921
L13G

To ATC

# Contents

# About the Author

Fred Greenbaum is Professor of History at Queensborough Community College of the City University of New York. A native New Yorker who now lives in Garden City he was educated at Brooklyn College, the University of Wisconsin and Columbia University and has taught previously at Brooklyn College and Queens College. Dr. Greenbaum's publications include *Fighting Progressive, A Biography of Edward Costigan* and, with Pedro Meza, *Readings in Western Civilization, Early Modern Period.* For sixteen years he has contributed articles in twentieth century America, including studies of Colorado progressives, Hiram Johnson, Samuel Gompers, John Dewey, Emmanuel Celler, "A New Deal for the United Mine Workers," the Anti-lynching Bill of 1935, and "Progressivism: A Complex Phenomena."

# Preface

It is hard to think of Robert Marion La Follette without envisioning the progressive movement and Wisconsin, for he is so thoroughly intertwined with both in the public mind. Ironically, he first came to national attention in the Washington of the 1880s as a regular Republican, albeit a little too independent to suit local Wisconsin political powers. He had held office for a decade before he became an insurgent and had been in politics almost twenty years before he focused his insurgency on a clearly progressive issue, the direct primary. Once he made his commitment his career was characterized by a consistency of purpose, and he emerged as the acknowledged leader of the national progressives. He publicized the need for direct democracy in order to prevent economic and political control by the powerful few and to enable the friendless and the dispossessed to obtain an equitable share of American bounty. Unlike more paternalist progressives, he welcomed the organization of society's underdogs so that they could secure their own goals.

His concerns in foreign affairs were the same as for the domestic scene. He opposed the use of government power to enrich the few at the expense of the many. And he demanded equitable treatment for small and weak nations as well as for the powerful and great.

Enormously ambitious, he sometimes confused a personal betrayal with a betrayal of principle, of the movement, or of the nation. William Hard, a friendly commentator, referred to his savage suspiciousness.[1] On the stump he turned his eloquence not only on his political enemies, whom he assumed to be actuated by corrupt motives, but on friends he had come to distrust. Such allies as Isaac Stephenson in 1908, Teddy

Roosevelt in 1912, and Francis McGovern thereafter learned the hazards of arousing his anger.

There could have been no possibility of fulfilling his ambition without his extraordinary, almost legendary, skills as a speaker. His subjects were always thoroughly researched, his drafts meticulously composed, and his presentation theatrically delivered with the flair of a born actor. His voice was an exceptional instrument, carefully cultivated. It was in an oratorical contest that he won fame initially; local pride in his victory enabled him to graduate from the University of Wisconsin and helped assure success in his first electoral contest. As a freshman legislator, his prowess in debate brought favorable attention from his party's congressional leadership. His ability to draw large crowds kept him before the public during the decade in which he held no political office. As governor he captured national attention by his dramatized challenge to the establishment. Thereafter the Senate, the stump, and the Chautauqua circuit were his pulpit, and, for hours, he wove spells over his audience.

In preparing a speech he chose a subject of interest to his audience, a subject that could be discussed fully in a single presentation, developed closely knit arguments, larded with factual material carefully personalized for the locale. His secretary preceded him to gather information on local products and rail rates. Statistics came alive as he translated overcharges in terms of taxes on an acre of farm land or the income of a laboring man, the price of wheat in relation to rail rates, the cost of food and supplies in relation to tariff duties; he appealed at the same time to altruistic and selfish motives, to class interests and disinterested citizenship. Classical in his rhetorical training, he stressed invention, but, although well versed in Shakespeare and literature, he eschewed literary quotes and emotional perorations in favor of achieving a total effect of sincerity.

As he mounted the platform, a chair, or a table, the viewer observed a man but five feet four inches in height, squarely built; his large leonine head showed flashing eyes, a square jaw, and a high square forehead, his hair piled above it in a pompadour. He began slowly, in a strong vigorous voice, vibrant and moving, widely ranged in pitch, varied in intonation and inflection; he changed voice quality when he wanted a telling effect. He knew the advantage of dramatic pause. As he warmed up he spoke more rapidly, loosened his collar and removed his coat, moved about the platform, particularly towards his auditors, and throughout used his body meaningfully and strenuously. He tossed his head, ran his hands through his hair, held his clenched fists above him while his head shook with intensity. His hands and fingers were always moving, his body a spring of steel. His mobile features portrayed every shade of emotion. He engaged his audience, answering queries readily, while asking questions which could be and were responded to in unison. If faces looked puzzled he departed from his manuscript and repeated the argument in a different form. He pretended that he lacked time to develop a point and elicited cries of "Go on, Bob." When he employed sarcasm it had a "bite like coals of fire." He concluded, dripping wet, his arms folded across his chest like a man who had done all possible, with a quiet, extemporaneous, heart to heart talk. When he ended by reading the roll of a representative's votes he imitated the monotonous tone of a reading clerk, then asked whether he had voted for his listeners or the special interests. He was a compelling personality who could hold a crowd indefinitely, for there was real conviction behind the technical facility.[2]

La Follette was a confirmed democrat, sensitive to the electorate, and particularly capable of zealous expression of its hopes and aspirations. But he was not a demagogue, pandering to public whim. At times he embraced unpopular issues in which he believed, even to the point of endangering his political survival. While he had a degree of flexibility, he was unwilling to compromise essentials, ever confident that in the long run his faith in the people would be rewarded by fulfillment for his programs and his ambitions. His refusal to follow the easy path often placed him in an isolated and exposed position. Although he attempted to guide the Wisconsin progressives in efforts to unify behind a single candidate and endorsed one of a number of competitors for nomination, he was unwilling to attempt to impose his will upon them, for it was contrary to his conception of leadership; had he made the attempt he probably would have failed, for his faction would not have accepted dictation. Consequently, opponents slipped in with a plurality of the vote.

A devoted husband and father, his children were raised to continue the progressive tradition. They were immersed in politics from an early age, and the whole family participated in discussions of issues and tactics. His personal concern for the welfare of his wife and children, as revealed in the family correspondence, is very touching. If anything he may have been an overly protective parent in some instances: his eldest boy, Bobbie, unlike Phil, was an indifferent student; when he first attended the university Bobbie was given dated post cards and asked for daily reports; Papa wanted the name and address of each of his professors to ensure scholastic diligence.

Although he is often pictured as essentially a dissenter, La Follette had a sophisticated grasp of domestic and international affairs and presented programs in both areas. If, throughout his career, he emphasized the threat of monopoly to popular government, it was not because he was politically naive. He realized that concentrated economic power in the hands of the few was incompatible with real economic, political, and social democracy. Then, as now, this was one of the most important problems confronting the country. His name would appear on any list of the greatest senators of the twentieth century. Yet, despite his successes, his career was essentially marked by failure. He failed to capture the one office he prized above all — the presidency. His long battle with the railroads ended in defeat, the lines restored to private ownership, with increased rates based partially on watered stocks. The commissions created by progressives to restrain economic concentration became instruments for corporate aggrandizement. The effort to restore competitive capitalism through anti-trust action collapsed; oligopoly, price leadership, and secret collusion are hard to prove in court, especially when the party occupying the White House requires campaign funds. On the contrary, corporations have come to dominate even agriculture. While powerful magnates have acquiesced in a generally higher standard of living and some aspects of a welfare state in order to retain their hegemony, the corporate tax, the income tax, and the inheritance tax have not sufficiently redistributed income or wealth.

Our attitude towards the world has not followed the course La Follette envisioned. Recently, Senator Fulbright echoed La Follette's concern with American arrogance on an international scale. Wilson's version of internationalism, anathema to La Follette, seems to govern our foreign policy.

Can greatness be assured only by success? Or can we find another standard of measurement for Robert Marion La Follette? Is a man great for effectively attempting to champion the many against the powerful few?

FRED GREENBAUM

*Queensborough
Community College*

# Chronology

1855    Robert Marion La Follette born in Primrose, Wisconsin, June 14, to Josiah and Mary Ferguson La Follette.

1856    Father dies.

1859    Attends Primrose district school.

1862    Mother marries John Saxton, moves to Argyle, attends Argyle district school.

1864    Attends Frank Higgins' private school.

1866    Moves to Fayette, attends John Parkinson's private school.

1867    Family returns to Argyle and then to the Primrose farm, La Follette remains in Argyle and supports himself in school as a barber.

1870-   Returns to Primrose to run the family farm and attends
1873    the winter terms at the Primrose district school.

1873    Moves to Madison, Wisconsin; prepares for college at the Wisconsin Classical and Commercial Academy.

1874    Enrolls in the sub-freshman class at the University of Wisconsin.

1875    Enters the University of Wisconsin.

1876    Buys, publishes, and edits the *University Press*.

1879    May, wins the interstate oratorical contest; June, graduates from the University of Wisconsin; September, enters University of Wisconsin Law School and reads law in the office of R. M. Bashford.

1880    February, passes the bar exam; November, elected district attorney of Dane County.

1881    December 31, marries Belle Case.

1882    Reelected district attorney.

1884    Elected to Congress.

1888    Tariff speech.

| 1889 | Appointed to the House Ways and Means Committee. |
|------|--------|
| 1890 | Defeated for reelection; returns to practice of law. |
| 1891 | September, offered bribe by Senator Philetus Sawyer. |
| 1894 | Manages campaign of Congressman Nils P. Haugen for Republican nomination for governor. |
| 1896 | Runs for Republican nomination for governor. |
| 1897 | February, "Menace of the Machine" speech at the University of Chicago. County fair crusade for the direct primary. |
| 1898 | Runs for gubernatorial nomination. |
| 1900 | Elected governor of Wisconsin. |
| 1901 | Vetoes "dog tax" and compromise primary bill. |
| 1902 | Reelected governor. |
| 1903 | Legislature passes ad valorem railroad tax, sends direct primary to referendum. |
| 1904 | Reelected governor. |
| 1905 | January, elected to United States Senate. Legislature passes comprehensive railroad commission bill. |
| 1906 | April, speech on the Hepburn Railroad Bill. |
| 1908 | May, filibuster against the Aldrich-Vreeland Banking Bill; June, seeks Republican Presidential nomination. |
| 1909 | January, begins publishing *La Follette's Magazine*; May-July, leads the fight against the Payne-Aldrich Tariff Bill. |
| 1910 | June, leads fight to rewrite the Mann-Elkins Railroad Bill; November, reelected to the Senate. |
| 1911 | January, Progressive Republican League founded. |
| 1912 | Seeks Republican nomination for President. Writes *Autobiography*. |
| 1915 | La Follette's Seaman's Act becomes law. |
| 1916 | Reelected to the Senate. |
| 1917 | March, leads filibuster against a bill to arm merchant ships; April, opposes American entrance into World War I; June, opposes enactment of the Espionage Act; September, speech in St. Paul leads to resolutions for his expulsion from the Senate and an investigation by the Committee on Privileges and Elections; October, opposes conscription. |
| 1919 | Irreconcilable in opposition to Versailles Treaty. |

1922    Initiates investigation into the Elks Hills and Teapot
        Dome leases. Reelected to the Senate.
1923    Tours Europe.
1924    Makes independent race for President with the Pro-
        gressive Party.
1925    Dies, June 18.

# CHAPTER 1

## Political Genesis

O N a cold Wisconsin winter day in 1856 Mary Ferguson La Follette drew her four foot ten frame erect as she stood in the Postville cemetery in Primrose Country, watching in sorrow as they buried her second husband. Alongside the large man's coffin was placed the tiny disinterred remains of her son Marion. Clutched in her arms was eight-month-old Robert, the youngest. At her side, barely able to understand what was happening was Josephine, not yet three. Ellen Buchanan, posthumous issue of the first marriage and now a young woman of fifteen, and the La Follette's older son, William, mourned with her. Josiah La Follette had bequeathed to his family one of the best farms in the country, but his wife once again was faced with the responsibility of running a farm and raising a family.

Robert Marion La Follette, an infant at the time of his father's death, could not have had a clear remembrance of his tall, heavy-bearded sire. Yet, inspired by his mother's reiteration that his father dreaded only that he might be forgotten, "his devotion to his memory was almost morbid." He embraced his unaffiliated religious liberalism, his interest in politics, his connection with the Republican party and drew upon his supporters to begin his career. In keeping with the La Follette tradition Josiah had been elected town clerk, assessor, and town chairman within five years of his migration to Primrose. His brother, Harvey, one of four who had preceded him to the township, held office after Josiah's untimely demise. His older son, William, was twice a Populist railroad commissioner in South Dakota.

Bob La Follette's heritage was typical of Wisconsin politicians, particularly of the progressives. Maternal and paternal lineage was from Northwest Europe: Joseph Le Follet migrated

*17*

from France, John Ferguson was Scotch-Irish; both fought as patriots in the Revolution, Joseph changing the family name to La Follette in honor of the Marquis de La Fayette. As prosperous farmers they were part of the old middle class, and Bob became a successful lawyer. A college graduate, La Follette was educated well beyond the norm. And true to American political tradition the family was intertwined with at least one other American political family; Thomas Lincoln and Jesse La Follette were neighbors in Kentucky, and the families may have been distantly related through the Lees.[1]

While his family was more prosperous than many of its neighbors, the short, agile, irrepressible boy did not have an easy childhood. They were, after all, pioneering farmers. At an early age he worked in the fields. While still young he walked a considerable distance to school through the extremes of continental weather. He absorbed corporal punishment from his teachers and his stepfather. Yet he had time for boyhood sports — favoring wrestling — childhood escapades like floating downstream on an ice raft, participating in school spelling bees, exhibitions, picnics, and above all acting and public speaking. As he grew up he enjoyed dancing and "always wanted to be the floor manager."

Mary La Follette sought to ensure her children's future by remarriage to a successful storekeeper from Argyle, John Saxton. Unfortunately Saxton, who was seventy to Mary's forty-five, was declining as a businessman; he soon drew upon the La Follette resources and sold portions of the farm. He was obsessed with rigid religious values and freely administered thrashings. His long Sunday biblical sessions, his insistence upon Josiah's damnation as an agnostic, soured young Bob's attitude toward religion. While Argyle had a better one-room school than Primrose, the children were placed in private schools whenever a good one was available. When the Saxtons returned to Primrose the thirteen-year-old boy remained in Argyle for two years, supporting himself by barbering in the evenings, and living with family friends. Humiliated when his teacher found him drunk, Robert returned to Primrose. He soon succeeded his brother in the management of the farm. At eighteen, about the time that news of the Panic of 1873 reached the harvesting farmers, La Follette leased the farm to his

MOUNT MARY COLLEGE LIBRARY
Milwaukee, Wisconsin 53222ɑ9

brother-in-law, Dean Eastham, and removed the family to Madison.

Bob had always intended to go to college. He had never been a disciplined student and, while well educated for rural Wisconsin, he was not ready for even the University of Wisconsin of the eighteen seventies. He prepared himself at Madison's Wisconsin Classical and Commercial Academy before entering the sub-freshman class of the University. Expenses were paid by teaching school, peddling books, and his mother's sale of eighty more acres of farm land.

When La Follette became one of the twenty seven thousand Americans enrolled in a four year college, he entered a politically dominated institution, headed by the moralistic philosopher, John Bascom, and staffed by an undistinguished faculty. Although a few professors attempted disjointed lectures or discussion, teaching was still by memorized recitation from textbooks. The campus was hardly a training ground for progressives. Nevertheless, with a total enrollment of 345 — eighty entering, forty graduating — there was considerable personal contact among students and faculty. Although modern scholars might not concur, the students were greatly impressed by John Bascom and other teachers.[2]

In Madison, shortly after his arrival, La Follette was profoundly influenced by Wisconsin Chief Justice Edward G. Ryan. Ryan had written a precedent setting decision sustaining a Granger law controlling railroad corporations. In his speech to the graduating class he warned against accumulation of wealth that paralleled conditions in the Roman Empire. He described "vast corporate combinations of unexampled capital, boldly marching, not for economic conquests only, but for political power." "The question. . .shall arise in your day. . .'Which shall rule — wealth or man; which shall lead — money or intellect; who shall fill public stations — educated and patriotic free men, or the feudal serfs of corporate capital?'" Forty years later the image of this "bowed figure, his fine almost feminine features, his wavy auburn hair, and the luminous impressive eyes which glowed as the old man talked. . ." remained vivid for Senator La Follette as he wrote his *Autobiography*.[3]

Yet Granger ideas were unsuited to most of the university

75-2085

students, rooted in the soil but climbing through academic training to higher social status.

La Follette's years at the university were crucial for his personal and political development. It was here that his personal charm created those long-term relationships which became the first base for his political apparatus. It was here that he developed the reputation as an orator that helped launch him on a political career. It was here that he first disclosed his enormous capacity for work, albeit not on his studies. It was here that he first met his wife.

Belle Case was a short, attractive sixteen-year-old farm girl with a bubbling personality when she first came to the university. A much better student than Bob, she graduated near the top of their class. She believed in the natural development of people and ridiculed social practices and conventions that cramped children's growth. In a series of undergraduate speeches and papers she developed her ideas and capped her work with a senior oration that won the Lewis Prize. Belle and Bob helped each other in preparation for major orations, saw each other regularly, and were engaged in their junior year, though they delayed announcement until their senior spring. They postponed the nuptials until La Follette earned the salary of a district attorney. Throughout their marriage Belle was his most valued confidant and participated in all important strategy sessions. In the first year of their marriage Belle became fascinated by Kent and Blackstone and later became the first woman to graduate from the Wisconsin Law School. While she never practiced law, a brief she wrote was presented to the Wisconsin Supreme Court; they not only won the case but broke new legal ground. During campaigns she delivered speeches, and when La Follette decided that his career required a personal magazine Belle wrote a regular column and edited the woman's page. "To write of my father without writing of my mother is an impossible task," their daughter Fola, insisted later. "They have been close friends and comrades in both the work and play of life to a degree that renders disassociation impossible, even in the phases of public activity which we are accustomed to think of as unrelated to the home circle. Their relation has always made our home and not father's office the center of all important conferences and discussions."[4] This able and attractive woman made an ideal mate for the ambitious Wisconsin politician.

La Follette was not only handicapped by inadequate preparation for college, but, like many of his fellows, by the need to earn a living. As a freshman and sophomore he taught school; at first his mother and sister cooked for a boy's club; later they took in boarders. During his freshman year he borrowed money to buy the *University Press*. He made it a financial success. He trebled the size of the paper, but, with aggressive solicitation, advertisements comprised forty percent of its space. He set type by himself, or with volunteer and low-paid help, and wrote many of the articles, particularly the gossip items. It afforded him the substantial income of seven hundred dollars a year and solved his undergraduate financial problems.

Running a newspaper did not prevent La Follette from engaging in an active university social life. He continued dancing, learned to sail, and became one of the chief college greeters and pranksters. La Follette particularly excelled in dramatics and brought these skills to oratory. He flirted with acting as a career, but John McCullough, a noted Shakespearian actor, advised him that he was too short, and this advice coincided with the necessity of a secure income. The focus of his extracurricular social activities was the Athenean Literary Society. Wisconsin had not yet embarked on a program of intercollegiate sports; consequently these literary societies were of great importance. Loyal to an allegiance barely two weeks old, the freshman La Follette played an active role in a clash with the politically dominant fraternities. Fraternity exclusiveness and social pretensions made them unpopular with the majority. When they manipulated the election of delegates to the Interstate Oratorical Association, the literary societies and independents called a second mass meeting which repudiated the previous results.

A good debater, La Follette was not comparable in reasoned argument to the studious Charles Van Hise, a future president of the university. But he was incomparable as an orator, and even his contributions to the weekly debates were heavily oratorical. Consequently, Van Hise represented the society in public joint debates and La Follette in oratory and declamations. During his last summer recess he toured with four Atheneans, alternating his readings and poetry with their quartet singing. His recitation of the Raven "could make your hair stand on end," one of his partners recalled and his "power of elocution and acting," a Sun Prairie editor commented, "would do credit to a professional." But his greatest triumph was his lecture on Iago at the Interstate Oratorical Contest at Iowa City, Iowa in May of 1879. With the diligence and attention to detail that were to become his hallmark, the speech was meticulously crafted, every phrase placed, every nuance of character shaded, every aspect of delivery determined; he drew upon all authorities available to him, Judge Braley on Shakespeare, Professor John Olin for style and delivery, and Professor David Frankenburger as a coach. He had no peer in the preliminary contests in Madison and Beloit. At Iowa City, at a time when oratory was a national pastime, he was competing against the best orators among the ten thousand students in the midwest. His analysis of Iago reflected the moral fervor that had attracted him to President Bascom. Iago, he argued, lacked emotion which was the native soil of moral life. He was compensated with intellectual acuteness for his lack of feeling, but the imbalance created deformity. La Follette's insights even impressed professional commentators. The oration was "a credit to the ablest Shakespearian critic," remarked a Milwaukee *Sentinel* reviewer. "It showed a delicacy of analysis that we look for only in maturity." The Madison *Democrat* placed his production among "the most notable of profound and finished analyses of Shakespearian creations." His performance carried the day. He returned to Madison to the kind of triumph that is today reserved for sports idols.[5]

His oratorical victory was to prove invaluable to him in many ways. It made him a statewide hero, greeted by politicians, feted by his classmates and honored in the assembly chamber of the state capitol; it provided instant recognition when he began his political career. Of more immediate importance it was partially responsible for his graduation. La Follette's world was always much broader than the university; he would rather attend a good lecture, court trial, or play than prepare for his classes, and his grades reflected his interests. The university was so small that each student was individually evaluated at graduation time. Some faculty thought that he should stay another year to make up failures. The faculty vote was tied, and Bascom broke it in favor of graduation. It would have been embarrassing to deny a diploma to the editor of the newspaper and the campus celebrity.[6]

La Follette's residency at the university did not come to an end. Following an earlier decision he entered a law school that had eight professors and fifty-two students. At the same time he read law in the office of R. M. Bashford, thus combining the old and new methods of preparing for the bar examination. Within seven months, drawing upon his many hours as a court buff, he passed the bar; applicants usually had completed a two year legal course. La Follette proved to be a good lawyer, diligent in preparation and gifted in the courtroom. But there were many fine lawyers in Madison, and establishing a practice proved to be difficult. To undertake marital responsibilities required an immediate assured income and an expanded clientele. La Follette hoped to obtain both through political office.[7]

# CHAPTER 2

# *A Bright Future*

R OBERT M. La Follette chose to run for district attorney of
 Dane County, a position traditionally reserved for young
candidates. For a novice Bob had many advantages: the
reputation of his father, his long residence and numerous
acquaintances, instant recognition for oratorical victory and his
speeches, orations and readings in the county. The youthful
incumbent, a drunkard, a procurer who associated with
gamblers, could not be renominated. Colonel Keyes, Madison
postmaster and long Republican boss of Dane County, had
helped to increase advertisements in La Follette's paper and
had presided over La Follette's victory reception. Thus, La
Follette was surprised when Keyes informed him that he was
supporting a candidate closer to him, Horace "Hod" Taylor.

While Elisha Keyes had been Republican state chairman, he
had relinquished the position in order to retain his postal
income and had become vulnerable to attack, particularly after
failing in his bid to become senator in 1879. In 1880 Keyes was
already fighting for political survival against a Milwaukee
business takeover led by Philetus Sawyer, John Coit Spooner,
and Henry C. Payne and could not be distracted by La
Follette's candidacy for a minor position.[1]

La Follette canvassed carefully, particularly in the country
districts, promising to save county funds by not hiring lawyers
to try cases. He drew upon his small knowledge of Norwegian
and his childhood contacts to enlist the support of the Scandinavians. La Follette led from the first ballot in a heated contest.
Except for the earlier intense seven ballot contest for sheriff in
which Keyes' confidante, Willet Main, was defeated, this was
the only extended rivalry. "Hod" Taylor and he gained
strength with each ballot. At a key point in the balloting, Eli

Pedersen, a Norwegian leader and a friend of Josiah La Follette, threw his support to him. After the fourth ballot La Follette was one vote shy of nomination. A move to make him the unanimous choice was greeted with vocal objections. Although La Follette was easily nominated on the ensuing ballot, Taylor's partisans remained firm and he retained two-thirds of his first ballot support.

As the campaign progressed La Follette appeared to be the most exciting Republican county candidate and received by far the greatest exposure in Keyes' organ, the *Wisconsin State Journal*. When the Democrats nominated the able and experienced R. M. Bashford, with whom La Follette had read law, the *Journal* commented: "The eloquent LA FOLLETTE will take care of him without difficulty, and will make a most excellent officer." The postmaster endorsed La Follette along with the rest of the ticket and the candidate, in turn, integrated aspects of Keyes' spreadeagle oratory into his own speeches. La Follette succeeded in overcoming the handicap of the preceding Republican administration and was elected, but by only ninety-three votes.[2]

District Attorney La Follette carried out his campaign promises. Although he was so inexperienced at his first prosecution that he did not know what arraigning the prisoner meant, he did not hire assistants to help him in his trials. More experienced lawyers donated their services; one estimated his contributions at about fifteen hundred dollars. In addition, he was an extremely zealous and diligent prosecutor. As a lawyer he had seen the protection of a client as a battle for truth. As a prosecutor he could see only the law and the criminal; he did not yet recognized a relationship between social injustice and crime. His cases were prepared with great care, his indictments flowed over with rhetoric and moral righteousness. While La Follette improved on his predecessor's record before the circuit court, the legend about his invincibility was not built there; his sixty-eight percent effectiveness was matched by his successor's sixty-nine percent. It was in the municipal court, in cases involving drunkeness, vagrancy, assault and battery, that La Follette overmatched his peers. In this arena he averaged twice as many convictions per year as his successor; and during his tenure governors pardoned twice as many of his

prisoners as of those of the public prosecutor of Milwaukee, who
ranked second. His moral standards appear to have been high,
even for the Victorian era. La Follette resisted political interference in his cases, obtaining a conviction in State v. Wilson,
despite efforts by Keyes to have the case dismissed, only to
have the governor issue a pardon. In one case he pursued Ed
Sanderson, chairman of the Republican State Central
Committee, who had been robbed while drunk and wanted to
cover up his spree. But in this case he embarrassed a member of
the "Milwaukee Ring" who was very unpopular among
Madison politicians and voters. On the other hand, La Follette
was somewhat lax in enforcing the sabbatarian laws, and
complaints were invariably filed by the Law and Order League
or indignant mothers. He did not obstruct the work of the
prohibitionists, permitting their lawyers to try most of the
cases, but he did not incur the wrath of the saloon-owner
controlled Personal Liberty League. La Follette had decided by
this time that he was going to seek the congressional
nomination and had no intention of alienating his beer-drinking
constituents by using unpopular paid informers. Under
pressure from prohibitionists he selectively indicted saloon-
keepers: a good politician could not become a fanatic
prosecutor.[3]

His two terms as district attorney marked more than his
political beginnings. In the fall of 1881 La Follette entered into
a partnership with his brother-in-law, Robert Siebecker, and
established a thriving practice, leading all Madison firms in
civil cases before the circuit court by the end of his second term.
On the last day of 1881, he rushed from a court case to the Case
residence in Baraboo, Wisconsin to marry the Spring Green
High School teacher, Belle Case. The Unitarian minister, who
performed the rites, omitted "obey" from the service. The
newlyweds joined Robert and Josephine Siebecker and the
groom's mother in the huge residence on West Wilson Street. A
year and a half later La Follette, a devoted family man,
personally prepared the house for Belle's return with the infant
Fola.[4] It was a responsible young man of substance who sought
a congressional seat in 1884.

La Follette had proven himself by running two thousand
votes ahead of the losing ticket in his successful campaign for

reelection. The time was auspicious to advance his career. Elisha Keyes, who had controlled Dane County, the heart of the district, was reeling from a series of political blows. The first came when he had lost to Senator Carpenter in 1879. Then, in 1881 Congressman Philetus Sawyer, a protégé of Postmaster General T. O. Howe and a lumber millionaire with close railroad connections, defeated him in his second bid for the Senate and began two decades of dominance in the state. When Keyes tried to use the assembly as a stepping stone to Congress, Howe replaced him as Madison postmaster with General George Bryant. Nonplussed, Keyes came to the congressional convention with an apparent majority of one, only to lose to George Hazelton. Furious, Keyes bolted, accepted his supporters' designation, split the Republican vote, and enabled the Democrat, Burr Jones, to be elected. Keyes had reached his nadir; he had fallen from power and had helped the Democrats regain control of Congress. Neither Hazelton nor Keyes was acceptable in 1884.[5] Someone had to be found who was acceptable to both factions, if not necessarily to the previous candidates.

Sam Harper, La Follette's intimate friend and future law partner, had little trouble convincing the district attorney that La Follette was that man, though Belle was reluctant to leave Madison. His most important ally was Ulysses Grant's friend, George Bryant, who had strong influence among the Civil War veterans. The Madison postmaster owned a number of large farms in Wisconsin and Minnesota and was a noted cattle and horse breeder. An astute politician, he was a good friend to the two young men, even advising La Follette's mother on the administration of her estate. He seemed to treat Harper and his companion as he would his own sons, and La Follette considered him to be his political godfather. For the next two decades he was to be at the center of La Follette's campaigns.

To win the nomination it was necessary to capture Dane and Grant counties. La Follette spoke the language of ambitious youth and could count on the fervent support of the younger element, including Bryant's employees. Bryant maneuvered an invitation from the Madison post of the Grand Army of the Republic for La Follette on Memorial Day, and the best young orator in the state delivered as expected. In the meantime

George Hazelton, who was ready to retire from active politics, was convinced by his friend, Bryant, quietly to solicit delegates for La Follette in Grant county, his home, and to throw his support to the twenty-nine-year-old candidate in the convention. Former Governor Lucius Fairchild, the state's most popular veteran, heeded Bryant's plea for aid. The Milwaukee *Sentinel,* reflecting that city's sentiment, found La Follette an acceptable candidate. As Bryant and Harper toured the district they overcame resentment that Dane county was fielding a candidate and advised La Follette to appear independent of Hazelton. Confident of victory, the candidate "imperiously" rejected attempts by Keyes' lieutenant, Willet Main, to compromise on the Madison delegation. Not only did it carry the city and country districts of Dane, but the La Follette faction defeated Keyes in his own ward for the first time in his career. "No more such fights for me," Willet Main confided to his diary. La Follette went into the convention with all the Dane county delegates and most of Grant county; he had a clear majority before the convention opened.[6]

His acceptance speech praised all his defeated competitors and emphasized issues that all Republicans could agree upon: the Republican party had inherited from the Democrats a nation in crisis; they had restored solvency to a bankrupt government; they had freed the slaves and had protected former bondsmen; and their protective tariff had saved American labor and industry. The Democratic press charged that La Follette had accused all Democrats of being thieves and traitors. La Follette found it necessary to counter this accusation, for even then he was relying on Democratic votes for election. Democratic efforts to create a split between La Follette and Keyes' supporters, by emphasizing the ease of his selection and his obligations to Bryant, were to no avail. The *Wisconsin State Journal* heartily endorsed him, commented upon the enthusiasm with which young Republicans viewed his candidacy, and stressed party unity. His incumbent opponent, Burr Jones, was an able candidate with a fine record but La Follette had the help of such seasoned campaigners as Bryant and Governor Fairchild. He campaigned so hard, however, that he became physically ill in late October, a pattern that was to cause him serious difficulty at the height of his career. At this point even Willet Main made a courtesy call. In a close election La Follette won by 491 votes and became the youngest member of Congress.[7]

La Follette was at the beginning of a very successful stay in the nation's capitol. Never having been east of Chicago, he accepted an invitation from Congressman Henry Casson to come to Washington to overcome his inexperience by first hand study and to gain an edge in committee assignments by becoming acquainted with Republican leaders earlier than other freshmen legislators. As a bonus it would keep him out of Wisconsin during the senatorial fight between Lucius Fairchild and John Spooner.[8] He faithfully attended all sessions, even those lasting all night, studied the rules, and read the *Congressional Record.* By the time his term began he was prepared for his role and had made invaluable contacts.

Belle found Washington comfortable. She fitted easily into the social whirl, made the proper courtesy calls, enjoyed the social functions, and always took pleasure in guiding constituents through Washington. The young couple delighted in window shopping at holiday time, but most of all they appreciated access to the theater and rarely missed a Baltimore performance by Edwin Booth or Lawrence Barrett. Only the inadequate heating in their quarters marred their first Washington experience.[9]

It was not long before La Follette endeared himself to the Republican congressional leadership and was marked as one of its most promising neophytes. While even then emphasizing the interests of farmers and laborers and resisting grasping corporations and promoters, he expressed party orthodoxy on national questions with passion, logic, and eloquence and soon reached a prominent position. Disappointed in an assignment to the Committee on Indian Affairs rather than to the one on public lands, he carried out his tasks with diligence and was recognized by the Indians as a champion of their interest comparable to Senator Matt Quay of Pennsylvania. But it was his congressional oratory that brought him to national attention. His first speech was a challenge to a large appropriation for rivers and harbors. He objected to the suspension of fifty-eight previous projects in favor of new undertakings, for it would allow them to "drag along subject to the destroying influences of heat, frost, floods, currents and tides." Since some of the works in progress dated back to the Republican forty-seventh Congress and the new proposals had been made by a Democratic Congress, Republican leaders were scarcely disturbed. And his speech received favorable national press coverage, even in Democratic papers.[10] His support of a tax on oleomargarine, to protect the public "from a fraudulent and unwholesome article of food," was well received in "America's Dairyland." His Jeffersonian paean to farmers brought him extensions of his allotted time: "The vital forces of every business. . .are drawn from and nourished by it. . . .Ownership of soil means ownership of home, and I tell you that government whose people build and own their own homes lays broadest and deepest its foundation." Subsequently he argued for agricultural experimental stations to improve the farmers' control over their operations and to tighten tariff loopholes to protect his tobacco growing electorate.[11]

The speech that brought La Follette to national prominence was his rebuttal of the Democratic Speaker's defense of the Mills tariff bill. Disturbed by John Carlisle's powerful response to Tom Reed's closing argument for the Republican opposition, he had attempted to convince Reed and William McKinley that a rejoinder had to be made. Both responded that he should answer it. And answer it he did. During set speeches it was the practice of congressmen to read, talk, and write, reported the Milwaukee *Sentinel.* "They commenced this with La Follette, Saturday, but in a very few minutes all papers were laid aside, writing suspended, the cloakroom deserted, chairs turned about and nearly every member present faced the speaker and gave him undivided attention until the last word was spoken." His colleagues granted him unanimous consent to extend his remarks from the five minutes allotted to the hour and a quarter his speech lasted. With careful statistical backing La Follette challenged Carlisle's evidence, emphasized the importance of gold discoveries and inventions in promoting prosperity, and insisted that the most marked advances were in industries that retained a protective tariff. When the Republicans gained control of the House in the next election La Follette was elevated to the Ways and Means Committee, the youngest Republican to be so honored since McKinley. And he had responsibility second only to McKinley for drafting the Tariff of 1890. He accepted as normal the practices of excluding Democratic committee members from the subcommittee deliberations on the tariff and relying upon manufacturers for information about schedules that affected them. La Follette still assumed that domestic competition would assure the lowest prices compatible with American wage standards despite prohibitive tariff schedules. And to ensure competition he supported the Sherman Anti-trust Bill.[12]

But La Follette did not always cooperate with the Republican power structure. With his election to the Senate, Philetus Sawyer, leader of the "Milwaukee Ring," centralized control of the Wisconsin Republican party. He used his position to promote his own financial interests: as chairman of the railroad committee (1883-87) and second ranking member of the commerce committee he furthered his lumber and railroad fortunes. Keyes had already been reduced as a factor. When former Governor Lucius Fairchild, the popular Civil War veteran, sought a Senate seat to advance his presidential ambitions, Sawyer quietly blocked his way. His candidate was John Coit Spooner, able counsel for major lumber companies and railroads, who, like his sponsor, had used politics for economic profit. After his election, Spooner rose to eminence as one of the best constitutional lawyers in the Senate. Henry C. Payne, a former supporter of Keyes and the leading corporate lobbyist for Wisconsin interests, completed the triumvirate.[13] Despite Sawyer's power in his home state, La Follette would not accede to his wishes involving Indian lands. During La Follette's first term in Congress, as a member of the Indian Affairs Committee, he killed a bill to permit the sale of timber from the Menominee Indian Reservation in Wisconsin, even though it was sponsored by a Wisconsin colleague and he was informed that the bill had been introduced at Sawyer's request; he thought the bill would make it possible to steal timber from the Indians. Sawyer did not intervene. Years later, when La Follette was far more secure in his position and a favorite of the congressional leadership, Sawyer wanted legislation to permit the Northwestern and St. Paul railroads to take as much land as they wished along their right of way. Despite continuous pressure from Sawyer and Payne, La Follette successfully

sponsored an amendment permitting the acquisition of a right
of way, railroad stations and other necessary railroad purposes,
but barring railroads from town sites and exclusive rights over
grain elevators and warehouses. While La Follette was
patronizing and paternalistic towards Indians, he sincerely
wanted to protect their rights. Until they had been educated
and had developed sufficient business acumen he wanted to
limit them to management of the proceeds from their holdings,
not "to entrust them with the power to dispose of their land."
La Follette challenged Sawyer twice more, when he refused to
support a Nicaraguan Canal proposal in return for a
contribution to the Republican national campaign, and when he
was active in recruiting Republican votes to help Democrats
defeat a ship subsidy bill. In the latter instance he had his only
harsh words with Sawyer as he ushered a congressman off the
floor to prevent the senator from coercing a change in his vote
by threatening to call in his loans.[14]

Despite essentially irreconcilable views on the relation
between government, business, and personal acquisitions,
Sawyer and La Follette remained on good terms throughout the
decade of the 1880's. And La Follette was not dependent in any
manner upon Sawyer for his renomination or election. He
obtained state patronage through Governor William D. Hoard
and jealously protected his federal patronage; he even
demanded the dismissal of the physician who had amputated
Fairchild's arm because the appointment had not been cleared
through him.[15]

Immediately after his first victory La Follette began to
organize for reelection. In each township his friends drew up
lists of twenty-five "active Republicans" and fifteen "fair
minded Democrats," as well as poll lists indicating political
affiliation and occupation. They dispatched speeches to
constituents; Belle addressed the envelopes, added garden
seeds supplied by the Department of Agriculture, and posted
the letters. The process was expensive and time consuming but
successful. Sam Harper organized Republican clubs and
recruited young partisans. La Follette was in demand as a
speaker during campaigns. "You cannot know how much we
need you" wrote one local worker; the congressman stimulated
the campaign and drew more than a full party vote.[16] Having

squeeked through the election of 1884 by 400 votes, he increased his margin to 3500 in 1886 and 3000 in 1888. In both instances he was renominated without opposition.[17] He was looking forward to the election of 1890 with confidence.

But when La Follette came home with the returns of election night he called up to his wife: "Well, Belle, Bushnell is elected to Congress from the Third District, and I am elected to practice law."[18] What had happened? The Republicans had compounded normal off-year reverses with their passage of a high tariff. McKinley and La Follette, the two men primarily responsible for this bill, were defeated despite apparently safe seats. 1890 was a disastrous year for Wisconsin Republicans. Only Nils P. Haugen was returned to Congress, and his margin was cut from 10,000 to 2500. The Democratic landslide swept Republicans from the executive mansion and from control of the legislature. Locally, German voters reacted to the Bennett law which, by requiring the education of children in English, apparently threatened parochial school systems, and they substantially increased their normally Democratic pluralities. In addition, La Follette had been so certain of reelection that he had made statewide commitments to campaign for a Republican legislature to reelect Senator Spooner and to help in other districts in the midwest in keeping with his national stature. As the campaign progressed Harper received numerous warnings, particularly in Scandinavian areas, contrasting Democratic vigor with Republican apathy, reporting slippage among labor and tobacco farmers, — strong Republicans resentful of the McKinley tariff. He was warned that no one could do La Follette as much good as he could do himself and was urged that the congressman return to his own campaign. But, certain that La Follette's speeches on the tariff would return dissidents to the fold, all were confident of victory by a reduced margin. Instead, Scandinavian voters, disaffected with the tariff, stayed home. La Follette was returned to Madison and began the only period of his married life in which he held no political office.[19]

# CHAPTER 3

## *Elba*

T HERE was no reason to expect defeat to lead to oblivion. La Follette remained an attractive political figure who had once again proved himself by running 700 votes ahead of his ticket. He had committed no blunders and had not yet created any important enemies. On the contrary, George Bryant, the most powerful politician in southern Wisconsin, was his sponsor. During this period McKinley was to rebound from defeat to become governor of Ohio and President of the United States. Yet, within a year, La Follette had become a pariah for the leaders of the Wisconsin Republican party.

In the early afternoon of September 17, 1891, La Follette sought out Robert Ogilvie at the Milwaukee Fair. Ogilvie, mistaking his purpose, invited him to see his horses. After looking at one, La Follette asked to see him privately. In a stall used for traps he confided: "Robert," he said, "I have been most damnably insulted." Unable to speak he sat there in tears. When he continued he told an incredible story — Senator Sawyer had attempted to bribe him.[1]

Philetus Sawyer, as bondsmen for two former Republican state treasurers, was liable for about a million dollars and might have had to pay $150,000 to $200,000 because they had been accused by the new Democratic administration of illegally holding back interest on state funds, a previously accepted practice. One of the accused, Henry Harshaw, was to be tried in Judge Robert Siebecker's court. Siebecker, a Democrat and the brother-in-law of La Follette, had been appointed by Governor Hoard over Harshaw's objections. Sawyer, sending a message on Harshaw's stationery, with the letterhead torn off, requested that La Follette meet him at the Plankinton House in Milwaukee. The essence of what transpired at this meeting is clear; its details became the subject for public contention. Sawyer offered La Follette money — $500 or $1000. Sawyer declared that it was offered as a retainer. La Follette said it had been offered as a bribe for a favorable decision by Siebecker, and only after he waxed indignant had the senior senator insisted that it had been meant as a retainer.[2]

That evening La Follette, still "very much agitated," "speaking under great stress," repeated his story to Governor Hoard and a friend. He sought their advice, as he was to do with a number of confidants and advisers in the following days. He was informed that disclosure would prejudice the treasurers' cases; they were friends and apparently innocent.[3] Others warned that Sawyer was so powerful that La Follette would only destroy himself if he made the interview public and even suggested that he refrain from informing Siebecker, though he sensed that was his duty. But La Follette consulted Judge Romanzo Bunn who confirmed his judgment, and he notified his brother- in-law. When Siebecker withdrew from the case the Chicago *Times* of October 23 reported its guess that an attempt had been made to influence the court. Although still not accused, Sawyer responded by telling his version of the meeting to an interviewer for the Milwaukee *Sentinel*. Faced with public disclosure of the incident, La Follette drafted his detailed account of the Plankinton encounter.'[4]

"Your letter, published in yesterday's Sentinel, sealed your political fate," wrote one sympathizer.[5] Another informed him that while 95% of the people would accept his veracity as opposed to Sawyer's, the same percentage "will be terrorized by the Senator's. . .millions, and he will be shielded at your expense."[6] While they could have anticipated the ensuing barrage of criticism in the Republican press, the personal hatred and ostracism that followed caused Harper to fear physical harm to his closest friend, and he kept him constantly in sight. La Follette went to his ranch in South Dakota to pull himself together. When he attended the National Republican Convention in 1892, formerly close congressional friends rebuked him. Belle was to compare the intense partisan hostility that he encountered with the hatred engendered by misguided patriotism during World War I; La Follette himself to the animosity he faced when first elected to the Senate.[7]

La Follette was faced with three choices: though a confirmed Republican, he could become a Democrat, and some of his opponents charged that this was his intention; he could drop out of politics; or he could fight back, a solution that best fitted his temperament. First he had to reestablish his Republican credentials lest it appear that he had been read out of the party. And fortunately the political situation permitted this. In late July of 1892 William McKinley came to Madison as a Chautauqua speaker through La Follette's efforts. McKinley, long a personal friend, was his house guest during his visit and attended a dinner with the politically and socially prominent Lucius Fairchilds. Secondly, H. C. Payne stepped down as chairman of the state central committee in an effort to repair wounds created by his treatment of Governor Hoard. H. C. Thom, a follower of Hoard, replaced him. When La Follette threatened to arrange his own schedule, Thom acceded to his demand that he speak during the 1892 national campaign.[8] Next, he forged an alliance for the long struggle ahead.

The center of his crusade was his own law office, La Follette, Harper, Roe, and Zimmerman. One partner, Sam Harper, was his closest friend from his freshman year in college until Harper's death in 1898. Gilbert Roe remained his friend and political confidant long after La Follette had left the firm to have greater freedom to campaign and Gil had moved his practice to New York. Alfred Zimmerman remained a factor in Wisconsin politics for decades after La Follette's death. Later, Alfred Rogers became La Follette's legal and political partner. The elder statesman of the Madison nucleus was General George Bryant. A Democratic President removed Bryant as postmaster and Roger Spooner, the former senator's brother, succeeded him as Dane County Republican chairman.

Congressman Nils P. Haugen, the sole survivor of the 1890 Democratic landslide, was a close political ally. Born in Norway, Haugen was then the leading Scandinavian politician, representing the second largest voting bloc in Wisconsin. (Scandinavians were extremely important to the Republicans, for many Germans were Democrats.) He had been a lawyer, a court reporter, a member of the assembly, and a knowledgeable railroad commissioner. He had grievances against the "Milwaukee Ring" because of insufficient electoral support and disputes over patronage. While he had been a regular Republican he was close to La Follette and the pioneer reformer, A. R. Hall. By 1894 he had developed an interest in corrupt practices legislation and a direct primary. Reluctant to run for governor until the very last, nevertheless he thought the triumvirate had been shaken by political reverses, the seventy-eight-year-old Sawyer had promised neutrality, and the depression had made the Democrats vulnerable. La Follette finally convinced him by polling 1200 university graduates. Young men, hitherto inactive in politics, they were a small, cohesive group, homogeneous in background (farmers' sons), prominent in their communities — since few citizens had even completed high school —, and an important new element in the coalition.[9]

Former Governor William D. Hoard was closely identified with the dairy industry. As chief executive he had become furious with Payne for lobbying against the Dairy and Food Commission in the interests of the meatpackers' oleomargarine subsidiaries. As chairman of the Republican state committee, Payne had not adequately supported the Bennett law, fervently sponsored by Hoard despite an awareness of its negative political potential. La Follette, on the other hand, had vigorously supported a tax on oleomargarine. George Bryant had successfully managed Hoard's initial preconvention campaign when, at the outset, not even the editor and publisher of Hoard's *Dairyman* had taken his own candidacy seriously. During the 1890's the dairy industry trebled in output, becoming the fourth most important occupation in the state, and Wisconsin emerged as the second ranking producer in the country.[10] Hoard's support of La Follette's crusade was of great importance.

Finally, Haugen introduced La Follette to Assemblyman Albert R. Hall. Hall was responsible for converting another fight against a political boss into an issue-oriented movement. A nephew of Oliver H. Kelley and a successful stock raiser, he had been identified with the Granger movement. He had served as speaker of the Minnesota assembly before he came to Wisconsin and had brought with him all of his knowledge of parliamentary procedure. Throughout the decade he fought a solitary crusade to abolish the granting of free railroad passes to politicians, a practice so universal that Haugen had accepted it earlier in his career. For this Hall was generally scorned as a demagogue and crank. He was not only a tireless campaigner but led the coalition forces in the legislature in many of their floor fights. La Follette was later to describe him as "Plain, modest, without guile. . . . He feared nothing except to do wrong. He made his way indifferent to abuse and misrepresentation. He did not serve the hour. He was not afraid to break new ground."[11]

Haugen was a reluctant candidate; as late as February, 1894, he discussed potential congressional committee assignments. While he was supported by the Chicago *Skandinaven* and obtained the withdrawal of Scandinavian candidates for lesser statewide offices, he campaigned little and did not carry his own bailiwick. La Follette, on the other hand, undermined one of his strongest opponents, "Hod" Taylor, by carrying Dane county despite the loss of Stoughton and Madison. He garnered an impressive one-third of the delegates for his candidate; but Haugen, with little second-choice strength and the quiet opposition of Sawyer, was defeated by the Marshfield business man, Major William Upham. The insurgents were permitted to choose the state treasurer, Sewall Peterson, and the inroads on the machine had begun.[12]

In the midst of the campaign, on April 21, 1894, La Follette's mother had died unexpectedly, a victim of pneumonia. Though seventy-six, she had attended a physical culture class all winter. For a time he seemed overwhelmed and helpless, for his filial feelings were intense, but he soon reaffirmed his fervor for life. Fola had been born two years after their marriage, but they had no other children at the time of Mary La Follette's death. In February of 1895 Belle gave birth to Bob, jr. Philip was born in 1897 and Mary in 1899. Belle could only continue her political activity because Fola assumed so much responsibility for the children. (Fola graduated from the university in 1904 and later left for New York to become an actress.)[13]

Governor Upham's tenure of office was disastrous. While a Democratic administration had succeeded in recovering $609,000 in the treasury cases, a quarter of a million dollars remained outstanding. Against the governor's wishes, bills

discontinuing the treasury suits were pushed through the legislature by Charles Pfister, whose father had been a bondsman
for one of the treasurers. Upham, a loyal Republican, ended his
chance of renomination with his signature. He was persuaded to
return to his business affairs despite a two-term precedent. This
gave enhanced credence to the insurgent campaign claims of
corrupt bossism.[14]

Preparation for 1896 began before the general election in
1894. Harper was elected president of the Wisconsin
Republican League and converted it into a center for political
education.[15] During this interim Hall prevailed in his insistence
on an issues-oriented strategy, that anti-pass and anti-machine
be paired as a platform; but once the 1896 campaign began,
anti-bossism again dominated reform rhetoric. The question of
tactics and the prime candidate remained to be resolved. In
January La Follette still continued to think of Haugen as the
candidate, and as late as June Haugen was willing to run. The
national convention changed the picture. Although La Follette
was forced by ill health to go south, Harper successfully organized Wisconsin for McKinley, while the "Milwaukee Ring"
worked for Thomas Reed. La Follette carried Madison and
Dane county and as a delegate to the national convention returned to national attention with his seconding speech for
McKinley and his exceptional nominating speech for a vice-
presidential candidate, Henry Clay Evans. La Follette could
attract most of Haugen's supporters, and the insurgents concluded that they could not win with Haugen. At one point they
considered running La Follette, Haugen, and Emil Baensch
with the understanding that delegates would be thrown to the
leading candidate. Haugen demurred and withdrew in favor of
La Follette, while Bryant feared a tactic that would look too
much like that of their opponents. Consequently, La Follette
announced that he was in the race to stay to the end, causing
consternation among many of his allies who had not been
informed. He was confident and determined: "I must win this
fight — it is more than politics to me."[16] As they went into the
convention La Follette and Baensch had an understanding that
the strongest of the two would receive the support of the other.
Sawyer's caucus chose Edward Scofield, a veteran and
lumberman, as its candidate.

When the convention opened in Milwaukee in August La

Follette led in delegates, and with Baensch the insurgents had a clear majority. Unfortunately, no arrangement had been made about when Baensch was to withdraw; some delegates were offered bribes, and Scofield was nominated. The La Follette forces moved to make the nomination unanimous and supported the slate and the platform, which included Hall's anti-pass resolution. Except for an attempt to aid Hall, La Follette's campaign emphasis was on the national ticket, — sound money and the tariff. He denied the "Crime of '73": Congress stopped coining silver dollars because they were being taken out of circulation by profiteers; wheat prices had fallen because of increased exports by Russia and India. And the depression was the result of the reduction of tariff rates by the Wilson Act (which was passed after the depression began).[17]

The presence of a friend in the White House enhanced La Follette's reputation but did little else. While he expected his share of the patronage, he lacked allies in the congressional delegation and could not convince McKinley to bypass normal courtesy. He and Haugen were unable to persuade the President-elect to choose Hoard as secretary of agriculture, though he was seriously considered. But La Follette did prevent Payne from entering the cabinet despite fervent support by Mark Hanna—McKinley's campaign manager— and the national committee. Ever suspicious of the motives of his enemies, he suspected that the offer of the comptroller of the currency had been engineered by Spooner in order to get him out of Wisconsin. Although McKinley assured him that Spooner neither made the suggestion nor objected, and that the President wanted him in a post next to cabinet rank, La Follette declined. His law practice was more lucrative, and the position did not appeal to his political ambitions. Tactically, his refusal was an excellent move for it set him apart from ordinary office seekers in the eyes of the Wisconsin electorate.[18]

Having failed to unseat the machine in two efforts with a campaign based on honesty and anti-bossism, La Follette realized it was time to take Hall's advice and shift to an issue-oriented campaign. While ideas had flowed so freely among the members of the coalition that they often did not know who was the originator, the group had acceded to La Follette's style, leadership, and sense of timing. Even now, he centered campaigns on a single issue, or a group of issues, until the Wisconsin Idea had been legislated.

A number of closely intertwined factors improved the climate for an issues-oriented campaign. The depression of 1893, a prolonged and devastating event, brought about a transformation in some of the urban-based reform movements. Good government and a war against vice and saloons had long been their concern. With the failure of standard economic reforms — reduced tariff and the repeal of the Silver Purchase Act — attitudes began to change. There was a declining faith in a self-adjusting system; social criticism found an audience in minds open to new ideas, searching for alternatives to the existing order. With bankers prosecuted as thieves and embezzlers, public respect for business leaders plummeted. At the same time, with one-third of the work force unemployed, it became difficult to blame poverty on character defects. Even Horace Rublee, publisher of the influential Milwaukee *Sentinel,* relinquished his Spencerian Darwinism in favor of more pragmatic analysis. New discussion groups were receptive to the university's social scientists, to Richard T. Ely's concept that society evolves from competition to cooperation. The New Woman developed a social consciousness by bringing club members in contact for the first time with young, poor, and working members, for declining funds created an increased need to administer charity by direct contact with slum dwellers, in an unfamiliar setting of poverty. Newly aware of the role of environment, they fought to improve working conditions for women and children, they campaigned to transform the urban environment, to obtain parks and playgrounds, night schools, sewing and cooking classes, boys clubs, hospitals, settlement houses, neighborhood clubs, and to make books available to the poor. And they began to demand access for women to opportunities formerly denied them. The Social Gospel movement spread from a handful of Protestant ministers to a point where the alliance of the religious establishment with the status quo was shaken. Protestant, Catholic, and Jewish theologians preached the New Religion from the pulpit, demanding a new citizenship, more involved in a sense of community responsibility. Ministers increased their social service, promoted cooperatives, and began to work with labor unions. Strikers found unexpected sources of support from among former opponents. Urban politics underwent a metamorphosis. Expansion of urban services had created a heavy load of debt for cities and towns, responsibilities that had to be met despite depression-induced reduction in income. Business principles in government and retrenchment did not prove to be adequate solutions when overweening public service corporations maneuvered to have their assessments reduced, refused to pay taxes while increasing their charges to the municipalities, or manipulated the state legislature to obtain exemption from municipal responsibilities in return for inadequate license taxes. The reformers now demanded redistribution of the tax burden to make it more equitable and to fund necessary public works. A community of consumers and taxpayers were contrasted with tax-evading, arrogant corporations. These campaigns bridged the social gap in a way the mugwumps had found impossible, and the ranks of reformers swelled with new recruits from among workers and trade unionists. When the corporations escaped urban wrath by appealing to the state legislature, where real power over municipal government lay, the urban reformers, spurred by the leadership of Milwaukee, organized a statewide lobby. Learning to deal with political reality, they abandoned non-partisanship and fought for control of the party machinery. In the summer of 1896 La Follette was joined by an important new ally, the Republican Club of Milwaukee (an immediate asset, but, as an independent power base, a future problem). The Milwaukee group came with its own urban-oriented progressive program and reinforced Hall's insistence upon an issue-oriented campaign.[19]

La Follette had found the central issue for his next campaign. Convinced that he represented the will of the Republican party and had been denied the nomination through corruption, La Follette sought a surer means of expressing the will of the party members than the caucus and convention. He found it in nomination by direct primary, a concept with which he had little previous familiarity but one that had long been bandied about and little practiced. It had been first implemented in Crawford County, Pennsylvania in 1842. Kentucky had adopted an optional state law, and the idea had been briefly considered by New York and California. Haugen had mentioned it in 1894, and Wisconsin Assemblyman Kimball had prepared but had not introduced such a bill in 1895. After his usual extensive research La Follette prepared his position in late 1896. And he had an excellent forum for his proposal. The Washington Birthday address at the University of Chicago had been delivered by McKinley in 1895 and Theodore Roosevelt in 1896. La Follette was chosen to offer it in 1897 — a mark of his growing stature. Harper and Hoard alerted Hoard's newspaper contacts about the importance of the event.[20]

Before an audience of "the scholarly element of Chicago," La Follette considered "the political machine, its evolution in our political history, and its menace to representative government." Republican government is based on the responsibility of the individual citizen, he asserted. Initially, prominent men had met in assembly to choose community representatives. With a broader electorate the caucus and convention system arose "to give the people a direct voice in self government." After the Civil War, an America occupied by an expanding economy confronted a new political machine in control of government, a machine which manipulated caucuses to frustrate irate citizens.

The modern political machine. . .is impersonal, irresponsible, extra-legal. . .without conscience and without remorse. It has come to be enthroned in American politics. It rules caucuses, names delegates, appoints committees, dominates the councils of the party, dictates nominations, makes platforms, dispenses patronage, directs state administrations, controls legislatures, stifles opposition, punishes independence, and elects United States senators.

It will offer, and violate, any platform pledge required to win, sacrifice any scapegoat, and then quietly reward him for his service. It is financed by those corporations which dominate our economic life in return for "its special franchise, its special power, its special exemptions, its exclusive privilege." The caucus cannot be reformed, he insisted. It invites corruption. It removes the nomination from the voter. An interested electorate can overthrow the machine if its will could be expressed at the primaries as clearly as at elections. The candidates should be designated by a petition of a fixed percentage of the previous vote, and then the party candidate chosen directly, through Australian secret ballot, at the polls. The Wisconsin Idea was taking shape. His speech was well received by his influential audience, printed in several Chicago newspapers and reprinted in some Wisconsin journals. Harper prepared a pamphlet consisting of the original, newspaper comments and a synopsis of a bill based on it; he offered it as a free non-partisan newspaper supplement. Three hundred newspapers accepted, and 400,000 copies were distributed.[21]

But the campaign had just begun. During the summer and fall of 1897 La Follette delivered county fair speeches based on the menace of the machine and including an analysis of current problems, particularly legislative inaction on important bills: Hall's anti-pass measure and James O. Davidson's efforts to force corporations to pay a fair share of taxes. He began in Mineral Point on July 4 and delivered his most publicized speech in Fern Dell on August 20. The Barabor *News* commented: "Mr. La Follette in his Fern Dell speech reached basic questions not usually touched upon in campaign seasons and beside which the tariff and the money questions are but bubbles on the surface."[22] He attracted huge crowds; at the Green County Fair he broke the record for attendance and gate receipts. Consequently, county agricultural societies, who managed the fairs and whose leaders favored him in any event, sent him more invitations than he could fill. Speaking on a platform before a grandstand he was compelling. He started slowly and built to an intensity sustained for hours. He often toyed with the audience, feigning a desire to halt at a key moment and eliciting a demand to continue. His audience was convinced of his sincerity, his honesty, and each person felt he was speaking directly to him. When he came to Sawyer's home town, Oshkosh, his enemies disrupted his performance with preparations for a horse race. Moving his wagon to block the track, he threatened to speak until sundown, preventing any races. He generated such political excitement that the *Journal* and the *Sentinel* printed his entire anti-trust address to the Milwaukee State Fair. He succeeded in making his proposal a bipartisam issue as newspapers lined up for or against him regardless of party.[23]

1897 marked the beginning of a new phase in La Follette's career. He had become clearly preeminent in his group and he was admirably suited for the self-righteous, issue-oriented crusade they had engendered. He was too politically potent to be considered a crank. On the contrary, local leaders assured him more delegates if he would speak. From this point, defeating the machine was only a means to implement his constantly growing awareness of the need for change — increasingly fundamental change.

In 1897, for the first time, his coalition maneuvered some of its Republican platform provisions through the lower house. Hall led the attack. He guided his anti-pass bill through the assembly, only to see it die. The assembly approved a resolution to investigate railroad income reports. And Davidson obtained passage of bills for more equitable taxation of express and sleeping car companies only to face a Scofield veto. Then an express agent informed La Follette that the governor was shipping personal items free, by frank, including one cow, crated — a cow to become famous in Wisconsin. Hall made these items reverberate through the assembly. The issues for 1898 were clear, but ousting an incumbent with at least a reasonable record was a difficult feat.

To make the attempt at least plausible, they launched a house organ, *The State*. Aware of the need for good relations with journalists, but facing a largely antagonistic press, La Follette sought an outlet for his views. (Actually, while they wrote hostile editorials, editors gave him important front-page coverage.) La Follette threatened to retire from politics if supporters did not raise money to buy a Madison weekly, *Old Dane*. The paper was purchased, ably edited by a young Norwegian and university graduate, John Nelson, and renamed *The State*. Its masthead emphasized protective tariff, trade reciprocity, sound money, equitable taxation, nomination by direct primary, punishment for bribery, a ban on railroad passes, prohibition of corrupt campaign practices, and economical and businesslike administration of public affairs. The journal prepared the public for the debate on selected campaign issues.

Nevertheless, La Follette was reluctant to run in 1898; the Republican Club of Milwaukee was determined that the governor be challenged. It published a bitter twenty-four page attack on Scofield, organized on a ward-by-ward basis for the convention, and, in an all-night session, pressed La Follette to ignore party custom and make the contest. Harper's death had robbed the coalition of a leader and an alternate candidate. Cognizant of friends' advice that a second defeat could eliminate him as a viable candidate in 1900, but aware of the need to keep his troops together, La Follette delayed a decision. He finally announced his candidacy with a new wrinkle, a statement of principles. The Milwaukee reformers endorsed him, adopted an acceptable platform he had drafted, and delivered a majority of Milwaukee delegates for insurgency. "For the next four weeks the war in Cuba will be a vacation on the sea compared to what we have here," his campaign manager, Gilbert Roe, predicted. La Follette came to the convention with more committed delegates than Scofield; but the uncommitted majority nominated Scofield despite bitter attacks by the Milwaukee Club and La Follette; the insurgents refused to make the nomination unanimous. Earlier, the coalition's platform had been adopted, and the rest of the slate was composed of men acceptable to them. The insurgents maintained a public stance of party unity, but privately insisted that Scofield's nomination had been purchased and cut the incumbent so that he ran behind the ticket.[24]

La Follette did not participate in the 1898 campaign. Overworked, he collapsed from nervous indigestion while trying a lawsuit and convalesced for six months. Ordered by his physician to a warmer climate, he and Belle went to San Diego, with side visits to the coast at La Jolla. Fola stayed next door with her Aunt Jo; Bob, jr., and Philip lived with Belle's mother for a year and felt spoiled by doting grandparents while they enjoyed the rural life of Baraboo. It was shortly after this that Belle gave birth to Mary. La Follette had come a long way from the young lawyer who had entered politics so that he could afford to get married. He now had a thriving law practice and lived in an imposing frame house, set back from the street, with a large lawn in front and a view of Lake Monona in the rear. The barn across the street, jointly owned with his neighbors, the Siebeckers, held his horses and a Jersey cow, and a hired man did the chores. The children grew up with a love of animals and riding.[25]

The next two years were marked by the growing strength of La Follette's "halfbreeds" and the disintegration of Sawyer's "stalwarts." The first addition to the insurgent ranks, and the most important, was Isaac Stephenson. The son of a lumbering contractor, at twelve he began as a cook in his father's camp. With hard work and some important contacts he became wealthy. A camp superintendent before the area was politically organized, he became a local official, moved up to the assembly, and then Congress, and served with La Follette with whom he enjoyed good relations. Stephenson's ambition to become a senator was blocked by Sawyer, Payne, and Spooner, who delivered the nomination to Joseph Quarles. Ready to accept a negative popular decision, he was infuriated at his rejection by those whose campaigns he had helped finance (he claimed to have spent $22,000 in one campaign for Spooner). "I began to realize for the first time the power and devious ways of the 'machine'." And he understood the need to end railroad and utility domination of politics and to regulate public service corporations for their own good as well as that of the public. Limited in his progressive vision, he reflected a significant element of the coalition. For La Follette he served not only as a needed source of funds but as an older friend and adviser. As the insurgents' financial backer Stephenson was more than generous. When La Follette proved initially reluctant to run again because of impaired health, lack of funds, and fear of a fatal third defeat, Stephenson offered to finance the campaign. At campaign's end La Follette returned all unexpended funds. In need of a newspaper he again approached "Uncle Ike." Although offered $50,000 towards the $163,000 purchase price of the Milwaukee *Sentinel* the "halfbreeds" could not raise the balance; it was purchased by young Charles Pfister. Stephenson then financed the creation of the Milwaukee *Free Press* and picked up its deficit for years. In all, it has been estimated that he expended $400,000 in the cause.[26]

Soon there were indications that La Follette was the coming man. The legislature finally adopted some of the platform pledges: an anti-pass law (with implementation postponed to permit another season of use), ad valorem taxes on railroad equipment, express and sleeping cars, and freight companies, an inheritance tax, a more permanent tax commission than enacted in 1897. Segments of the Wisconsin Idea still lacking were a railroad commission, more equitable railroad taxation, and direct primaries, but the insurgents became noticeably less hostile towards Scofield.

Another sign was the support of Wisconsin's most powerful congressman, Joseph Babcock, and of his friend, the able Emanuel Philipp; the congressman had been denied a Senate seat by the triumvirate. With his district in La Follette territory, continued opposition was dangerous. He offered a truce through a mutual friend, Henry Casson; La Follette accepted, reaffirming his position on issues and obtaining access to Babcock's patronage. In a compromise Philipp became Milwaukee County chairman, Theodore Kronshage of the Milwaukee Club, secretary. La Follette solicited Babcock's advice and responded privately to charges. Supporters of the two were not always easily reconciled.[27]

Babcock and Philipp acted as conduits from La Follette to the Milwaukee business community. La Follette gave assurances to Marvin Hughitt, president of the Chicago and Northwestern, and in a letter to an old friend, Thomas Gill, attorney for the Wisconsin Central, that he was not hostile to business and only desired equitable taxation. Corporations remained neutral or gave him financial support. Without changing his platform, he and *The State* deemphasized railroads and stressed taxation of express and telegraph companies.[28] A week before his announcement he wrote to Roe: "It looks pretty certain for the nomination even at this time. I have been engaged in the mollifying business."[29]

What of the ruling triumvirate? Spooner opposed the truce but remained in Washington. Sawyer had died in March. Payne was ill. Babcock remained quiescent and declined to run for the national committee, neutralizing *The State*. Charles Pfister, about to assume "stalwart" leadership was preoccupied with a street car scandal and a civil suit. There was no central opposition.

Consequently La Follette could present himself as the only statewide aspirant, as a man whose time had come, as a harmony candidate. Three years of stressing issues permitted him to change his program to mollify the new without antagonizing the old. In his 1898 letter soliciting support he had proclaimed: "The issue is between the people, in overwhelming majority, and a small but powerful minority which profits in maintaining existing conditions. . . .The end of machine control is at hand." In his comparable letter of 1900 he emphasized the long struggle to advance principles, their incorporation in the party platform, and his assurance from statewide conservative counsel that the party would "nominate a man known to be in accord with these principles." While confident, he left nothing to chance, organizing caucuses, making deals for delegates, dispensing patronage, answering innumerable letters, dispatching tens of thousands of campaign pieces, and paying canvassers through wealthy local supporters. Zimmerman sent funds to "fix" caucuses in Waukesha, the home of an opponent, A. M. Jones, and the irreconcilable Scofield. With the sweep of the Waukesha and Oconta caucuses even local opposition collapsed and his strongest opponent withdrew. "It is astonishing how many friends La Follette has now and has had all over the state," Alfred Rogers commented wryly to Gil Roe. "I do not believe he ever had an enemy in this whole state."[30]

La Follette took a long rest before beginning the campaign. The Democratic party was divided by William Jenning Bryan's candidacy and fielded a weak opponent in Louis Bomrich. In a presidential year, running a harmony campaign, La Follette emphasized national issues. And that placed him in the anomalous position of defending imperialism. Initially, he knew nothing of the Philippines and could find little information in the *Congressional Record*. He denied that McKinley was an imperialist, and insisted that our involvement in Cuba was the result of "pure, lofty, disinterested devotion to the cause of freedom," and that Bryan had voted for the treaty. The United States was in the Philippines only to maintain a stable government in a diverse, multilingual area occupied by 84 tribes, 69 of which were uncivilized. Aguinaldo, he asserted, represented only a tyrannical minority. America was acting in the Jeffersonian tradition of expansionism to spread enlightened liberty. On domestic issues, he reiterated that prosperity depended on the gold standard and protective tariff. He denied a relationship between trusts and tariff; combines had arisen in free trade England and Standard Oil was not protected; after, all, Republicans had passed the anti-trust law. The only state issue that he emphasized was the direct primary. As predicted by the new state chairman, George Bryant, the entire ticket won by 100,000 votes.[31]

# CHAPTER 4

## *The Wisconsin Idea*

A young family moved into the sandstone governor's mansion on Lake Mendota; Mary was only two. The children had a stately house to play in, with a large, lovely lawn extending to the lakeshore. It had a center hall, a library on the left, a drawing room on the right, and a dining room across the width of the house at the end. There were eight bedrooms and two baths on the upper levels. The executive mansion was located on the opposite side of Madison from their old home, physically and politically. Consequently, though it had been the custom for the neighboring women to call on the governor's wife, few called on Belle.

The two centers of Madison were the capitol and the university, on opposite ends of State Street. More than any one else La Follette was responsible for bringing these two worlds together. He drew upon the resources of the university for many of his programs and informally exchanged ideas with members of the faculty. At one white tie and tails affair for important university guests, Bob, jr. and Phil opened an unused heat register to hear what was being said at the dining table below. Black dust descended onto the white tablecloth. The children were surprised when their father treated it lightly.[1]

While the physical aspects of the job were pleasant, La Follette's tenure as governor was anything but smooth. He was elected after a harmony campaign during which a broad sampling of Republican leadership was consulted. But there was nothing harmonious about conditions in Wisconsin at this time. Forty-five percent of the farms were mortgaged. Eighty percent of the population owned ten percent of the wealth and one percent of the population owned half of the state's property. Political and economic power was concentrated in the hands of a few corporations and privileged firms paid little in taxes. Harmony did not include embracing the status quo. Years of struggle lay ahead.

The inauguration went well, but the lack of cordiality between Scofield and his successor was an omen of the future. La Follette was the first Madison resident to be inaugurated since Reconstruction. Traditionally dressed in a Prince Albert coat, he was conducted to the overflowing assembly chamber by the local militia and out-of-town officials. Students greeted him with the University of Wisconsin yell. The state's largest inaugural ball was held that evening at the university gym with many faculty in attendance. Belle donned a silver grey embroidered crepe gown, high-waisted with a square neck. She wore no jewels; only a soft bow of silver gauze graced her dark hair. The governor managed the grand march but was awkward and uncomfortable in the quadrille.[2]

La Follette was much more in his element as he broke precedent to deliver his inaugural address in person. In these remarks, and in future gubernatorial papers and presentations, he elaborated the Wisconsin Idea. The media focused national attention on the state, on his statements, his struggles, his setbacks, and his successes. Reformers across the country sought office in order to emulate his administration of Wisconsin. His speech began on a non-controversial note; he was consistently to support economy and efficiency in government. He praised his predecessor's employment of business methods, cautioning that much remained to be done. Rarely thereafter did he mention items that could be agreed upon by the whole party. For twenty-two pages he discussed the need "to secure uniformity of assessment and enormously increase the tax upon classes of property which now escape wholly or in part." Uncooperative corporate officials and negligent assessors should be penalized. The citizen, he continued, shifting to nominations, could only "preserve his sovereign right to an equal share in government" if "assured an equal voice in his party ballot. . . . It is here government begins, and if there be failure here, there will be failure throughout." No business could survive, he asserted, under the equivalent of the caucus and convention system, where self-selected agents, responsible to no one, made vital decisions. A primary would attract better candidates than the machine servants, he insisted, and a second choice provision could prevent minority victors. Having presented his most controversial items, he advocated improved rural schools, improved commercial roads, and women in state positions. He assured big business that he was not opposed to size, which was necessary, but combinations to control prices, stifle competition, and create monopolies. The quality of his speech received favorable comments, but its content brought mixed reactions.[3]

While both sides later expressed public surprise at the fight that followed, each had expected a conflict. Senator Spooner had no faith in La Follette's harmony campaign even as he spoke for the Republican candidate. Alfred Zimmerman, Bob's former partner, anticipated legislative opposition to the primary bill only a month after the election. Always suspicious, La Follette began to plan for the session with his picked leaders. The "stalwarts," who had found him easy to approach during the harmony campaign were deeply offended as his private secretary, Jere Murphy, unceremoniously blocked access. Emanuel Philipp condemned the unprecedented secrecy and conspiratorial tone of the new administration: "Two men would be talking in a corridor and a third would approach; instantly there would be warning glances exchanged and the two would separate, to be seen again a few minutes later continuing the conversation."[4] La Follette's conception of a strong executive who prepared carefully for legislative battles was strange and frightening to his more conventional opponents. And the traditional tactic of buying legislative votes infuriated him. But conservative opposition to the administration primary bill was largely based on political philosophy, not purchased votes. La Follette always found it hard to believe that those opposing his reforms could be just as honest and sincere as he was. He sprayed all of his opposition with the stench of the corrupt minority, and they responded accordingly. As articulated by the respected Milwaukee *Sentinel* and by conservative floor leaders, his opponents decried the expense of primaries, its weakening of party organization, the possibility of minority rule, the difficulty farmers had voting at harvest time and the infringement upon the personal right to assemble (an effective argument with German voters). Similarly, they criticized La Follette's insistence on a railroad ad valorem tax for the tax commission had suggested either an increase in the license tax based on gross receipts or an ad valorem tax on the value of property. The ad valorem tax would have brought in a greater revenue and was more equitable, for most state revenues were raised in that manner, but the nature of La Follette's attack was unwarranted. Always theatrical, he dramatized his displeasure at rejection of the ad valorem tax by vetoing a bill to license dogs, chastising the legislators for refusal to levy equitable taxes on corporations while pretending to "relieve the farmer or city home-owner of a small measure of increased tax upon his realty by imposing a license fee upon his dog." Showing rural bias, he pointed out that city dwellers could escape the additional levy by relinquishing their dogs; farmers had no such option, for the watch dog guarded their domestic animals. An equally emphatic veto of a compromise primary bill followed. With La Follette directing all the action from his office, the administration bill had narrowly passed the assembly. Hectic senate lobbying, using persuasion, economic pressure, and corruption, as La Follette so graphically described in his *Autobiography*, prevented passage. The senate substitute limited application to county and village elections; they rejected assembly modifications. La Follette denounced the bill as a sham passed by corporate and machine tools who violated the party platform. Angrily, the "stalwart" majority censured the governor for "abusing the Senate." The administration had failed to redeem its pledges, but the lines had been drawn for battle.[5]

While La Follette was not uncompromising, he was not willing to accept an ineffective half measure in order to build a legislative record. He feared such laws would reduce the pressure for adequate legislation and would never accomplish the purpose for which they had been drawn. He felt the public could only be educated to accept a limited amount of change at one time, so he presented his program piecemeal. But he insisted that each step forward be a complete step in itself. The problem became one of the proper tactics to achieve his ends. It did not take him long to realize that his goals were too threatening to his adversaries to obtain effective legislation through compromise. The alternative was to return to the people, present his case, and overwhelm the opposition. This required not only his reelection, but the election of a compatible legislature. Such a contest perfectly suited the personality and public image of "Battle Bob." Although he felt he successfully separated his public and personal relations with his opponents, his embittered enemies and former friends hardly agreed.[6]

The La Follettes have tried to portray the "stalwarts'" campaign of 1902 as a formidable effort; in fact it was nothing of the kind, and the La Follette camp was aware of this. It lacked adequate leadership and focus. Senator Spooner, unable to prevent a self-defeating fight against La Follette's renomination, had announced that he was not seeking reelection. The conservatives could not rally around their most popular figure, and, desiring his reelection, they could not replace him with an active candidate. The governor's supporters could not reject so esteemed a Wisconsin representative, even if he had opposed their program. Consequently the platform commended his career, expressed regret "for his announced determination not to serve the state another term in the Senate," and offered to reelect him "should he now find it possible to reconsider his decision and express his willingness to stand as a candidate in harmony with the sentiments and in support of the platform of principles here adopted by Wisconsin Republicans." The statement emphasized the "halfbreed" commitment to ideals and put Spooner on the defensive without denying him support.[7]

It was true that the Wisconsin "stalwarts" had great authority in Washington — Payne was Postmaster General, Babcock ran the congressional campaign committee, Henry Casson was sergeant-at-arms, and Spooner was a close presidential advisor; unfortunately, the fight took place in Wisconsin. Payne used federal patronage against La Follette, but his major focus was the unprecedented nomination of an accidental President, and since La Follette supported Roosevelt, Payne had to emphasize other states.[8] Besides, La Follette had sufficient gubernatorial patronage. While Pfister had a great deal of money with which to run the "stalwart" campaign, so did Stephenson, and the incumbent spent it more wisely. Pfister rented the eleventh floor of a Milwaukee office building; the progressives, promptly labeling his group the eleventh story league, used it as an excuse to move the convention to Madison. When Pfister tried to buy editorial support from hundreds of newspapers, John Hannan uncovered the story for the Milwaukee *Free Press*. The "stalwart" candidate, the able but colorless John Whitehead, had failed to excite the electorate in 1900 and did no better in 1902. The Washington "stalwarts" had advised conceding a traditional renomination to La Follette and concentration on the legislature. By running an inept campaign against a dynamic and popular governor, who had completely recuperated from a severe illness, they gave La Follette a rationale for his intended legislative purge.

With his 144-page Voters' Handbook and eight-page supplement *The Battle Only Half Over*, La Follette blanketed the state with his version of the previous session; roll call votes emphasized legislators' stands on taxation and the primary. He easily won renomination, was reelected over the conservative David Rose, aided by "fair minded Democrats," but lost more Republican votes than he gained Democrat and ran 10,000 votes behind the ticket. The "halfbreeds" won an impressive majority of the assembly and twice as many new senators as the "stalwarts," but since half the Senate was held over from the previous session La Follette fell just short of a senate majority.[9]

Speaking to a largely new and inexperienced legislature, La Follette once again took the initiative in a three-hour message, hammering home the issues of direct primary and ad valorem taxation of railroads and introducing the issue of a regulative railroad commission (coinciding with President Roosevelt's efforts to tighten the Interstate Commerce Act). Once again, he sought to put his opponents on the defensive by chiding them for neglecting to follow a mandate to accept the tax commission recommendations, accusing them of superficial examination of the ad valorem bill and of having succumbed to railroad lobbyists. He identified himself with the people and asked the legislators whether they would be identified with the people or the railroad interests on election day. Brushing aside the supposed difficulty of ad valorem assessment, he insisted that railroad value was readily determined as collateral for loans or for sale. Presenting an exhaustive expert compilation of statistics comparing rates between Milwaukee and 136 towns with lower rates in Iowa, he set favorable terms for the debate over railroad regulation. When his figures were disputed as too selective, he produced a special 178-page message with ten pages of supplementary tables comparing rates for every station of Wisconsin's two major railroads with those in Illinois and Iowa. Although Emanuel Phillipp entered an equally comprehensive rebuttal, La Follette was to have greater success convincing voters.[10]

But the battle was not yet to be engaged before the electorate. The first field of combat was a divided legislature: the "halfbreeds" controlled the Assembly; the "stalwarts" maintained a slim margin in the Senate. La Follette devised the tactic of rallying support and preparing public opinion by sending repeated messages at strategic instances. Early encounters led to a standoff. The "halfbreeds" could not attempt to block Spooner once he had reconsidered and become a candidate, for his career in Washington was a source of state pride; therefore, they took the initiative in his reelection. On the other hand, faced with a tax commission report that they should have paid $2,788,530 on an ad valorem basis rather than the $1,600,379 that they paid in license fees and buffeted by a vigorous campaign for a commission, the railroad managers attempted delaying tactics; unsuccessful, they retreated and withdrew their opposition to tax reform. But paired with tax reform was a companion bill to have accountants check the accuracy of reported railroad income. State auditors were to find evidence of over a million dollars in rebates upon which no taxes had been paid; after a court fight the state collected payment.

In an effort to catch his opponents off balance La Follette immediately presented a direct primary bill. The measure was swiftly pushed through the Assembly by the new speaker, Irvine Lenroot, then thirty years old with but one legislative session of experience. First, the bill was deliberately stalled in the upper house. Then John Gaveney, Keyes' son-in-law, added a popular referendum to provisions applying to state and national office, delaying implementation and giving its adversaries another chance to defeat it. Lobbyists descended upon Madison until they were more numerous than legislators. Babcock assumed leadership and promoted Spooner's plan to allow the primary to pass with a referendum clause. Reluctantly, the "halfbreeds" found it necessary to accede to this proposal.

On all other issues the "stalwarts" won pyrrhic victories. An imposing lobbying effort, including a convention of shippers, defeated the railroad commission. But La Follette was only preparing the issue for the 1904 election and the shippers' lobby was discredited with disclosures that they received rebates and favors from the railroads. And his unsuccessful effort to legislate a railroad rate freeze was generally thought to have prevented increases and to have caused some reductions. Other casualties of the session were anti-lobby, anti-rebate, grain inspection, and telephone regulation bills.[11]

By the end of the session no one could doubt that La Follette would seek reelection. Many of his proposals had been defeated, and he had identified his political career with his political program. Without him at the head of the ticket a vigorous "stalwart" campaign against the primary might have been successful. At first glance the election appeared to have been a rerun of 1902. Once again La Follette was the central issue, and he attracted deep commitment or furious antagonism. None of his adversaries had his charismatic appeal. Two attractive and competent candidates were advanced, each of whom had prior identification with the La Follette coalition: Emil Baensch and Samuel Cook. They ran a harmony campaign; Baensch used as his slogan: "FOR ROOSEVELT, BAENSCH AND PARTY PEACE."[12] Once again the campaign was issue-oriented and as much a struggle for control of the legislature as the governorship. There the similarity ended. This time the opposition was well led by Babcock. La Follette retained the advantages of incumbency but had to overcome strong prejudice against a third term. On the other hand, this time the progressives had more holdover senators and the advantage in that contest. Both sides were heavily committed, and feelings were intense. "The men of means and Employers are about as crazy as were the Millerites who gave up their homes and all under insane delusions," wrote one La Follette supporter. "I have never known so much bitterness or determination among the 'big ones' so called in this Co." They "have their employees frightened badly." Factory workers were afraid to come to La Follette rallies, he reported.[13] The "stalwarts" turned out an army of federal officeholders and railroad employes in an effort to garner votes for their candidates. State officeholders, most particularly the ubiquitous game wardens and inspectors of illuminating oil, matched their activity. The progressives found Democratic chairmen trying to keep "fair minded" Democrats away from the Republican caucuses, but in some counties conservative Democrats were aiding the "stalwarts."[14] John Strange observed that "Cook is using money like 'a drunken sailor,'"[15] while La Follette headquarters was besieged with pleas for funds with which to pay workers.[16] But the "halfbreeds" had a unique weapon: Robert M. La Follette. After his 1903 Chautauqua lectures "Fighting Bob" returned to the county fairs, reading statistics, comparing railroad rates for that county with lower rates elsewhere. Later, he criss-crossed the state seeking delegates and challenging antagonistic legislators. Here he introduced a new device, one that shocked supporters as well as opponents — the roll call. La Follette pictured the roll call as wholly impersonal and not bearing on any individual. "I have no personal feeling against those who do not agree with me but pursue this course solely from a sense of duty to the public," he informed one opponent while suggesting an appearance at the meeting would be embarrassing.[17] It is hard to imagine a candidate listening while La Follette listed his votes, implying greater concern for the interests than his constituents, and agreeing that it was all impersonal. It was a highly effective technique, pitting "Battle Bob," the champion of the people, against the vested interests. His personal efforts were backed by a superb organization. He started with a list of 1500 militants who would quickly contribute their time or money; a second compilation of 10,000 unquestioned supporters; and a catalogue of 100,000 or more to whom a reasonable appeal for aid could be made. These indexes were revised and enlarged, broken down into the smallest political unit, the school district, and one man in each district was responsible to distribute literature and mobilize the vote. In his speeches, and in more than a million pieces of literature, La Follette emphasized only a few issues: equity required that the railroads pay an additional million dollars in new and back taxes, that a railroad commission should equalize Wisconsin freight rates with those in neighboring states, and that the voters should endorse the primary election. By emphasizing the huge rebates granted to favored shippers, La Follette undermined the defense of the railroads and their shipper allies. Babcock was forced to divert his energies to combat a favorite son challenge to his renomination; this was followed in the general election by support for his Democratic opponent, reducing a normal 8000 to 10,000 Republican majority to 385. Despite Philipp's "Red Book" disputing La Follette's rate figures, despite the "stalwarts'" aggressive and extensive campaign, the governor met with considerable success. Of the 533 votes needed for nomination the incumbent had 515⅓ uncontested delegates. Unfortunately, in such a hotly contested election every available technique was employed by both sides, and there were numerous delegate challenges.[18]

Both sides were convinced that they had a majority. The state central committee, which decided delegate contests, was dominated by La Follette partisans. In the proceedings that followed, enough La Follette delegates were seated by unanimous vote (including the "stalwart" members) to give La Follette a majority. This was conceded on May 7 by a Milwaukee *Sentinel* dispatch to the Chicago *Tribune*.[19] The results were not acceptable to the "stalwarts" and they accused the "halfbreeds" of voting Democrats (probably true at least in Dane county) and of mounting phony challenges so that delegates could be stolen by the central committee. To publicize their case, the "stalwarts" met at the opera house the day before the Madison convention and demanded that the rights of delegates be respected the following day. Amid rumors of violence the "stalwarts" gathered at the opera house an hour before the opening of the convention in the university gymnasium and marched the mile to the session, four abreast, preceded by two American flags. There they were met by an unprecedented scene. They were diverted, individually, though a barbed-wire passage, to a small side entrance and overawed by burly attendants. Dignified party wheelhorses felt humiliated as each had to present credentials countersigned by the state central committee. Inside, a heavily guarded eight-foot wire fence separated spectators from delegates. The "halfbreeds" were determined to prevent any seizure of the convention. Acting on a rumor that M. B. Rosenberry was going to seize the gavel after presenting the minority report on the delegate contests, Rosenberry was surrounded by three "heavies" and only the intercession of Bryant enabled him to make his motion. Irvine Lenroot, as chairman, ruled the motion out of order. He was sustained, and the majority report on the credential challenges was passed. The Baensch delegates walked out and retired to a new convention at the opera house. The Cook delegates joined them after the nomination of La Follette. Former governors Upham and Scofield, Senators Quarles and Spooner, and Congressman Babcock highlighted a convention that chose Cook as its nominee after the withdrawal of Baensch.[20]

Each convention sent four delegates to the Republican national convention, prepared to nominate President Roosevelt. Receiving short shrift from the Republican national committee, the members of the La Follette contingent decided not to present their case before the credentials committee; they just filed the reasons for their decision and returned to fight in Wisconsin where they had the advantage.[21]

The "stalwarts" petitioned the Wisconsin Supreme Court to issue a writ restraining Secretary of State Walter Houser (a "halfbreed") from designating the La Follette ticket as the regular slate, claiming that the Republican national committee had authenticated the "stalwarts" as the regular Republicans. On October 6 the court rejected their plea without commenting on the authenticity of either convention. The state law, it declared, left the decision to the state central committee. At this point Cook withdrew, Scofield replaced him, and, with the death of Payne, Roosevelt finally called off any fight against La Follette. He ordered that their names be coupled during the campaign, for harmony was in their mutual interest. Most "stalwarts" shifted their support to the Democratic candidate, a move Roosevelt suggested should have been done earlier rather than endanger the national ticket.[22]

While the court fight was still in process, Lincoln Steffens' favorable account of the governor appeared in *McClure's*. By his own account Steffens arrived in Wisconsin expecting to find the state run by a demagogue. As he questioned both sides he began to see La Follette much as La Follette saw himself. Through July, as Steffens was writing his article, the La

Follette faction fed him information: Belle suggested that Stephenson be given proper credit, and Gilbert Roe, who now lived in New York, conferred with the journalist. When Belle saw one of the final drafts of the manuscript she wrote to Steffens that his article "is something I have longed for, yet hardly daring to hope for and really never expected. To have you turn your searchlight on Wisconsin politics is better than anything our guardian angel could do for us." Nevertheless, she had some suggestions for changes: While Hall should receive proper emphasis for his work on the railroad planks, La Follette did not just borrow his ideas; he had supported these principles during his congressional career. Gilbert Roe requested that the use of game wardens be deemphasized for they did their job properly and their activities were not against the law, unlike political campaigning by federal officials. To aid La Follette's campaign, Roe suggested that Steffens remove references to La Follette's ambitions beyond the executive mansion. Steffens headlined his article: "Wisconsin: a State where the People have restored Representative Government." There is trouble in Wisconsin, he announced. La Follette will not play the game. La Follette was a good politician who used patronage to build a machine to fight bad business men. He traced La Follette's career sympathetically and showed the techniques used to prevent his program from being enacted. The article reached the newstands in late September, was sold out by October 2, and enhanced La Follette's growing image as a national figure.[23]

On the eve of the elections La Follette dealt a final blow to his adversaries. Drawing upon a federal refund of a Civil War debt to remit state property taxes for the second year in a row, he refuted charges of extravagance. Despite his appeal to both Social Democratic and Democratic voters, he lost so many "stalwarts" that he ran 100,000 votes behind Roosevelt and 50,000 votes behind the state ticket. But the electorate approved of the primary. The governor showed gains only in the more recently settled, poor, rural north and west, among Swedish and Norwegian voters. He continued to fare poorly among the Germans and lost considerable strength in the more prosperous southern counties. The bitterness engendered by his political tactics and program brought a higher percentage of voters to the polls than in any other election from 1900 to 1914.

Nevertheless, the "stalwart" faction was shattered for the time being, and La Follette's wooing of Bryan Democrats eliminated the Democrats as a viable force in Wisconsin for a decade.[24]

On January 12, 1905 the triumphant governor addressed a legislature that he controlled for the first time, for only three "stalwart" senators had been reelected. He reported with pleasure that the tax changes during his first two terms had yielded sufficient revenue to reduce the direct tax levy. Ad valorem taxes had been so much more lucrative than license fees that he suggested their application to electric railway and lighting companies with the income returning to the locality. To complete his revenue program he called for a mortgage and graduated income tax. He sought to make the tax system more equitable with a larger share imposed on those who benefited most from society.

Once again, a large portion of his address, forty-one pages, was devoted to the subject of railroads. Protesting against high and discriminatory rates which favored the competitors of Wisconsin cities and which promoted consolidation of businesses, he called for the establishment of a regulatory commission to investigate all shipper complaints, which would take the initiative to examine rates where shippers feared railroad retaliation. Since interstate railroads made greater profits on their Wisconsin mileage, he was certain that rates were excessive. A uniform accounting system would be mandated so that profits could not be hidden. Effective publicity would limit the need for enforcement. And overcapitalization, a particular ploy of railroad promoters, could be prevented by requiring commission approval for new issues. Consumer interests would be protected by commission employment of experts. The legislature had before it a comprehensive regulatory program.

But La Follette had not completed his presentation. Railroad employes who suffered industrial accidents were to be compensated. Corporations were not to be permitted to make political contributions; trusts and lobbies were to be controlled; the civil service merit system was to be extended and a civil service commission created. Rural common schools, which he knew from experience functioned poorly, were to be replaced with central schools to which students would be bussed.[25]

Once again La Follette was frustrated in attaining his goals, but this time the delay was temporary. The progressives could not agree on a candidate to replace Senator Quarles. To no one's surprise "Uncle Ike" Stephenson felt he was entitled to the position. He reminded the governor of his contributions to the party and insisted that "stalwarts" were more likely to support him than any one else.[26] La Follette advised Stephenson to come himself or to place someone completely trustworthy in charge of his campaign. He agreed with Stephenson's opinion "that it would be unwise and unsafe for me to declare that I would under no circumstances accept the senatorship." He warned that "halfbreeds" would abandon a candidate who depended on "stalwart" votes.[27] As more and more candidates entered the race La Follette grew increasingly perturbed. He feigned illness as an excuse to cancel Chautauqua engagements. He repeatedly refused the position while the Milwaukee *Sentinel* was predicting he would maneuver a stalemate that only he could break. Finally, without ever testing Stephenson's contention that he had enough "stalwart" support to carry a caucus vote, La Follette accepted the designation, conditional upon passage of his program. Stephenson was clearly disappointed, but the relationship remained friendly. La Follette continued to court him; Stephenson needed La Follette if he were ever to fulfill his ambition of serving in the U.S. Senate. Despite his own desires, when it was rumored that La Follette had called the special session in December to relinquish the seat if Stephenson could be elected, the wealthy old logger urged him to go to Washington.[28]

La Follette delayed resigning as governor pending the acceptance of his program. Expert advisers and legislative leaders drafted his most important measure, the railroad commission bill; authorities of national stature were consulted. W. H. Hatton, who was instrumental in writing the bill, conducted open hearings, and guided the proposal through the senate. To indicate the depth of his commitment La Follette threatened to resign from the Senate and run for the commission when opponents pressed for an elective rather than an appointive commission. Aided by a special address by William Jennings Bryan, long a friend of the governor, the bill received unanimous approval of both houses although it included regulation of telegraph and telephone companies and was far more stringent than any existing national legislation. La Follette was disappointed that the commission could not prevent over-capitalization by regulating the issuance of securities. In other proposals he met with marked, if not perfect success. The legislature passed civil service reforms for state officeholders but failed to extend them to local officials; and incumbents were required to pass the same tests as candidates, forcing the removal of a few of his own appointees. It limited lobbyists to appearances before legislative committees. It strengthened corrupt practices provisions. La Follette followed Roosevelt's lead in the area of conservation and showed foresight in his concern for the ecological relation between waterways and forests. He obtained a forestry service and set aside 250,000 acres. By having waterpower resources surveyed he showed an early awareness of the future of electricity. He also understood the need to protect the consumers of electricity. To prevent monopolization of water power sites he provided for nullification of a franchise if a dam had not been built within four years. He failed to obtain a second choice provision for primaries to prevent a minority candidate from being nominated. His call for a special session to complete his legislative program was unavailing, although he did obtain an investigation of insurance companies. A true Australian secret ballot was defeated.[29]

As La Follette's gubernatorial career was drawing to a close, the La Follettes decided not to return to their former home but to look for a farm. After considerable hesitation about the high price, $30,000, they finally purchased Maple Bluff Farm, sixty acres of working farm three and a half miles from Capitol Square, with twelve hundred feet of Lake Mendota shoreline, a view of the city, a dairy herd, and eleven acres of orchard. After a particularly successful season of Chautauqua engagements in 1906 the senior La Follette bought eight Shetland pony mares and a stallion and ordered stationery headed "La Follette Brothers Shetland Pony Farm." The family grew so attached to the animals that few were sold and the operation was never profitable, but it imparted to the two boys a disciplined sense of responsibility. A second personal decision was to leave the younger children at a boarding school until a suitable family home could be found in Washington.[30]

As he prepared to embark on a new phase of his career, "to participate in that great work, which was to deal immediately with the problems President Roosevelt has courageously pressed upon Congress for solution," La Follette could look back on his accomplishments with satisfaction. He had enacted the bulk of the Wisconsin Idea. He had introduced corporate taxation based upon physical evaluation. His railroad commission had been given more power and made more effective than its national counterpart. It could initiate investigations or examine a complaint, set absolute, not only maximum rates, based on physical evaluation; rates dated from the commission order, even during a court challenge; the burden of proof rested with the railroad, and it could not discredit the commission with reversal obtained by introducing new material without due notice. Responding to Philipp's criticism, rates could be adapted to industrial conditions, available to all under the same circumstances. Uniform accounting and the service of experts made the commission particularly effective, and the reduction of rebates partially compensated the railroads for lower rates. The commission could act upon complaints of inadequate service, restoring a common law requirement that, he had argued as early as 1887, had fallen victim to railroad combination and arrogance.[31] And regulation did not injure the economy; in fact, Wisconsin's economic gains exceeded the national average. As La Follette said: "The object of our legislation was not to 'smash' corporations, but to drive them out of politics, and then to treat them exactly as other people are treated. Equality under the law was our guiding star."[32]

La Follette set new political standards and patterns that were widely emulated. To him, the party platform was not a political catch-all to garner votes and then to be forgotten. "They are the party's promise to do specific things. They are the voter's guide in determining with what party he will affiliate. They constitute a written contract deliberately entered into with every man who casts his vote for the candidate of his party. Neither the party nor the official representative of the party can with honor repudiate that contract."[33] After finally gaining control of the party mechanism which would have enabled him to determine nominations he kept his commitment to a direct primary, and his candidate lost in the first contest for governor. The second choice provision never proved successful, and divisions among progressive factions enabled minority "stalwart" candidates to slip in. Primary contests were a commonplace, for the anti-boss rhetoric of the progressives and the separate power bases of members of the coalition made it impossible to impose any man's will on their wing.

After all, the progressive movement was not so much a unified impulse as it was a convergence of differing philosophies at a given time on given issues. It was agreed only that giant corporations had assumed too dominant a role in political and economic life, that the ordinary citizen must be protected from this overweening power, and that his input into the political process must be restored. With widely different political philosophies, some supporters withdrew at an early stage, satisfied that their program had been enacted; others, identified with the movement well beyond its peak, and continued to disagree with their peers in general perception and specific legislation.[34] To complicate matters, by recruiting men of high calibre to state service (partially through increased salaries), by drawing upon experts from the universities, industry, and government, La Follette introduced men of an independent character who could not be controlled. Nils Haugen, who was appointed to the tax commission, successfully insisted upon full valuation for property tax even though La Follette did not want its application to ordinary farmers, whom he always favored. For the railroad commission La Follette chose the head of the university's transportation department, B. H. Meyers, an able Democratic lawyer, John Barnes, and the Commissioner of Industrial and Labor Statistics, Halford Erickson. He forged a close relationship with the university. Academicians, such as John Commons, attended regular Saturday lunches with the governor and key legislators and served as advisers; and the university was well enough funded to attract national scholars. An important innovation of La Follette's tenure was one for which he was not particularly responsible. Since about half the legislature of 1901 had only a common school education and only a fifth some

post-high school training, Charles McCarthy, a Ph.D. from the
university, created a legislative reference library. The legislator
would spell out his concern and the library would draft the bill,
supply precedents, indicate states with similar laws and collect
newspaper clippings on the operation of the existing laws. "It
might almost be said that, when we look at the Wisconsin of
today," wrote John R. Commons, "we see what many other
states will be ten years from now."[35]

CHAPTER 5

# "Rattling of Dry Bones"

L A FOLLETTE'S reputation preceded the junior senator to the nation's capitol. Walter Wellman wrote in the *Review of Reviews:* "He has become so accustomed to battle that it is doubtful if he can be happy in the repose and calm of peace; hence the prediction, so often heard of him, that when he gets going in the United States Senate there will be a rattling of dry bones."[1] The Senate was dominated by the arch-conservative Nelson B. Aldrich of Rhode Island; La Follette's long-time antagonist, John Spooner, was a major figure in the hierarchy. President Theodore Roosevelt had a progressive reputation and his rhetoric stimulated the progressive movement. Yet, La Follette found no solace in this quarter. Roosevelt considered him to be "not evenly balanced and dangerous to the general welfare of the country and the party."[2] Despite Governor La Follette's endorsement of his administration, Roosevelt's patronage had been placed at the service of "Battle Bob's" enemies. Dissimilar conceptions of legislative goals and tactics were to cause early differences between these two leading progressives. Roosevelt looked over the composition of the legislature, examined his patronage and publicity resources, and then accepted the best bill he could pass during a given session; La Follette, drawing upon his Wisconsin experience, refused to accept any measure that he felt would not be adequate to do the job. Fearing the blunting of public pressure by watered down enactments, he preferred no legislation until the membership of the body could be altered sufficiently to pass a satisfactory bill.[3]

Nevertheless the La Follettes received a cordial reception. Spooner presented La Follette's credentials to the Senate in accordance with custom; and patronage was settled acceptably — Spooner received the western district and La Follette the eastern. Roosevelt greeted them at a White House reception for the diplomatic corps as old friends; they had met when he was the civil service commissioner, and he had been their guest in Madison. While many of their former acquaintances had left, others were still in office and remained friendly. But Washington had changed. Socially, "While there seemed to be more wealth, there was less display, and good taste more generally prevailed; homes were more artistic; dress more becoming; manners quieter; voices lower." It was less picturesque and colorful, more conventional, and less democratic. Apartment houses now seemed to dominate the architecture of the city. It was much more quiet and convenient than the boarding house of their congressional days. They took a large apartment at the Ontario, where occasional sounds from the zoo added to their sense of isolation. After finding a satisfactory maid and another apartment to serve as the Senator's office, the La Follettes found the situation fully comfortable.[4]

As an experienced legislator La Follette was aware of the importance of committee assignments. When asked about his preference he made just one request, a place on the Interstate Commerce Committee, where his expertise on railroads could be of service. Instead, he was made chairman of the committee to investigate the condition of the Potomac River front. "I had immediate visions of cleaning up the whole Potomac River front until I found that in all its history the committee had never had a bill referred to it for consideration, and had never held a meeting." He was placed on three committees with enough routine to keep him busy; claims, Indian affairs, and pensions. Once again, he used the assignment on Indian affairs to block the Indians' exploitation.[5]

But he first made headlines as a senator in 1906 in the debate on railroad legislation. As a congressman he had been a vocal supporter of the law to create the Interstate Commerce Commission and he had just completed an extended bout with the Wisconsin railroads after which they came under strict control and had to pay equitable taxes. In the intervening years the Interstate Commerce Commission had been stripped of much of its authority by the Supreme Court. Of the sixteen decisions by the high tribunal involving appeals from commission rulings the court had overturned fifteen and sustained one. In 1897 in the maximum freight case the ICC had been deprived of the right to determine rates. In 1902 Congress had tried to at least prevent rebates with the Elkins Act. Now, under pressure from the public and the President the Hepburn Bill had passed the House and had been released by a reluctant Senate Committee on Interstate Commerce. La Follette felt the measure to be wholly inadequate. Through the intercession of Lincoln Steffens he had an extended interview with Roosevelt, explaining its deficiencies and soliciting support for corrective amendments. The President observed that no such bill could pass Congress, and La Follette was left to his own resources. He decided to depart from the senatorial custom of freshman silence and to make a major speech on the subject.

His first speech as a senator had considerable impact. Although he began the same day as reports were being received about the San Franciscan earthquake, nevertheless, he spoke to overflowing galleries for two and a half hours on April 19, three and a half hours on April 20 and completed the speech on April 23. The constitutional opposition to the bill rested largely upon the procedure for testing ICC orders. This was the wrong emphasis, he asserted. "The authority of the Commission may be so limited that the procedure for the enforcement of its orders will be relatively of little importance. . . . To permit the railroads to control the commerce of the country is, in the final analysis, to permit the railroads to control the country." The sovereign has the right to require common carriers to render service upon reasonable and equal terms. Effective regulation required the prohibition of preliminary injunctions to prevent corporate efforts to delay judgement. Courts should be limited to procedural, not substantive judicial review, for the ICC knew more about the facts and, if citizens must accept a jury's decision on facts a corporation could not have the facts tried over again in court.

At this point he noticed the rapid diminution of Republican Senators in the chamber. Mindful of the deliberate snub administered to Albert Beveridge of Indiana for a similar indiscretion, La Follette ignored a possibility that occurred to his wife at the time, that his colleagues were taking a luncheon break after an exciting debate between Albert Hopkins and Benjamin Tillman, and rebuked the assemblage. "Mr.

President, I pause in my remarks to say this," he interpolated, "I cannot be wholly indifferent to the fact that Senators by their absence at this time indicate their want of interest in what I may have to say upon this subject. The public is interested. Unless this important question is rightly settled seats now temporarily vacant may be permanently vacated by those who have the right to occupy them at this time." His self-righteous indignation was warmly applauded by visitors and invoked a threat to clear the galleries by the chair. Colonel Hannan thought that his friend had committed a political mistake, but by late afternoon of the first day the senators were listening with at least one ear, and attention increased as the speech unfolded.

Resuming his speech, La Follette asserted that the Sherman Act alone could not eliminate trusts; the alliance with railroads must end; competition had been undermined with rebates, discriminatory rates, pools, traffic agreements, and combinations until ninety percent of railroad mileage was controlled by six sets of financiers. After adverse court decisions the ICC had requested that Congress empower it to investigate the reasonableness of rates on its own initiative or that of shippers (who were reluctant to risk retaliation). The attempt to control rebates with the Elkins Act had been followed only by increased charges. The Hepburn Bill "will not solve the transportation problem"; it only patched holes created by judicial decisions. The Senate should not accept the argument that this bill was all that could be attained but should clothe the government with regulatory authority to the limit of its constitutional power. Large shippers were only concerned with equal rates, but equal levies could still be too high; the government must protect its citizens against excessive taxation, whether by railroads or itself. Recommendations by the ICC had been ignored. The bill permitted it to act only upon a complaint; it should act on its own initiative, he maintained, or a public body be created to act for consumers. Without evaluating railroad property reasonable rates could not be set; levies based on overcapitalized stock confiscated the property of the public. Without the ability to determine equitable classification of freight effective charges could be altered. Without power to set minimum as well as maximum tariffs railroads could favor a company by reducing tolls. Without authority to determine when differences in conditions warranted unequal long and short haul rates, courts would continue to render ineffective provisions against such discrimination. Railroads should not be permitted to discredit the ICC by introducing testimony in court that had been withheld from the commission. The bill lacked safety provisions, did not eliminate free passes, and did not cover express companies. Investments should come from new capital, not high tolls. Railroad profits, he insisted, were inordinate; freight charges exceeded the Prussian system, and passenger fares were twice as high. "Sir. I say to the Senate here to-day that nothing, *absolutely nothing*, can prevent the ultimate government ownership of the railroads of this country except a strict government control of the railroads of this country." The public must be protected from this natural monopoly, he concluded.

Senator Joseph Foraker of Ohio questioned La Follette's interpretation of ICC recommendation, and the freshman Senator refuted the veteran with quotes from official reports. The bill's sponsor, Senator Jonathan Dolliver, was convinced in debate that equitable imposts could not be adequately determined without physical valuation and supported him on that issue thereafter. La Follette's efforts to amend the bill received considerable Democratic support but little from Republicans. He failed to obtain maximum hours' provisions, to prevent railroads and railroad officials from acquiring coal and asphalt lands and eliminating independent competitors. In disgust he offered an amendment he thought self-evident, prohibiting judges from hearing regulatory cases involving railroads in which they held a pecuniary interest, only to see even this proposal rejected. Unable to obtain Roosevelt's support he still asserted that it did not comply with the President's 1901 recommendation of "just rates" or his 1904 request for "reasonable rates." Ironically his efforts were important in creating a climate that contributed to the bill's passage. Displeased with the result, he wrote to Roosevelt insisting that the statute was written for shippers, not consumers. That summer he read the roll in sixteen states and, returning to the battle in the next session, succeeded at least in passing a bill to limit the hours of continuous service of railroadmen to sixteen hours.[6]

During the debate on the Hepburn Bill La Follette had mentioned the problem of Indian lands and had sought an amendment to protect the tribes' surface holdings when they leased mines to railroads. He was suspicious when the Senate committee amended a House bill to extend leasing of coal sites belonging to the Choctaws and Chickasaws to permit their sale. La Follette checked with the director of geological survey and found that 413,000 acres of superior bituminous coal had been located on this property and that railroads controlled the leases for 112,000 acres ostensibly held by private coal mining companies. His opposition to the amendment in committee and on the floor was unsuccessful, but public airing prevented immediate action.[7]

At the same time La Follette convinced the President to support a joint resolution withdrawing public coal, oil, and lignite land from public sale. In the absence of congressional action Roosevelt withdrew a million acres of coal sites from the market during the summer. When Congress convened La Follette introduced a comprehensive measure to protect all government-owned coal lands. Roosevelt supported an administration proposal as La Follette's bill stalled, much to his chagrin. Senators feared that his measure would retard state development, the President informed him: "I am very anxious to get some substantial measure of relief this session, and we can then amend and improve it as may be found necessary in the future far more easily than if we had nothing on the statute books." La Follette protested that the administration proposal left too much to executive discretion, but Roosevelt refused to be bound by La Follette's bill and responded that his new Secretary of Interior, James Garfield, felt the administration's vehicle would accomplish more. Disappointed, La Follette continued to press both for the protection of Indian rights and for the preservation of coal reserves.[8] Despite disputes about the means to be used to achieve their ends, La Follette continued to support Roosevelt and publicly defended his reputation well into the next administration, though privately he expressed reservations about his trimming once the dispute with Taft had begun.[9]

While making his mark in Washington, La Follette was

instrumental in bringing about a split in the Wisconsin progressive camp. Lieutenant Governor James O. Davidson had succeeded the senator. A poor Norwegian immigrant, Davidson had been a tailor, a store clerk, a store owner, and had risen through political ranks until, from 1898, he was the highest ranking Norwegian officeholder in the state. As governor, he had led many progressives who had fulfilled their progressive goals and looked towards a period of retrenchment and the healing of party wounds. La Follette and some of his closest associates wanted to carry the movement forward, and the Senator drafted Irvine Lenroot, a young legislative leader who preferred to run for Congress. Davidson had a good progressive record, and had performed well as governor, and La Follette had difficulty rallying even his own supporters. William D. Connor, the powerful state chairman, joined Davidson. Haugen remained silent; Stephenson imposed neutrality on the Milwaukee *Free Press* and refused to finance the campaign. La Follette could not canvass since he was forced to raise funds on the Chautauqua circuit and exposed himself to charges of bossism. Lenroot was Swedish and could not attract Norwegian votes only one year after the two countries had separated with bitterness. La Follette's only solace was that Babcock was defeated in the general election.[10]

More important than Lenroot's defeat was a weakness that it disclosed in the progressive movement. If one of their issues was bossism, how could the progressives resolve conflicting ambitions and differing assessments of candidates' strength? Who was to determine the proper progressive response to an issue? How could they prevent the election of minority conservative contestants if they could not unite behind a progressive? How could they prevent a progressive aspirant from making a deal with conservatives? These questions plagued the movement throughout La Follette's career.

Hoping to heal some of the wounds of the previous year, when Spooner resigned in 1907 La Follette threw his support to "Uncle Ike." Stephenson indicated he was content to cap his career by serving for the remainder of Spooner's term, providing his opposition withdrew. Unfortunately, La Follette's inability to control the ambition of Lenroot and William Hatton was interpreted by Stephenson and his

followers as lack of real support. Stephenson felt the heated opposition to his candidacy released him from his pledge; La
Follette did not agree. Although the two senators cooperated,
Stephenson was satisfied with their accomplishments in
Wisconsin and would not join La Follette in his efforts to spark
a national progressive movement: "I did not choose to purify
the politics of other states." There was an open political break
between two men who had once been drawn to personal
intimacy through politics. The wealthy incumbent was opposed
for reelection by two progressives, State Senator William
Hatton, so quietly aided by La Follette that many supporters
were not informed, and Milwaukee District Attorney Francis
McGovern, who had his own urban power base. Stephenson obtained a plurality in the preferential primary and was
investigated for spending $107,000; in the absence of fraud he
was elected only to be frustrated by the Senate for two years
while the subject was rehashed; though narrowly seated he
became embittered by La Follette's unnecessary harrassment.

In the meantime, Davidson defeated La Follette in every
encounter. He was renominated without opposition. The convention rejected La Follette's campaign planks, defeated the
second choice primary, and elected Stephenson's campaign
manager chairman of the state central committee. La Follette
campaigned in Herman Ekern's independent race for reelection;
Davidson supported his successful opponent. Pundits predicted
La Follette would be in trouble in 1910.[11]

Reverses in Wisconsin did not deter La Follette from his
larger goals: a national progressive movement that he would
lead from the White House. In the meantime he settled himself
more permanently in Washington. He left his apartment for a
rented furnished house, brought the children east with a
companion and teacher, and added to the household two young
Wisconsin neighbors, who relieved Belle of household chores,
and his secretary. He took issue again with a White House
resident whom he largely supported, for he hoped to forge a
progressive consciousness. Now he spoke with the authority of
an established senator widely reported as a possible presidential candidate. But he had even less support from fellow
Republican senators than during the Hepburn debates. And he
was even more determined for he hoped to defeat rather than

improve a bill. The measure was the Aldrich-Vreeland proposal to issue to national banks $500,000,000 of emergency currency based upon state, municipal and railroad bonds; it had been moved for passage in response to the financial panic of 1907. In mid-March, 1908, La Follette presented ten pages of evidence to establish the role of interlocking directorates in centralizing banking and industry. This legislation was unnecessary, he insisted, for the country was prosperous and the currency was sufficiently elastic. Bankers really wanted a source of money for inflation and speculation. J. P. Morgan had precipitated the current American financial stringency by raising interest rates, reducing commercial loans, and funneling funds into the stock market. The panic had been created to chastise Roosevelt for demanding improved railroad regulation, urging the restraint and prosecution of capitalists for violating the law, and "announcing the novel doctrine that criminal statutes were for the rich as well as the poor." Morgan then used financial distress to acquire the Tennessee Coal, Iron and Railroad Company and to attack individual companies while protecting speculators.

Thorough revision of banking and currency laws was needed "to meet the evil practices which are undermining the integrity of bank management"; instead, the makeshift Aldrich bill required the treasury to accept unstable municipal and railroad bonds unacceptable to prudent bankers, as a basis to issue emergency currency. It would provide an entering wedge to base rates on watered railroad capitalization regardless of the physical value of the line. Banks could still make loans to their directors, he pointed out, and bank officials were not to be punished for wrongdoing.

Aldrich moved to meet some of La Follette's objections. Even before his speech Aldrich had removed the railroad bond provision and the Madisonian predicted that it would be returned in conference. He accepted two La Follette amendments: to prohibit banks from investing in corporate securities where they had interlocking directors; and to examine the volume of emergency bank notes outstanding. But the Senate decisively rejected criminal penalties for officials who invested bank funds in corporations in which they were directors.

When the bill returned from the House-Senate conference

committee La Follette was not surprised to see not only the
restoration of railroad bonds as collateral for currency, but the
elimination of his two amendments. Under parliamentary rules
a conference report could be debated but not amended. Unable
to defeat the measure, La Follette decided a filibuster could
mount enough public support to prevent a vote. Starting with
the aid of only two Democrats, W. J. Stone of Missouri and the
blind Thomas Gore of Oklahoma, he undertook a spectacular
but one-sided battle.

Although he had just recovered from influenza, on May 29,
1908 he filibustered for a record breaking nineteen hours in a
sweltering Senate chamber with the galleries "packed to
suffocation" while "long lines of people stood in the hot
corridors waiting for a chance to get in." Most of the Senators
vacated their seats to obtain relief from the heat, returning only
for quorum calls demanded by the filibusterers to rest the
speaker for six-minute spells, yet the walls of the Senate floor
were lined with fascinated Representatives, clerks, and congressional employes. Repeating arguments made before, La
Follette insisted that the bill would increase the tendency to
concentrate wealth, and digressed to discuss the tariff, railroad
regulation, and physical valuation. Periodically he sent word to
his daughter, Fola, that he was "feeling tip top." At about
11:30 P.M. a page brought him his usual glass of milk and egg;
he took a big swig; "take it away," he spat out, it's "drugged."
Ptomaine induced severe dysentery; he was only enabled to
continue by fleeing to the toilet during several roll calls in the
next two hours.

Aldrich, though seventy, never left the floor and never
rested. With the aid of unprecedented rulings by the chair,
sustained by his automatic majority, and some doctoring of the
*Congressional Record*, he outmaneuvered his opponents and
was in a position to break the filibuster when fortuitous circumstances intervened. After Stone had spoken for six hours Gore
took the floor for two hours. By arrangement Gore was to relinquish the floor to Stone who would hold it until La Follette
resumed. La Follette was in his committee room preparing
speech materials when the blind Senator turned to Stone and
yielded the floor; but Stone was not in his seat. Efforts by
Senator William Heyburn of Idaho to obtain recognition and

continue the filibuster were unavailing. La Follette returned to find the Senate in uproar, the roll call begun, and the contest terminated.[12]

With national attention focused on him as a result of the filibuster, La Follette turned his attention to the convention. In 1907 his closest advisers urged him to seek the presidency, and he did not have to be prodded. When Nils Haugen advised that his efforts were premature, he was no longer invited to conferences. La Follette's relationship with Stephenson was somewhat strained when the wealthy lumberman made only a small contribution to his war chest. Gilbert Roe called him the greatest democrat since Lincoln in the *Independent*. In an interview in *Everybody's* La Follette set the tone for his campaign: he was fighting to rid the government of agents of special privilege; he opposed those who sought unfair business advantages and wished to develop natural resources in their own interest rather than the public interest. Legislation for the special interests, he warned, produced wealth, but impoverished people, wealth to corrupt government and the courts "to get more resources, more profits and more power."[13] Congressman Henry Cooper presented the Wisconsin version of a campaign platform to the convention — it included physical valuation, direct election of senators, public inspection of campaign expenses, a tariff commission, tariff revision with rates based on the difference in the cost of production here and abroad, trust control, exemption of labor from anti-trust laws, and prohibition of injunctions in labor disputes — but it received scant attention.[14] Roosevelt delivered the nomination to William Howard Taft, and La Follette began to look towards 1912. While La Follette endorsed Taft and campaigned for the ticket, he was not entirely satisfied with Taft's candidacy; after all the Democratic candidate was his good friend William Jennings Bryan about whom he would say no ill. In offering his support he reserved the right to criticize defects in the platform. He questioned Taft's stand on physical valuation and obtained a hedging response from him. He questioned the candidate on the tariff and thought he had a firm commitment for downward revision. By mid-October La Follette was so involved in editing his journal that he offered to distribute 100,000 copies of the first issue, supporting Taft, in lieu of campaigning.[15] Referring

to La Follette's addresses Lincoln Steffens wrote to Tom
Johnson: "Take the Senator's speeches in support of Taft, but
in praise of Bryan, . . .he would come pretty near carrying the
state for Bryan."[16] The rotund and gregarious Secretary of
War, having distinguished himself in appointive judicial and
administrative posts, easily won his first elective test.

# CHAPTER 6

## *Trials of a Large Man*

F EW men have come to the presidency as well prepared as
William Howard Taft. He had had a distinguished judicial
career. As governor of the Philippines he had brought the
rebellion to an end while winning the respect and admiration of
former insurgents. Roosevelt had employed him as a foreign
affairs trouble shooter, and he had been an effective secretary of
war. His deficiencies were not yet noticeable, although his
lassitude was in marked contrast with the energy of his predecessor. He proved to be politically inept, while Roosevelt was
one of our most skillful practitioners. Roosevelt had advised
him to cooperate with Aldrich and Joseph Cannon to enact his
proposals; to many it appeared that he became their captive.
Taft saw his role as a consolidator, his task to complete and
perfect Roosevelt's program. The electorate had been aroused
by Roosevelt's rhetoric, by muckraking articles, by the fervor
and accomplishments of progressives on the state level — in
Wisconsin, Oregon, Missouri, New York and Colorado — and in
many municipalities; an insurgent cry for more direct
democracy and greater equity echoed north, south, east, and
west. La Follette's roll call had taken its toll in New Jersey and
Kansas. Progressive Republicans had been elected from Idaho,
Iowa, South Dakota, and Kansas. Jonathan Dolliver, Moses
Clapp, Albert Beveridge and Norris Brown ceased vacillating
and joined his crusade. Together with a resurgent Democracy
the progressive Republicans challenged the political establishment. Instead of cooperating with the minority in his party, —
men who were more in sympathy with his program than Aldrich
and Cannon, — Taft tried to stifle the opposition to the
congressional leadership, and the Republican party was torn
apart.

As the year 1909 began the La Follette family changed quarters once again, moving to a four-story English basement house on Wyoming Avenue. The senator occupied two connecting rooms on the first floor as an office. The second floor contained the two parlors and the dining room. The younger children and La Follette's secretary, Nellie Dunn, were settled on the third floor; and Bob and Belle lived at the top. For the first time the Senator felt secure enough to ask Belle to furnish the house "completely and comfortably and in good taste." They began to entertain more extensively and more liberally, for La Follette had an adequate income, and the house became the center of the progressive Republican caucus.[1]

A second change of importance was La Follette's decision to publish a personal journal. As the Milwaukee *Free Press* slipped from the progressive ranks, along with its owner, La Follette saw the need for a political organ. The publication was to be one of national scope, in keeping with the ambitions and importance of its originator. "La Follette's will be a magazine of progress, social, intellectual, institutional," he announced on the front page. "Engrossed in material development" of "a continent of vast riches" the nation permitted great industrial organizations to gain control of "politics, government and natural resources." In the "struggle between Special Privilege and Equal Rights. . .This magazine recognizes as its chief task that of aiding in winning back for the people complete power over government — national, state and municipal. . .". In the second issue he added:

IT WILL BE CONSERVATIVE WHEN GOOD THINGS ARE TO BE CONSERVED.
IT WILL BE RADICAL WHEN BAD THINGS ARE TO BE UPROOTED.

Belle was to edit the "Home and Education" department, and progressives of national reputation would be contributors. The first issue started auspiciously with articles by Jonathan Bourne and Lincoln Steffens. While later issues reflected the activities of the progressive movement, the magazine was always subordinated to the advancement of La Follette's career.[2]

As inauguration day approached, a small group of senators met at the La Follettes' new residence. The senator recognized the importance of organization if the progressive Republicans were to be effective. He had objected to Senator Eugene Hale's request for unanimous consent to consider a naval appropriation bill on the day it was introduced. That Sunday, February 13, a few progressive Republicans discussed the proposed legislation with dissident naval officers. They were determined to examine the location and maintenance of the nation's navy yards from a military and not a political point of view. La Follette insisted that a board of experts and not a political secretary of the navy should make these decisions. He objected to a naval committee dominated by senators from states with navy yards: "We are administering a trust fund and I know of no principle which would recognize the disposal of a trust fund by those who have some interest, political or otherwise, in its disposal." While their amendments failed, an alliance had been forged.[3]

As the district scrutinized the incoming first family, La Follette commented that since Washington no man had been proven so qualified to be president. Taft was honest, able, tactful, forceful; he was pledged to carry out Roosevelt's policies. He raised one pregnant question. Would Taft "press forward along the numerous progressive lines followed by President Roosevelt, or retreat on some few reactionary positions which might be assumed as Rooseveltian by certain perfectly honest minds"? He did not expect sensationalism, but he did want "unflinching resolution in carrying forth the campaign against vested wrong and intrenched privilege. . . necessary to the gathering of the fruits of the Roosevelt planting and watering."[4]

The inauguration of the new president proceeded amidst portents of problems to come. The close relationship between Roosevelt and Taft seemed strained during the period preceding the inauguration; Nellie Taft had long resented the dominating influence of the rough rider and constant implications that her husband could not have been nominated and elected president on his own. After the inauguration she broke precedent by sitting beside her husband during the trip to the White House, a place usually reserved for the outgoing executive. Roosevelt was to leave for Africa, at least partially to prevent talk that he was dictating to his successor. Even lion hunting was tame for him, and retirement could not long hold an attraction for a fifty-year-old dynamo, especially when he disapproved of some of the actions of his hand-picked successor.

Even the weather sent a warning. A pleasant light snow of the early evening became a blizzard during the night; seventy-mile-an-hour winds yanked telegraph and telephone wires from poles. The storm isolated the capital from the country, as the administration was to be soon thereafter. At dawn the storm intensified and then calmed; but snow, continuing to fall, caused the lead horses in the procession to rear and back. While Teddy waved to the spectators, deep in slush, Taft did not even acknowledge their presence, as if courting popularity was demagogic. Finally, the ceremonies were moved inside the Senate chamber, arrangements which frustrated the patient crowd that had endured the elements.

As the Tafts settled into the White House some changes were immediately apparent and others were soon to be observed. Gone was Teddy's athletic boisterousness, his high pitched voice, the sounds of the children skating through the house. Gone was an energetic president who had sought to enhance the power of his office. Replacing him was a massive and lethargic Ohioan, six foot two and three hundred and thirty-two pounds, a man so large that a special tub, created for him, seven feet long and forty-one inches wide, weighing one ton, had been moved from the battleship North Carolina to the White House. An aggressive executive was being replaced by a man of judicial temperament whose new eminence fulfilled his wife's and brother's ambitions rather than his own. As the new president said with a chuckle on inauguration day: "I always said it would be a cold day when I got to be President of the United States." As if to mark the end of an era, the stable had been converted to a garage, and a White Steamer replaced the state carriages.[5]

That Taft had courage was soon apparent. He immediately tackled a question that even Roosevelt had shied away from, fully aware that "The readjustment of tariff schedules. . .always creates division in the party proposing it." He called a special session of Congress to carry out the Republican party platform pledge of tariff revision. There could be no doubt that he intended to work for reduced schedules. As early as Roosevelt's campaign of 1904 he had called for tariff cuts. In his speech accepting the nomination he had phrased his position in a manner suited to La Follette: "The tariff in a number of the schedules exceeds the difference between the cost of production of such articles abroad and at home, including a reasonable profit to the American producer. The excess over that difference serves no useful purpose, but offers a temptation to those who would monopolize the production and the sale of such articles in this country, to profit by the excessive rate." He had reiterated his pledge in La Follette's presence in a campaign speech in Milwaukee. As the special session assembled the progressives eagerly anticipated a great state paper outlining downward revision of the tariff. When the clerk completed a two-minute message calling for quick disposition of the matter to avoid disturbing business the progressives were stunned.

Anticipating a fight La Follette outlined his position. The tariff was intended to protect high wages and infant industries while domestic competition kept prices down. But monopoly had replaced competition, and immigrants accepted a lower standard: "the protective tariff has failed to protect American labor against the competition of the former, while enabling the manufacturers to raise prices of necessaries which the American workman requires as consumer." In the steel industry men were working seven days a week, twelve hours a day, with a twenty-four hour stint when they changed shifts every other Sunday. "If this is the necessary fruit of protection, it might be better to admit free of duty the pig iron of England whose 'pauper' labor works only eight hours a day." In addition the United States was now an exporting nation, and tariffs were raised against our goods. Tariff reductions would not hurt U.S. exporters; it would only force them to charge as little in the U.S. as in Europe; and it would help reduce European tariffs against us. The new political reality was that Democrats had their own protected industries despite free trade rhetoric and many Republicans were unhappy about sheltering monopolies. It was time to remove the tariff from politics. When Judge

Elbert Gary presented comparative costs of production of pig iron, Andrew Carnegie had laughed at his figures. It was time for a permanent committee of experts to examine corporate records and turn "on the light of a searching investigation of the whole tariff subject."[6]

As a revenue bill the tariff originated in the House of Representatives. But even before work on the tariff had begun, Taft was confronted by a struggle between the congressional establishment and insurgents within his own party. "Uncle Joe" Cannon, the hard-swearing, spittoon-using speaker of the House (who wore hand tailored suits of hand woven material, properly rumpled so as not to offend his constituency), had established a virtual dictatorship over the House of Representatives through his control over appointment to committees and domination of the Rules and Ways and Means Committees. He determined whether a congressman could be effective for his constituents, whether he could make a record, and whether his bills would ever be considered. As the special session opened he found that the dissidents within his own party, in combination with the Democrats, could command a majority. The progressives wanted election of the committees by the House, regional distribution of the committee of rules and a calendar day in which committees were called by alphabet to present bills. Roosevelt had convinced Taft that Cannon could not be defeated and was necessary to the success of the administration; the President intervened in favor of the speaker and antagonized the progressives. In the meantime, Cannon made deals with enough Democrats to offset Republican defections — eight New York congressman were delivered by a Brooklyn leader with ties to Standard Oil and by an upstate glove manufacturer, one represented the Chicago packers, two the Louisiana sugar planters, and Georgia lumber interests made their contribution; all were seeking favorable schedules — and the thrust was deflected with a minor compromise, permitting a calendar day to consider committee business alphabetically. It was not until March of 1910 that George Norris outmaneuvered the speaker and stripped him of much of his power, and then thwarted an attempt to dislodge Cannon from his chair. (La Follette was not impressed by this victory. It was good for morale, he felt, for it had shown that trusts could be defeated, but monopolies would control the caucuses that chose the members of the rules committee.)[7]

Sereno Payne, the chairman of the Committee on Ways and Means, was knowledgeable on tariff matters, but he was an orthodox Republican who followed orders. All schedules were determined by a majority of the Republican members, composing the subcommittee, who then voted as a bloc. When the subcommittee reported petroleum as a free list item, Cannon forced it to be changed to a 25% duty, only to lose the schedule to a Norris amendment from the floor. The Payne bill, as it passed the House, suited the President. The House insurgents were not pleased, but did not organize opposition. The bill satisfied neither faction in the Senate.

Aldrich's finance committee met in secret session, aided by New York customs appraisers, listened to the interested parties, and came up with 847 amendments to the Payne bill, most of them increases. The Rhode Island senator requested immediate consideration of his handiwork — 300 pages and 733 complex paragraphs. La Follette protested that customarily the committee submitted written justification for each change and allowed sufficient time for careful study. Aldrich's motion carried, with a provision that the Senate meet, without recess, from 10 A.M. to 11 P.M. The progressives requested that many paragraphs be passed over for future consideration, and they divided the schedules for closer study and active debate. Because of the length of each session it was necessary to prepare arguments for the next day's debate after midnight. Jockeying for advantage began even before the finance committee reported; La Follette and Aldrich debated whether the McKinley committee had held secret meetings after public meetings. With the bill's introduction Aldrich encountered a smashing broadside by La Follette and Dolliver, denouncing the measure and routing its author in debate. How did Aldrich handle a specific item like gas retorts, La Follette queried? How did he determine cost of production here and abroad? Did he accept statements of interested parties or investigate further? How was a reasonable profit assessed? As Dolliver and La Follette attacked him, they read excerpts from Taft's campaign speeches promising tariff reductions, Aldrich denied that the Republican party had ever committed itself to downward revision. He rejected any separate consumer interest, for consumers were also producers. His words were echoed by his partisans.

Taft was shocked. Aldrich and Cannon had pledged that they would cooperate in tariff revision. He feared Aldrich was ready to sacrifice the party. He had repeatedly emphasized to both progressives and conservatives that he intended to fight for his pledges and would veto an unsatisfactory bill. Nevertheless, he had rejected conservative Vice-President James Sherman's suggestion that he withhold all patronage until he obtained his tariff. To the progressives' dismay he remained silent as the bill was debated. Efforts to enlist his support elicited promises, vacillation, and promises reiterated. The insurgents, already discontent with the President, began to smolder.

Jonathan Dolliver, who had closeted himself with hired experts for three days, launched the assault on specific schedules on May 4. Unaccustomed to attacks by one of the most caustic wits in the chamber, Aldrich lost his composure with Dolliver's charge that the cotton schedule had been written by a group of New England cotton manufacturers. The Boston *Transcript* called his three-hour speech "The most damaging criticism of Republican tariff making. . .in recent years." Aldrich wilted as the progressives, with La Follette as the chief strategist, dissected schedule after schedule: Dolliver and La Follette examined textiles (New England cotton mills were earning 8% and still wanted higher duties. La Follette reported); Bristow attacked the lead, paint, and sugar schedules; Albert Cummins scrutinized linoleum, oil cloth, and steel and concluded that steel could be reduced $9.00 a ton and still pay 6%; Beveridge kept tabs on Aldrich, with the figures constantly before him. All the progressives backed each other in debate. But Aldrich, accepting only a few insurgent amendments, had an automatic majority.

Progressive exasperation with the President became a rift during consideration of an income tax measure introduced by William Borah and Joseph Bailey to replace the House inheritance tax provision stricken in the Senate. Taft, who had previously stated that an income tax bill could be drafted to circumvent earlier Supreme Court objections, traded votes against the income tax in return for Aldrich's guarantee of a corporation tax. The progressives felt betrayed. An income tax would make the treasury less dependent upon the tariff for revenue, La Follette wrote, and schedules could be raised or lowered as the tariff commission decided. A corporate tax on net income, he argued, was inadequate, for a prosperous corporation could avoid payment by increasing salaries for directors, by issuing more bonds, and by paying more interest.

Taft accepted "old guard" assurances that the tariff would be improved in the conference committee. Except for the chairman, Sereno Payne, all the conferees appointed by Aldrich and Cannon were diehard protectionists. Payne was so disgusted with the proceedings that he threatened to walk out and was only kept in line by the intercession of the President. Taft indicated to La Follette that he would press for reduction in the conference committee, and La Follette, in a fifteen-page letter, itemized the schedules that should be reduced; if the rates were not greatly lowered, he insisted, the bill should be vetoed. By this time Taft, who had become personally repelled by the progressives whom he considered demogogic, felt much more comfortable with the "old guard." After forcing changes in the lumber and glove schedules he thought he had won a victory. But the progressives would not let him rest.

La Follette continued his attack on the conference report. In a voice grown hoarse with constant use, he castigated the completed bill as worse than the one that had emerged from the finance committee. To support his contention he submitted figures obtained from the Bureau of Statistics. He charged the wool trust with raising prices on clothing in anticipation of higher schedules so as to increase their income $120,000,000 a year. "The debate is running down." Belle wrote to her sister-in-law. "That is, there is no chance of ever awakening any opposition. There is a kind of deadness in the situation that makes it foolish to try to liven it." La Follette was denied the chance to take a parting shot at the bill by moving his name down the list of speakers and consuming the remaining time with irrelevant speeches. Taft's effort to woo progressive support was largely unsuccessful. No longer the lone man in the Senate, La Follette was so personally moved by insurgent support that he could not bring himself to speak about it.[8]

La Follette did not waste the concluding tariff speech he had prepared. He spent a long hot summer on the Chautauqua circuit, earning funds to publish his magazine while spreading progressive gospel. He stood on the platform in his white collar, white shirt, white tie, white duck pants, white canvas shoes, holding his black alpaca coat in his arm, attacking the special interests, the congressional leadership, and the tariff, stopping in Washington state to aid in Miles Poindexter's Senate campaign, and contacting leading progressives wherever he went. "I hardly know why the time seems so precious that we spend together and so vacant when separated," his wife wrote. "I have always the sense of waiting for your coming." While he was home, often with guests, the children — Bob, Jr. was 15, Phil 13, and Mary 11 — engaged in the discussion as equals. Their father constantly reminded them to prepare themselves for the struggles against the world's oppressions and afflictions.[9]

During this summer La Follette refrained from any direct attack on Taft; but an open break was imminent. On September 17 the President made a speech in Winona, Minnesota; he analyzed both the strengths and weaknesses of the bill, then, in an ill-chosen phrase, he concluded it was the best Republican tariff ever passed, and, therefore, the best tariff. Commenting on his remarks, George Norris agreed it was the best tariff ever, but it was still wholly inadequate to "the exigencies of the age."[10] His fellow progressives were not as gentle. Henry Allen of Kansas proclaimed that from now on he was looking to Africa for 1912; the editor of the *Saturday Evening Post* committed his magazine to insurgency; Dolliver wrote to La Follette about the consequences of inevitable battles with the President — he was confident that La Follette and Clapp could survive an onslaught from Pennsylvania Avenue, but he was concerned about Beveridge.[11]

Progressive confirmation of suspicions about Taft was not their only setback that summer. Francis Heney, the crusading San Francisco district attorney who had prosecuted the Oregon land fraud cases, and Tom Johnson, a pioneering reform mayor of Cleveland, were defeated in bids for reelection. La Follette commented:

The lesson is this, the corporations are never beaten. . . .The government will slip back into their hands the moment the vigilance of the people is relaxed, the moment the issues can be confused. Johnson has had them beaten time and again, but they never ceased the fight. The people must be as ceaseless in their struggle for the right as the forces of plutocracy are sure to be for the wrong.[12]

If there still had been any possibility of rapprochement between Taft and the progressives after the Winona speech, the events of autumn assured bitter conflict.

A struggle over differing views of conservation that had been brewing during the Roosevelt administration came to the surface, and it crystallized many of the grievances of those who had been close to Teddy. James Garfield, son of a former president and Roosevelt's secretary of interior, and Gifford Pinchot, head of the forest service, had been most closely identified in the public mind with the "rough rider's" conservation program. When Roosevelt passed the torch to Taft he had been promised continuity of personnel and programs; unsolicited, Taft had offered to retain Roosevelt's cabinet heads who wished to continue. Once inaugurated, Taft chose an entirely new cabinet. Richard A. Ballinger, the stocky, square-headed, self-made man from the state of Washington who replaced Garfield, had anti-conservationists among his closest political friends. Ironically, he had been brought into the Roosevelt administration by his predecessor, a college acquaintance, in order to reorganize the muddled land office. He came to the capital with a reputation as a crusading city attorney and mayor, who fought corruption and vice (but who had not shown an interest in social struggles). Ballinger raised the office to a level of unparalleled efficiency, revitalized its activities, and defended Roosevelt's measures before an anti-conservation Western congress. At the time he returned to private affairs Garfield seemed to have been pleased with his work. This was not true of the tall, gaunt aristocrat with a drooping moustache, Gifford Pinchot. Ballinger had not only been employed to apply business principles to the land office, as he had done to the government of Seattle, but to replace a policy of land sale with one of land management. Unfortunately, Ballinger did not advocate leasing of government land. As a western progressive he feared that leasing would favor large, established corporations at the expense of their small, independent rivals. In addition, by keeping new sources off the market, land management would enhance the value of corporate holdings. On the other hand, he did not advocate giveaways. His desire to sell mineral and timber lands at their properly appraised market value conformed to public positions taken by President Roosevelt. Ballinger wanted the sale of timber lands, except for the national forests, and he clashed with Pinchot over the foresters' use of the Forest Management Act of 1898 and over a mineral and coal land report. Until Ballinger's resignation from the land office the two faced each other as chiefs of rival bureaus with rival purposes.

Under Roosevelt, lines of command were not always clearly defined. Because of his personal friendship with Roosevelt and Garfield, Pinchot had been able to develop a broad program of conservation reaching beyond his own bailiwick in Agriculture into Interior. Ballinger felt Pinchot's encroachments were bad management practice and prevented interference with his staff. Roosevelt's concept of the law was very broad, and he and his two collaborators had withdrawn about a million and a half acres of public land containing possible water power sites from public sale although he lacked specific congressional authorization; after all, Congress had not prohibited it. Ballinger made some of this land available for sale on the grounds that its withdrawal had not been authorized. Pinchot pressured Taft, who feared a split with Roosevelt; many of the sites were withdrawn again, somewhat reduced in surplus acreage, and Ballinger added a few sites that had been overlooked. While the water sites caused friction, it was coal lands that proved to be crucial.

Ballinger followed Roosevelt administration policy and promoted a bill to separate title to the land from mineral resources below the surface; while he preferred the sale of resources, he accepted leases and tripled maximum valuation. It was his bad fortune to be cast as the villain in the saga of the Cunningham claims. These claims to coal lands in Alaska were deficient in some respects. First they were filed under the general mineral laws which did not apply to Alaska. Clarence Cunningham was so anxious to prove that there was no prior collusion with the Morgan-Guggenheim interests, with whom he and his partners had a subsequent agreement, that he unwittingly disclosed illegal prior collusion among members of his group in filing their individual claims. As a result, Louis Glavis, an intense young investigator for the land office, prevented the titles from being cleared. Cunningham approached Ballinger, at this point a private citizen and retained his services as a lawyer specializing in land law. Ballinger interceded, but recognizing deficiencies in his case, recommended that he refile under the 1908 law, which was loosely interpreted, and thus solve his problems; Cunningham did not wish to come under the law's regulatory features. Throughout the controversy Glavis delayed his report; he was not satisfied with invalidation. He had already convinced his superiors of that point. He envisioned these claims as similar to the Oregon land fraud cases, prosecuted by Frank Heney, and wanted indictments. Glavis was reassigned, ostensibly for working too slowly; although his successor requested more time a hearing was scheduled. At this juncture Glavis took his case to Pinchot who arranged a meeting with Taft. Presenting his case like a prosecutor, Glavis implied that Ballinger had acted in collusion with Cunningham. Taft and Ballinger were furious at the attack on the secretary's integrity; after an investigation the President exonerated Ballinger and fired Glavis for insubordination. At the same time he asked Pinchot to stay out of the controversy and not to resign. But Pinchot or his staff kept leaking information to the press, hoping to create an incident. Glavis wrote an article for *Collier's* which ignited a barrage of progressive attacks on the administration. The editorial leads were more damaging to Taft than the text. "ARE THE GUGGENHEIMS IN CHARGE IN THE DEPARTMENT OF THE INTERIOR?" its cover asked. A congressional investigation became inevitable; to prevent a whitewash, Pinchot asked Dolliver to read a letter to the Senate attacking Ballinger and disclosing the forester's role in supplying material to Glavis and the press. The embattled Taft had desperately tried to avoid a break with one of Roosevelt's favorites but, on January 7, 1910, Pinchot achieved the martyrdom he had courted.

The progressives tried to use the hearings to discredit the administration. George Norris had outmaneuvered Cannon and the House, not the speaker, chose the delegation. E. H. Madison, a progressive Republican representative, assumed a judicious posture during the hearings and wrote a masterful minority report which greatly influenced public opinion. But Louis Brandeis, counsel for Glavis, provided the devastating headlines. With meticulous skill he showed that the summary and opinion written by Attorney General George Wickersham had been predated and that Taft's memorandum exonerating Ballinger had been drafted in the secretary's private office by his friend and subordinate, Oscar Lawlor. Administration denials of the existence of the memorandum made its consequent disclosure even more damaging. While no corruption was ever to be proven, Taft's credibility was destroyed.[13]

La Follette accepted Pinchot's version of the controversy. Pinchot, he felt, was following Roosevelt's policy of protecting potential water sites and Ballinger was abandoning this policy. "Back of them are two great opposing forces. On the one side is an army of citizens who are determined upon the wise conservation of our natural resources and the protection of the rights of the public in these resources. On the other side are the hosts of Privilege, bent upon securing at any cost, for private exploitation, the natural resources that still remain in the hands of the public." "True conservation consists not in hoarding our resources, but in using them properly," he added in a later article. This generation is entitled to the advantages of our mineral wealth, but the benefits of this development should "inure not to a few men, but to the rightful owners — all the people of the United States." Like Glavis, he wanted to protect Alaskan coal from the Morgan-Guggenheim syndicate, to prevent duplication of the anthracite industry, where railroads used their transportation monopoly to gain control of the fields. Why should the United States permit a corporation to build railroads from the mineral fields to the sea and pay Morgan ten dollars a ton when it could produce its own for four dollars? No private corporation would permit it. Drawing upon the Isthmian Canal Commission experience (often cited by progressives), he suggested a board of public works to build a railroad from the coal fields to Controller Bay, to acquire all Alaskan railroads, to develop public utilities, and if necessary to establish and operate wharves, docks, and steamship lines. Mines should be leased with at least one mine retained for military needs; the surplus from government operated mines should be sold and would serve as a yardstick by which to judge prices. In the early years of this government lead mines had been leased, he reminded his fellow senators. Had the policy of leasing mineral lands been continued we could almost defray the costs of government, and the nation would not be threatened by trusts and monopolies.[14]

When the focus of the Taft administration shifted to the question of railroads La Follette took a central role in the debate. At first he found much to praise in the administration measure. The functions of the ICC would be enhanced, he wrote. It could issue an order changing rates; it could "determine and prescribe individual and joint classification of freight," the basis of rate making. Yet, its authority to suspend new rates until an investigation proving their reasonableness was completed might be nullified by an accompanying sixty-day limit, he warned. To ensure fair rates the shipper was permitted to opt for an available alternate route. Initially he favored the commerce court for it could expedite appeals from ICC orders and would prevent railroads from seeking friendly judges. From the beginning he felt there were provisions that required critical study. When he completed the analysis he decided the bill was inadequate. During the Ballinger-Pinchot contest he had become close friends with Louis Brandeis, who had assisted the district attorney in the New Haven merger case which had been started by Roosevelt and dropped by Taft, and the two examined the bill. In the Senate, La Follette attacked a series of provisions which, when combined, threatened to destroy the applicability of anti-trust laws. The first permitted railroads to acquire controlling interest in other corporations if they already had a twenty-year lease; a second provision limited pursuit of such cases before the commerce court and the Supreme Court to the attorney general; and a third would have prevented the Supreme Court from hearing the facts in a Sherman Act case if the commerce court and the attorney general agreed that the acquired corporation had not been in substantive competition. With meticulous detail, supplied by Brandeis, he traced the New Haven acquisition of competing electric inter-urban lines, railroads, and steamship lines until it had established a monopoly.

Other aspects of the bill were as obnoxious to him. He feared it would "fasten irrevocably upon the commerce of the country the burden of transportation charges to pay interest and dividends upon all the watered stocks and bonds" engendered by corporate greed.

Although reasonable rates had been implied in the original interstate commerce act, there was still no machinery to determine reasonableness, no physical valuation. After the Mann-Elkins bill passed, with innumerable progressive amendments, La Follette was more impressed with what the progressives prevented than what they incorporated in the measure — traffic agreements had not been legalized and anti-trust laws were not to be waived. In a lengthy analysis he found many improvements, some positive additions, and some seriously negative provisions. As a whole, he felt the bill was a step forward and he voted for it.[15]

One other major bill concerned La Follette before he returned home to seek reelection — the creation of a postal savings bank. While La Follette firmly supported the principle as a safe depository for small savings, free of manipulation, he did not support the Senate bill until amended by progressives and rejected the presidential version as passed by the House.[16]

Both factions in Wisconsin viewed the Senatorial campaign as an opportunity. The La Follette progressives hoped to recoup after a series of setbacks and the "stalwarts" wanted to unseat their chief opponent. To defeat the senior senator the conservatives raised a campaign chest of over $114,000. Taft hoped to eliminate a gadfly and potential rival and lent them administration support. Vice-President Sherman, initiating the campaign, addressed the "Taft Republican" convention. Unfortunately for the conservatives' plans only Davidson had a chance of contesting La Follette's reelection, and he would not run for a faction led by W. D. Connnor. With their most popular candidate leading their ticket and championing the popular side of the current controversies — the Payne-Aldrich tariff, the Ballinger-Pinchot affair, and "Uncle Joe" Cannon — the La Follette progressives tried to regain lost ground. "Battle Bob" could not campaign because of illness; consequently, thirteen progressive leaders of national repute came to Wisconsin to campaign for him at their own expense; in fact, Albert Cummins canceled $7500 in Chautauqua dates to speak. Richard Lloyd Jones wrote a political puff for him in *Collier's* which appeared three days before the primary. As La Follette had expected, his victory in the primary was overwhelming; he defeated Samuel Cook 142,978 to 40,791. The progressive victories for state office in the primary and general polls were so sweeping that his opponent's alternate strategy of denying him legislative election was thwarted by a progressive margin. Francis McGovern was elected governor. The defeat of Henry Cochems by the socialist, Victor Berger, only slightly tempered the general celebration. Throughout the nation Taft was repudiated. Progressive Republicans were elected and reelected while Democrats defeated enough conservatives to give the opposition control of the House. Taft was headed for defeat in 1912.[17]

# CHAPTER 7

## "A One Eyed Galoot"

A S the progressive Republicans, riding a tide of progressive victories and administration defeats, returned to Washington, with one eye on the 1912 national convention, they decided to effectuate a plan long discussed — the creation of a league of progressives. While it was their hope to incorporate Democratic progressives in their organization — such as Louis Brandeis, Frederick Howe and Ben Lindsey — they found it necessary to name their group the Progressive Republican League, lest they be accused of forming a third party and undermine their credibility in their own states. The league was underwritten by Clarence Jones and Rudolph Spreckels, each of whom promised $25,000 a year for five years. La Follette drafted the declaration of principles in his Washington home during the Christmas recess, and after signed endorsements by senators and congressmen the league was launched from the same quarters on January 21, 1911. One name noticeably absent from the prospectus was that of Theodore Roosevelt.[1]

Even while the "rough rider" was still in Africa, Gifford Pinchot and James Garfield had tried to enlist him in their controversies with Taft. But the ex-President would not commit himself. Upon his return his criticism of Taft was private and confidential, and, at first, very mild. Assuming that Taft would be renominated and that any Republican was better than a Democrat, the former President tried to pull all factions of the party together. Responding to pressure from Pinchot to lead the New York progressives, Roosevelt revived a direct election measure which had had the support of Governor Charles Evans Hughes and administration representatives — only to meet defeat. Urged by his allies to carry the fight to the convention, Roosevelt announced his candidacy for the temporary chairmanship. At this point Hughes accepted a seat on the Supreme Court, and Taft deserted his former chief and probably joined the enemy. The executive committee refused to nominate him. Furious, he took his fight to the convention floor and won. Subsequently, he became increasingly critical of Taft in private conversation. But even after his progressive speech at Osawatomie he attempted to unify the party. Much to La Follette's displeasure he campaigned for his conservative friend, Henry Cabot Lodge. But he also stumped for the progressive, Albert Beveridge. Discouraged by the defeat of most of the men he had supported, unwilling to oppose a president who had been one of his closest friends, and uncertain about the strength of the progressives, Roosevelt encouraged members of the league, but would not join.[2]

La Follette maintained an awkward relationship with the colonel during this period. In the eyes of the public the two were members of the progressive wing of the party. The senator had publicly lavished praise upon the ex-President, while privately he criticized him for playing to both sides, for hedging and straddling. Similarly, Roosevelt refrained from public criticism of La Follette and during the next year repeatedly endorsed many of his proposals and accomplishments; yet, he had always considered him radical and had sided with his enemies during the difficult early struggles in Wisconsin. Along with other progressives, La Follette journeyed to Oyster Bay to visit with Roosevelt upon his return from his African and European tours. While Garfield and Pinchot were unhappy that their hero would not lead their crusade, La Follette saw Roosevelt as a seemingly reluctant candidate — just as he was. "To be entirely just," he wrote to Jonathan Bourne, "in some ways I think he sees more liberally. But he is far from being broadly and fundamentally democratic."[3] "He will say something first on one side of the issue, then to preserve the balance he will say something on the other side of the issue," he informed Judson Welliver. "That is constitutional with him."[4] As the driving force behind the league, La Follette sent drafts of the league's statement of principles to leading progressives, including Roosevelt.[5] Roosevelt advised caution; states developed at different rates, and they did not want to shock honest men into opposition. He was neither a trimmer nor a dictator, he wrote, but wanted to lead people without driving them. It would not be a public service for him to join the league, he concluded.[6] La Follette agreed that many states were not ready for the full program. "So it was in Wisconsin at every step of our advance. There were sections of the state which were not abreast of other sections. But we brought them into line by an organized campaign of education. So it seems to me we must press forward the reform work in the states where it is most needed. If we wait for them all to be ready, it will be a generation before we get very far with our legislative program."[7] "Roosevelt won't take the lone chance," William Allen White commented. "He fears being regarded a one eyed Galoot."[8]

La Follette was willing to "take the lone chance." Even prior to Taft's nomination in 1908 La Follette's supporters were looking to 1912, and at no point did they lose sight of their goal.[9] When it became obvious that neither Roosevelt nor Cummins would hazard a race, La Follette offered his candidacy, apparently willing to make the sacrifice. "I stand ready to go to the front and take all the chances on beating the administration and any near progressives who would take a mournful delight in probating my political estate," he wrote to Fremont Older, provided that he was sufficiently funded. "The progressive cause is the only hope of the country. It should not be permitted to foozle because no one has the courage to go up against the Administration forces and the solid South."[10] He maintained the stance of a willingness to support either Roosevelt or Cummins, knowing that neither would run, while offering to make the fight himself; after all, personal ambition could not interfere with the movement.[11] La Follette had no illusion about Roosevelt. Pinchot had brought word from Oyster Bay of quiet support, for the ex-President feared that endorsement might seem like another attempt to name a candidate. "He is willing to have some one do the Light Brigade act, stop Taft, and get shot about the right time," La Follette wrote. Roosevelt would not take the risk "but would be very glad to administer upon the estate of the man who does undertake the job." Yet, he confided to Older, "I am not so certain that we are to make a losing fight."[12] He had an immense faith in the composite judgment of the people which was "always safer and stronger than the judgment of any one individual

mind." While the people had been betrayed by their representatives, they had never failed in any great crisis in our
history. There was no danger from "the ignorance or want of
patriotism of the people," but from the corruption of public officials by businesses. "The real cure for the ills of democracy is
more democracy." The people would gain "absolute control of
their own government. If constitutional obstacles are encountered, constitutions will be amended. . . . The people are
the conservative body of this country. They are to be trusted."[13]

He undertook his campaign for the Presidential nomination
with ample funds, a viable progressive organization, and confidence that the people, once able to speak out, would rally to
him and his program.

One of his first mistakes was to choose a campaign manager
who did not have similar confidence in his ability to win. In accepting the appointment W. H. Houser asserted his belief in La
Follette and promised to do anything requested. But, he wrote
"I doubt if you can be nominated, or elected if nominated — the
interests are not yet subdued." At crucial points he took the
senator at his word and promoted what he considered to be the
interests of the cause rather than his candidate and unwittingly
advanced the Roosevelt strategy.[14]

As insurgents throughout the country were organizing in
order to prevent Taft's renomination, La Follette continued to
focus national attention on his activities in Washington. At the
start of the new Congress the progressives captured headlines
by refusing to attend a caucus to choose the successor to
Aldrich and then opposing the election of Senator Jacob
Gallinger as president pro tempore. La Follette followed with a
demand for proportional representation on committees, for his
faction composed one-fourth of the Republican delegation in the
Senate, a far cry from La Follette's days as a lonely dissenter.
Unsuccessful in this undertaking, he offered a resolution to
reinvestigate the election of Senator William Lorimer, who had
been seated despite progressive protests, on the basis of new
information about a slush fund. A substitute motion passed
which created a committee that was sure to vindicate the
Illinois senator; although its report exonerated Lorimer, the
facts developed in the hearing caused his ejection from the
Senate.[15] Having tasted victory La Follette continued to

publicize his position on important current issues.

In the Standard Oil case the Supreme Court modified the Sherman anti-trust law's prohibition of monopolies by applying a standard of reasonableness, that corporations violated the act only when they were in unreasonable restraint of trade. While the court held that Standard Oil was violating these guidelines La Follette was deeply disturbed by the decision; he printed Justice John Harlan's dissent in his magazine with favorable comments. There had been no organized corruption in American government for its first eighty decades, he argued, it appeared "when the corporations . . . began to tunnel mountains, to bridge great rivers, to build great lines of roads, to start great industrial enterprises. . . . From that hour to this its virus has been spreading into every fiber of our political system." Scandals commenced "when the corporation had to go to their state legislatures to get franchises, and to Congress to get special privileges and land grants." The new decision not only overturned earlier cases and made it more difficult to prosecute trusts, but it eliminated guides for the business world and rules of law for the courts. The Court could "exercise a power over the business interests of this country more despotic than any monarch of the civilized world over his subjects"; one corporation will be told its combinations in restraint of trade are reasonable, another that they are unreasonable. He offered a bill to list unreasonable restraints on trade, to place the burden of proof on the corporation, not the prosecutor, and to permit the injured party to add his suit to government proceedings by simply proving the amount of the loss.[16]

Having challenged the Supreme Court La Follette confronted his rival, Taft. In his criticism of the Canadian Reciprocity Treaty he did not speak for a unified progressive caucus, for many of his fellow insurgents supported the mutual reduction of duties. He endorsed reciprocity with Canada, he asserted; his objection was to this particular treaty. It took from farmers the few benefits they received from protective tariffs. Tariffs, he insisted, should be based on differences in cost of production. Nevertheless duties on foodstuffs were to be eliminated although Canada had a lower cost of production and the United States had a surplus of grain. Manufacturers would receive free raw materials from Canada plus entrée into Canadian markets.

Farmers would receive greater competition and could only benefit if cheaper raw materials produced lower prices for finished products, a dubious prospect in monopolized industries. The treaty required "the farmer to surrender his market at an enormous loss to secure valuable concessions to a few prosperous special interests . . . the railroads, the milling interests, and the beef trust." Joined by the majority of the "stalwarts," some of whom were protecting regional economic interests and some of whom saw this treaty as the entering wedge of general tariff reduction, La Follette helped defeat the treaty. Undaunted, Taft called a special session of the new Congress, controlled by the Democrats. The treaty passed, but La Follette outmaneuvered the president who found it necessary to veto three bills lowering schedules. "Battle Bob" made political capital of Taft's inconsistency; the President had vetoed reductions favoring farmers with the excuse that there was no report by the tariff board, while he placed the full force of the administration behind a Canadian Reciprocity Bill the tariff board had never considered. Ironically, the arguments in favor of the treaty convinced the Canadian Senate that the agreement endangered the country's economic independence, and it rejected the measure.[17]

La Follette challenged Taft when he vetoed statehood for Arizona with a warning against the potential tyranny of the majority if judges could be recalled. Progressives united behind La Follette; many who questioned the wisdom of judicial recall believed states should be permitted to experiment. The President, La Follette charged, himself exalted by the votes of the 'popular majority' . . . declares that the people cannot be trusted to rule." Taft permitted citizens to "play at self-government" up to a point, but really believed "in government by a select few." For his part La Follette was committed to direct government. The initiative and referendum had permitted citizens to demand good laws and repeal bad ones. "The recall will enable the people to dismiss from the public service a representative whenever he shall cease to serve the public interest. . . ." Representative government could only fail when "the representative proves incompetent or false to his trust. . . . The citizen is entitled to halt "the evils of misrepresentation and betrayal."[18]

Always looking for new techniques of publicity, La Follette decided to write his own campaign biography, serializing it for maximum exposure, and investing the income in his uphill struggle for nomination. At first he negotiated with *Hampton's*, but, wary of the magazine's financial condition, he tried to get a commitment of steady payment and publication to completion. Relieved to be free of his contract when *Hampton's* was sold, La Follette dealt with the *American Magazine*, hoping to receive the same $15,000 fee. After some annoying delay the contract was signed; it was agreed that Ray Stannard Baker would help him with the writing. Through the fall of 1911 he gathered information, particularly taxing the memory of early political associates. With favorable reception of the articles he asked his New York lawyer, Gilbert Roe, to negotiate a contract for their publication as a book.[19]

The *Autobiography* recounted the log cabin to success story already well known to readers of articles about La Follette, a common image for contemporary politicians, an account neither wholly accurate nor inaccurate. What was missing from the Lincolnesque portrait was the family's social and economic position in early childhood. Like most politicians, La Follette came from a comfortable middle-class background, though his father's death caused some hardship. His description of his early political career was very dramatic, but it was faulty in its details. Remembering the earlier power of the Keyes machine and the later opposition of Keyes, he forgot that when he entered politics Keyes was already fighting for survival and could not concentrate on a candidate for district attorney. Recalling his solitary courage in the Senate, he projected this role back to his days in the House by emphasizing his refusal to obey Sawyer and playing down his protected position as a fair-haired boy of the congressional establishment. A good portion of the book dealt with the education of a progressive, how an orthodox Republican gradually became aware of the danger to America that corporations posed. He described his constant effort to inform the electorate while he fought to further political democracy. His autobiography, stopping before his difficulties with Roosevelt, carried him to the 1912 campaign; that tale was told after the break and added to the earlier articles when the volume was published.[20]

Publicity was important, but the Progressive Republican League's organizational efforts were crucial. At first it experienced difficulty, but soon favorable reports began to filter in. Roosevelt's articles and speeches praising La Follette and the Wisconsin progressives for sane legislation gave it a boost. By early October George Record reported the failure of Taft's western trip; by convention time "most Republicans will see that he cannot be re-elected."[21] Amos Pinchot wrote to James Garfield about the Wisconsin leader: "People are beginning to ask whether after all he is not a pretty safe kind of man. I believe that if we can raise money enough to finance a vigorous campaign we can defeat Taft."[22] By this time Garfield may have thought this possible, but he was determined to nominate Roosevelt.

James R. Garfield was close to the colonel and completely devoted to his interests. He had long hoped that Teddy would oppose Taft and seek the nomination himself. He was projecting his own desires when he wrote to Gifford Pinchot in March that "it would be absolutely impossible to do anything with or for La Follette in Ohio"; he predicted that another candidate could capture three-fourths of the delegation and insisted upon flexibility.[23] By October Roosevelt was not yet ready to take the gamble, but La Follette's progress whetted his appetite. On October 9 he sent for Garfield; they devised a strategy to keep Roosevelt's options open, without hampering the election of progressive delegates in opposition to Taft, but which would not advance La Follette's candidacy. Progressive Republicans were scheduled to meet in Chicago the following week to plan the fight against Taft. "I shall go to Chicago and urge the program of constructive measures and a real progressive candidate — leaving to each state to select progressive delegates," Garfield confided to his diary. "It would be useless to urge La Follette everywhere."[24] In Chicago he found that La Follette was favored and that his views would not prevail. He decided not to make a fight lest it appear that he was representing Roosevelt. He tried to modify the endorsement. He wrote in his diary that it was not a pledge, and that unpledged delegates, or delegates committed to other progressives, could be chosen where La Follette was unacceptable. He informed La Follette of his stand and sent a copy to Roosevelt.[25] Ominously, Roosevelt's organ, the *Outlook,* echoed Garfield's position.[26] For their part La Follette and Houser felt they had obtained a clear endorsement in Chicago.[27]

Still without a clear commitment from Roosevelt, but determined to force him to accept the nomination as the only unifying leader of the progressive movement, Garfield set out to prevent the endorsement of La Follette at the Ohio progressive convention. In his efforts he was aided by such newly converted Ohio "regulars" as national committeeman Walter Brown and Dan Hanna, son of Mark Hanna. Every place he turned he envisioned overwhelming support for Roosevelt and resistance to La Follette. He converted almost everyone to whom he spoke, only to find opposition at a later date. He repeatedly confided in his diary that he had convinced John Fackler and W. H. Houser, only to reverse himself in future entries; Fackler continued to press for a clear endorsement of La Follette. E. W. Scripps and Milton McRae insisted that more progress could be made with a candidate than with a statement of principles; consequently Garfield had little use for the Scripps press and noted that it worked for profit and not principle. Yet, when progressives from ten counties met in Cleveland on November 17, Garfield succeeded in preventing an endorsement of La Follette. As he reported in his diary, Roosevelt's article in *Outlook,* timed to appear the day before the meeting, was crucial to the outcome of the conference; the ex-President's attack on Taft's trust policy touched off speculation that he was entering the fray. Garfield immediately reported to Oyster Bay about the success of his efforts. Returning to Youngstown, he attended the banquet of the Garfield Republican Club and listened to a speaker call for Roosevelt to enter the race. By the time the Ohio State Conference of Progressives met on January 1, 1912, a well orchestrated chorus was singing a prelude to a Roosevelt candidacy. Supporters of the Sagamore Sage in the La Follette organization were insisting that the colonel would not run, but La Follette must avail himself of Roosevelt's potential strength through the Garfield formula. Nevertheless, La Follette felt confident that he had the support of the majority of delegates. He did not reckon with his own campaign manager, Walter

Houser, and, as Alfred Rogers concluded, Houser made a mess of it. Houser had never expected La Follette to be nominated, and while he preferred his candidate, he thought Roosevelt was acceptable. In early December he saw the "regulars" deserting Taft for Roosevelt; some of these new progressives were not ready to support La Follette, he reported. He did expect to win their endorsement by January, and he agreed with Scripps and McRae about the importance of personalizing issues through a candidate. Yet he was not convinced that Garfield was wrong under the existing conditions. Consequently, he was finally worn down by the constant badgering of Garfield and accepted a compromise. The convention adhered to a presidential candidate dedicated to progressive principles and declared La Follette to be "the logical candidate to carry them to successful fruition." But it had endorsed Roosevelt as well as the senator by tying the two names together in a manner that La Follette had clearly tried to avoid, in phrases that pleased Roosevelt. The next day Frank Munsey's Washington *Times* declared Roosevelt to be the progressive candidate and that La Follette was ready to withdraw.[28]

While undermining La Follette in Ohio, and wherever he could reach nationally, Garfield convinced Gifford Pinchot to press La Follette to accept a campaign in harmony with Roosevelt; Pinchot was joined by his brother Amos, Gilson Gardner, and Medill McCormick. By Christmas of 1911 McCormick had escalated and was proselytizing for his withdrawal in favor of the colonel. La Follette remained adamant, and Pinchot considered seeking unity through a Roosevelt endorsement of La Follette's candidacy. That scheme was soon discarded in favor of a conference of financial backers, who would put pressure on the Wisconsin senator. La Follette, fearing that any such discussion would be interpreted as preliminary to his withdrawal, refused even to confer with any other candidate. When "Battle Bob" received the support of William Kent and Charles Crane, Gifford Pinchot refused to abandon his candidacy without group approval. Without Pinchot the others felt they could not act.[29]

But support for Roosevelt continued to rise. While a few questioned his progressive commitment and record in office,[30] the ex-President could enlist dissident regulars and could tap sources of campaign funds that were not available to La Follette. And, in states like Colorado, Roosevelt was simply more popular than the senator, even in progressive counties. Aware for some time that they could not carry the state for La Follette, and at best could obtain a divided convention delegation, the Colorado progressive Republicans predictably followed the lead of Ohio.[31]

Once La Follette had accomplished the unexpected, once he had brought the progressives to a point where they could anticipate victory, they became willing to desert him in order to achieve it. Despite continuing evidence of his viability as a candidate, such as the warm reception given a two-hour speech by an overflow crowd at Carnegie Hall on January 22, McCormick, Pinchot, and Gardner sought a way to let "old Bob down easy" so that they could openly embrace Roosevelt's definite, though unannounced, candidacy. (He had already decided upon a draft of the call for his candidacy to be issued by six progressive governors.) The pressure upon La Follette continued to mount. A week later, after another conference, he still refused to step aside, and Pinchot still felt he could not act without approval of the progressive caucus. When the Chicago *Daily News* reported that La Follette had agreed in conference to withdraw, the candidate had Houser issue a statement that he was in the race "until the gavel falls in the convention announcing the nominee."[32]

But La Follette was about to supply his followers with an excuse to abandon him.

December and January had been very trying months for him. His physical resources had been taxed by innumerable speeches and campaign stresses. Simultaneously there was increasing evidence that, as he had feared, Roosevelt had used him as a stalking horse and intended to replace him as the progressive candidate. So many insurgents who had urged him to make an apparently hopeless race were now trying to ease him out that he did not know whom he could trust. Even his campaign manager had failed him at a most crucial point. Albert Cummins of Iowa, who had refused to sign an initial call for La Follette's candidacy, confirmed La Follette's suspicions by entering the race. Personal affairs added to his problems. At the beginning of January he suffered from ptomaine poisoning which weakened him through most of the month. Under constant pressure, he found it difficult to sleep. On January 29, he had no sooner survived the latest effort to oust him than he and Belle had taken their youngest daughter, Mary, to Providence Hospital; a critical operation had to be performed for the removal of a gland near the jugular vein. La Follette considered canceling an engagement to speak before the Periodical Publishers' Association in Philadelphia on February 2, but was persuaded that his absence would give credence to rumors that he planned to withdraw.[33]

The Senator had not had time to polish his very large draft. On the train to Philadelphia he cut the speech so that it could be delivered in little more than half an hour, but the manuscript had not been retyped. He had intended to trace the relationship between the special interests and government, the need to define unreasonable restraint of trade and to create a commission to investigate such restraint, and to determine real corporate value so as to determine reasonable profit. Only the press, he felt, could illustrate the intricate sources of power. "But what do we find has occurred in the past few years since the money power has gained control of our industry and government? It controls the newspaper press" through a community of interest. Only the periodical press was still free. But he warned them that in the future the centralization of advertising could be used by the money power to gag the magazines. In itself, the subject of his speech might have offended his banqueting audience. When he entered the hall at eleven o'clock the dinner had been in progress for three hours; Wilson had just completed a brilliant address, well suited to the occasion. La Follette was suffering from indigestion and had drunk only some tepid chocolate, which nauseated him, and had had a drink of whiskey to combat fatigue. His initial reception was warm, but the toastmaster looked aghast when he produced his thick manuscript. He tried to explain his use of a manuscript by commenting that he did not want his remarks misconstrued, and he immediately lost the audience of editors and publishers. Sensing the situation he tried to recoup by restructuring his speech at the podium but was much too tired to succeed. Speaking extemporaneously, and then returning to his manuscript, he repeatedly covered the same ground and prolonged the agony for about two hours. As the speech dragged on Governor Woodrow Wilson, who had started taking notes, stopped writing, and his long face reflected his recognition of the gravity of La Follette's failure. "It was a shocking scene," wrote his Wisconsin ally, Henry Cooper, on the back of his dinner invitation. "He lost his temper repeatedly — shook his fist — at listeners who had started to walk out too tired to listen longer,— was abusive, ugly in manner." The hour was late. His delivery was poor. The evening was a disaster. Accompanied by his son-in-law, George Middleton, La Follette went directly to his room, spoke neither to Lenroot nor Steffens, walked into the bathroom, and vomited. That same evening he caught a train back to Washington to join Belle at the hospital where Mary was to undergo surgery.[34]

Fortunately Mary recovered from the operation. But La Follette's campaign never recuperated from the speech. Those, like McCormick and Garfield, who had long worked to replace him with Roosevelt, quickly seized upon the opportunity to declare that La Follette had broken down. The Pinchots, reluctant to repudiate their pledge of support but certain that Roosevelt was more likely to unseat Taft, finally were able to rationalize their open advocacy of the "rough rider." Gifford Pinchot attempted to give La Follette advance notice of his forthcoming public shift, but La Follette would not see him lest the public mistake Pinchot's endorsement of Roosevelt as one in which he concurred. On February 17 Pinchot wrote an explanation to La Follette; the letter was not made public until April 13. La Follette had undertaken a hopeless race in order to advance the progressive cause, he insisted, knowing that he might prepare the way for another but could not win it for himself. The decision of the Ohio convention had been endorsed by Houser, yet La Follette, on his own, had decided not to cooperate with candidates of a similar persuasion. Such a course would lead to the renomination of Taft and could only be justified if Roosevelt were not a progressive. Since Roosevelt was the only progressive candidate who could be nominated, he was backing him, despite his continued respect for La Follette's accomplishments. To make matters worse Houser informed interested progressives that La Follette was not himself and was uncharacteristically demanding personal loyalty; George Record interpreted a telephone conversation with the campaign manager to mean La Follette was withdrawing and the press trumpeted his statement. As the news from the East flashed across the country, the hesitant trickle of his supporters towards Roosevelt became a swift moving flood, carrying away even those who, like Hiram Johnson and Irvine Lenroot, had remained loyal until the fateful speech.[35]

As he had stated from the beginning of his campaign, La Follette was in the race until the close of the convention, and he restated his position in no uncertain terms. On February 5, resisting enormous pressure to sign a statement of withdrawal, he "REQUIRED" Houser to issue a release that he was taking a short rest and then would resume his campaign.[36] "In twenty years of fighting for the progressive cause," he informed the readers of his magazine, "I have not halted or turned aside to find the easy way. I have steadfastly refused to make combinations which would in any way involve the issues in uncertainty."[37] And many of his friends remained with him. He retained control over the Wisconsin delegation; Rudolph Spreckels and Charles Crane continued to finance his campaign, but Crane's contributions were on a reduced level. And Senator Asle Gronna of North Dakota reaffirmed his support: "Senator La Follette may have broken down temporarily. His friends, nevertheless, will support him to the end," he declared. "With a few weeks' rest he will be himself again, and I can not see why there should be any necessity for thinking about throwing our strength to any other man."[38]

The first primary was to be in North Dakota in late March, and there La Follette had the advantage. Senator Gronna's organization was at his disposal, while Roosevelt, only recently a declared candidate, entered after a series of setbacks in southern conventions; the Taft forces had acted swiftly to commit a solid South before the "rough rider" could make headway. Roosevelt sent many of his most prominent progressive supporters to North Dakota, but with the state progressive machinery behind La Follette, he allied himself with Congressman Louis Hanna's "stalwarts." La Follette campaigned personally in the state for four days. He responded to Gifford Pinchot's depiction of him as a disabled engine: "my fire box is all right, my drive wheels strong, and my sand box isn't empty." La Follette won a sweeping victory.[39]

Elated, he wrote that he hoped to carry Nebraska, South Dakota, half of Minnesota, Oregon and "with that lead, land California"; he felt it was possible to come to the convention with more votes than Roosevelt.[40] "The backwash of the Roosevelt wave is setting in," he commented hopefully. "His supporters are beginning to feel the strength of the opposition to him from real progressives."[41] As expected, La Follette easily carried Wisconsin in the next primary. In the meantime Taft added northern conventions to his southern totals and edged Roosevelt in the Massachusetts primary. Disturbed by the trend, Roosevelt cried fraud in state after state.

But in April the tide turned. Although La Follette spoke to large and responsive crowds and felt confident of victory in Oregon and Nebraska he was dealt a double defeat on April 19. Roosevelt had captured the progressive organization in both states and defeated La Follette in both primaries. By the time of the California primary, relations among former allies had become strained. Roosevelt's supporters insisted that La Follette was splitting the progressive vote. Once again La Follette was well received; even some of his former supporters were more than just cordial. Once again, Roosevelt won. And the pattern repeated itself in Ohio, New Jersey, and South Dakota. After Roosevelt swamped Taft in his home state, many thought the race was over. But one-third of the seats had been contested, and the Republican National Committee, which would decide the contests, was dominated by Taft. La Follette, optimistic as ever, expected the convention to be so evenly divided between Taft and Roosevelt that his thirty-six votes "may hold the balance of power, name the candidate and make the platform."[42]

The campaign had left him with a fierce anger towards Roosevelt; he was convinced that he could have carried all the progressive states won by the rough rider had he not been deserted, and there would have been no progressive split to open the way to a Taft nomination. The two progressive candidates had disagreed on tactics and issues but there had been a mutual need to cooperate in order to advance their respective careers and to promote progressivism. Despite growing disillusionment with the ex-President, La Follette had been guarded in his criticism even in private remarks, for he courted his support. Once Roosevelt emerged as a candidate all of their earlier differences, all of the more recent irritations were magnified, for La Follette felt he had been ill used. And as the Sagamore Sage defined his New Nationalism the Senator found that he disagreed with its central thesis, with the colonel's perception that trusts were inherently efficient and concentration, under government control, must be permitted in order to improve the nation's international competitive position. Roosevelt had never been a trust buster, he insisted, and was as acceptable to the interests as Taft. When he became president trust capitalization was $3,784,000,000; when he passed the reins of office to his hand-picked successor their paper value had grown to $31,672,000,000, 70% of it water. Formation of monopolies was a criminal conspiracy in violation of federal statutes and the common law, punishable by fine and imprisonment. The court injunction was an additional weapon available to a crusading official. "If in the earlier stages of trust formation, the Executive had used all the power of this great government to enforce the anti-trust law, it would have saved the people the payment of hundreds of millions of dollars wrongfully taken from them in excessive transportation rates, and in exorbitant trust prices which they had to pay for the necessaries of life." Neither a decent platform nor promises were sufficient. "The citizen should ask what the candidate has actually done toward solving the problems that confront us; whether his course of action gives the assurance of profound conviction. . . . " By this standard of measurement he did not consider Roosevelt a truly progressive candidate.[43] Consequently, he could take no action that might advance Roosevelt's interests.

On the eve of the convention La Follette wrote to his law partner, Alfred Rogers, who, as a Wisconsin national committeeman, would pass on the validity of delegate challenges. It was better if Taft won on the first ballot, he insisted, than that "our votes would be held responsible by fool progressives over the country for the defeat of their candidate. . . . The bluffer shall be kept as far from the wire as possible."[44] During the tense sessions of the national committee, in which most of Roosevelt's challenges were rejected by his own supporters,

Rogers was considered pro-Taft by the New York *Times*. Nevertheless, he voted in favor of at least some of Roosevelt's claims.[45] Of the 254 contested seats fewer than a hundred could be considered seriously; Gilbert Roe, La Follette's former partner and lifelong friend and adviser, estimated that no more than sixty-five had any substance. Roosevelt had a legitimate claim to a maximum of 49 contested seats, he continued. Roosevelt insisted that 72 contested delegates were unquestionably his because he needed that many to control the convention. Neither Taft nor Roosevelt had a legitimate majority, Roe concluded.[46]

Even after the decision of the national committee to grant the Roosevelt forces only 19 of the contested seats, Taft's control of the convention was not hopelessly irreversible. La Follette telegraphed his private secretary, John Hannan, that he wanted to make it clear in his speeches that he would only accept the nomination if a progressive platform were adopted. His main purpose was to distinguish his brand of progressivism from Roosevelt's, but the glimmer of hope remained.[47] Roosevelt, on the other hand, felt he still had a real chance at the nomination. His delegates supported him with a religious fervor. His managers had been in contact with wavering Taft delegates. Federal officeholders needed a winner to hold their jobs, and Taft did not fit that description. But they could not be expected to jeopardize their standing with the regular faction unless Roosevelt could show them that he was going to win the nomination. Roosevelt had to devise a tactic to stampede this group into his camp.

Taft's managers had chosen their candidate for temporary chairman carefully. It was to be Elihu Root, Roosevelt's former Secretary of State whom he had often praised. When widely respected Herbert Hadley, Governor of Missouri and Roosevelt's campaign manager, declined the honor of opposing Root, Roosevelt hit upon a new strategem. A supporter of La Follette would be offered support. Gilbert Roe refused. Francis McGovern, Governor of Wisconsin and the titular head of the Wisconsin delegation, was more amenable. In the eyes of the convention his candidacy would indicate a united front between the two camps and might influence just enough votes to carry the all-important first roll call. McGovern would then rule in

favor of Roosevelt in the case of the seventy-two contested
delegates, and it would be all over. For the ambitious
McGovern this represented an opportunity for national recognition that he could not pass up. While he was committed to La
Follette, Roosevelt appeared to be an acceptable progressive
candidate, and his supporters constituted the bulk of the
progressive wing of the party. He could not accept La Follette's
vehement opposition to the colonel.

La Follette had reasons to question Roosevelt's commitment
to the progressive cause. As a progressive governor La Follette
had seen a supposedly progressive president make common
cause with his "stalwart" opponents. As a senator he had often
criticized Roosevelt's compromises, bargaining away provisions that he felt essential to effective legislation, resulting in
laws inadequate to accomplish the purpose for which they had
been drafted. Nevertheless, he had supported Roosevelt
consistently. He had many reasons for refusing to make
common cause with his convention rival, for it really meant
preparing the way for his nomination. He believed that the
movement had outgrown the need to compromise and to accept
a charismatic candidate who could neither fully understand the
essentials of progressive programs nor be counted upon to
stand firm when conservative opposition mounted. He was
disturbed that Roosevelt had attracted George Perkins and
Frank Munsey as his closest advisors, for they represented the
very interests that La Follette had opposed throughout his
career. But more than anything else he harbored very strong
personal feelings against the ex-President. From the time of his
return from Africa the senator had suspected his motives;
almost alone, La Follette had been convinced that Roosevelt
was seeking renomination. To watch Roosevelt's friends undercut his candidacy from within his own organization when a
word of support from Oyster Bay might have ensured his own
nomination made him furious. The possibility that Roosevelt
was using him as a stalking horse cast a shadow upon his whole
campaign; when the colonel emerged from the background La
Follette was determined that his rival should not succeed.

The proposal that the Wisconsin delegation back its
chairman for temporary chairman of the convention was
presented to the delegates. From any angle they were in a

quandary. Unless the progressives succeeded in electing a temporary chairman who would rule in their favor, Taft would have a first ballot nomination; La Follette had an outside chance only if the convention was deadlocked. But a convention choice of McGovern, with the resultant rulings in favor of Roosevelt's seventy-two delegates, would probably have led to the New Yorker's nomination, and La Follette was determined not to extend any aid to the man who had undermined his campaign. Speaking for La Follette, Houser opposed any action, such as support for McGovern, which could be construed as an alliance with Roosevelt, or which would further his nomination. It was agreed that they would consult with the North Dakota delegation. A motion by McGovern that it would be to La Follette's advantage to name the temporary chairman passed by a voice vote, and John C. Blaine immediately said that he regretted that action. They decided to confer with La Follette the following day. La Follette endorsed Houser's presentation, and when warned that the delegation would split if he remained adamant, he asked that the split come on the first ballot, otherwise the delegation should remain with him to the end. John Hannan informed the group that Gilbert Roe had been approached by Roosevelt's emissaries prior to McGovern to create the appearance of collusion between the two candidates. McGovern protested that Hannan had not raised any objections when he inquired before committing himself. The vote was carried by La Follette by the margin of fifteen to eleven. Nevertheless, when the proceedings opened, Henry Cochems, who had presented La Follette for president in 1908, mounted the rostrum and offered McGovern in nomination. Seconding speeches were made by a series of Roosevelt's supporters. Finally, Walter Houser strode to the platform. Earlier in the campaign he had issued a number of statements that had proved injurious to La Follette's campaign. Everyone expected a seconding speech. "This nomination is not with Senator La Follette's consent," he declared. "We make no deals with Roosevelt. We make no trades with Taft." Roosevelt's ploy had failed. Root was chosen over McGovern, 558 to 502, with only 18 votes more than half the convention. The Wisconsin delegation had split: the majority had voted for McGovern, and the rest had scattered its votes for honorary candidates. But on the equally important motion by Governor Charles Deneen of Illinois to bar the contested delegates from voting on any of the contests the Wisconsin delegation had voted solidly with Roosevelt.[48] The selection of Root effectively ended the contest.

Now that it was apparent that Roosevelt could not obtain the Republican nomination, he prepared to bolt the convention. The only question that remained was finances. Amos Pinchot described the scene that evening in the colonel's suite, with twenty followers staring at George Perkins and Frank Munsey conferring while the candidate paced, until both walked towards him, placed a hand on each of his shoulders and said: "Colonel, we will see you through."[49]

Realizing that disaster was imminent, some of Taft's supporters sought a compromise candidate, with Governor Hadley as the most likely choice. Roosevelt refused to consider any proposal unless his seventy-two delegates were seated, which would have obviated the need for compromise; Roosevelt would then probably have been nominated. Consequently, Taft was chosen by a majority of the convention, while 344 of Roosevelt's delegates refused to vote. When Roosevelt prepared to have himself selected by a new party of his creation he found that many of his entourage who held office and had something to lose would not follow him: most of the governors and senators who had endorsed his candidacy chose to remain with the Republican party.[50]

La Follette was disturbed by the turn of events. Republicans had prevented George Perkins of the House of Morgan from becoming Roosevelt's Hanna. But Roosevelt, he thought, might have shattered the prospects for a progressive Congress; he was entering candidates against progressives who would not support him and was promising not to oppose reactionaries who endorsed him. "I agree with you that everything should be done to prevent true progressive republicans from joining the Roosevelt party," he wrote to Rudolph Spreckels. "His success means disaster to the progressive cause and to the country."[51]

Throughout that summer *La Follette's* attacked Roosevelt. Reiterating charges raised during the fight for delegates, La Follette accused Roosevelt of making forceful and positive speeches on subjects not in dispute while treating progressive principles in general terms; "he does not go to the real rock of the existing evils" such as overcapitalization; he blamed the middleman, but not the trust and tariff, for the high cost of living. Louis Brandeis, a Wilson man, wrote an article challenging his labor stance; his platform did not include the right to organize, and he supported trusts that had bad labor records. Spreckels, who had campaigned for La Follette and then endorsed Wilson, wrote that the ex-President had Wall Street's approval, while Wilson was not favored by the special interests. During the closing months of the campaign La Follette ran the last chapters of his autobiography in which he described, in most unpleasant terms, the colonel's activities during his campaign.[52]

"He cannot support Taft, and he must oppose Roosevelt," Belle informed their cousin. "But he does not intend to endorse Wilson. It is his purpose to build up and unify the progressive republican strength, ready for any work that comes to them to do."[53]

La Follette had been impressed with Wilson for over a year. In early 1911 he had commented that the governor's successful fight to elect James Martine to the Senate had redeemed the choice of the preferential primary; he approved of Wilson's public statements on initiative, referendum, and recall in commission government. As the fight for the Democratic nomination narrowed down, he made it clear that he favored the New Jersey governor over Champ Clark and Oscar Underwood; afterwards he commented that the convention had chosen the most progressive candidate available to it. He expressed reserved praise for Wilson's acceptance speech; it was not ambiguous, particularly on the tariff, even if it was insufficiently specific and somewhat restrained. But the 1910 Democratic Congress had not established a progressive record, and he feared that Wilson could not accomplish much, even if elected.[54] "Now about Wilson," he wrote to Roe. "I am moving slowly. He has been a progressive (of a certain kind) about eighteen months. For my part I have had an experience quite fresh in my mind, of depending on half baked progressives of the republican brand. And it justifies me in going a little slow on a democrat progressive who hasn't shed his milk teeth yet." Besides, he had not yet asked Bryan to visit.[55]

As Wilson elaborated the New Freedom, La Follette was

pleased with his compatible analysis of the central theme of corporate concentration. Wilson's economic adviser was Louis Brandeis, with whom the senator had honed his views on public issues over dinner at his house almost every time the lawyer visited Washington. They had particularly emphasized the questions of trusts and railroad regulation. Both rejected the New Nationalist contention that monopolies were a result of efficiency. Both insisted that competition created productive companies and that monopolies were the result of unfair methods of competition, methods that must be eliminated. In his speeches, Wilson emphasized the inefficiency of trusts, which carried the burden of watered stock and uneconomic plants purchased at outlandish prices to complete the monopoly. They feared competition, he asserted, and prevented it by foul means. He categorized the New Nationalism as a new partnership between trusts and the government; such a partnership already existed, with corporate domination, and the New Freedom intended to dissolve it. La Follette was sufficiently attracted to consider declaring for the Democrat as a private citizen, but in the end he just permitted his readers to glean his preference from his editorial bias; his supporters in Wisconsin openly declared for the Princeton historian.

As the campaign drew to a close La Follette characterized Wilson's campaign speeches: "The lucidity and intelligence of the political exposition was an intellectual treat of the first order; while the nobility of sentiment, the feeling for democracy and for America struck home to the susceptibilities of the audience like an experience of religion." His election reflected the people's distaste for special interest domination under Roosevelt and Taft. He hoped that the President-elect could overcome his reactionary caucus and produce progressive legislation. In any event, the progressive Republicans would support him when he was right and oppose him when he was wrong.[56]

Even before the new administration took office La Follette experienced an unexpected political bonus. Shaken by events, the old guard decided to make concessions to the progressive mood of the electorate. La Follette and Cummins were added to the Republican steering committee. Of the five bills that emerged three had been previously introduced by La Follette and a fourth proposed concepts he had been advocating since his maiden Senate speech. The Republican caucus endorsed bills to limit injunctions, to supply legislative reference and drafting services, to regulate women's hours and conditions of employment, to create a tariff commission, and to provide for physical evaluation of railroads as the basis for rate making. While all of these bills incorporated principles for which he had been making a spirited fight, the item closest to him was the physical valuation bill. As its leading advocate since 1906, he was placed in charge of the subcommittee to which Representative William Adamson's measure was referred. While he could no longer prevent the legitimizing of previous excessive capitalization, he and John R. Commons worked daily, into the early morning, perfecting a bill that would prevent rewarding future overcapitalization. Had this principle been acted upon when he first offered it, he told the Senate, shippers would have saved $400,000,000. Before anyone bought a business he would want its physical plant evaluated, he reminded them. Yet for years the ICC had been expected to set reasonable rates without it, despite their repeated requests. Physical valuation should be based on original cost to date, as already employed in Wisconsin and Washington, for it showed true investment as opposed to watered stock. He rejected such intangibles as good will for that could only be included in a competitive situation, and carriers were monopolies. The bill, once considered so radical, passed unanimously.[57]

# CHAPTER 8

## Progressives and a Minority President

THE advent of the new administration brought about marked changes in Washington. In place of the jovial and personable Taft was the austere and aloof Woodrow Wilson, a president who felt most comfortable addressing people en masse across a rostrum, not individually in close proximity, and who believed that he could move a nation to a new morality through his oratorical prowess. Ascetic in taste, Wilson dispensed with the pomp of the traditional inaugural ball and cancelled it. His inaugural address was a statement of progressive purpose, a call for national revitalization nourished by nonpartisan contributions (a wise appeal from a minority president), an effort to attract progressive followers of La Follette and Roosevelt.[1]

It was not only Wilson's progressive rhetoric that distinguished his administration from his predecessor. His relationship with the legislature was in marked contrast. Where Taft had relied upon the congressional leadership, Wilson saw himself in the role of parliamentary party leader and strongly asserted himself through the congressional caucus. As a result a remarkable variety and quantity of legislation was passed in a relatively short time.

Administrators of cabinet rank serving Roosevelt and Taft had been largely recruited from those who earlier had occupied sub-cabinet positions. Extended Republican executive dominance had made this all but inevitable. Wilson's cabinet was composed largely of men who had no previous administrative experience on a national level. The only exception was Secretary of Interior Franklin Lane, a member of the Interstate Commerce Commission. The most prestigious position, Secretary of State, went to three-time Presidential candidate,

William Jennings Bryan, a personal and political friend of La Follette. Two congressmen, a newspaper editor, a college president, a judge, a labor leader, and two lawyers sat with the President. All had progressive reputations, even if not all sustained their reputations in office. Wilson had considered Brandeis for two separate posts but had bowed to heated opposition.[7] This administration had the potential of earning La Follette's support.

The strongest member of Wilson's cabinet was Secretary of Treasury William Gibbs McAdoo, a pragmatic political amateur, and his future son-in-law. While La Follette was to have specific differences with McAdoo, they had much in common. Like La Follette he had faith in the ability of the people to make decisions: "The 'common people' . . . have, through this instinct or common sense a comprehension second only in its accuracy to mathematics or an exact science," McAdoo insisted, providing only that they were properly informed.[3] Like La Follette and Brandeis he felt that trusts were not the product of economic necessity but of the greed of promoters, and their further expansion had to be prevented to restore healthful competition. Trusts did not bring about increased wages, he continued; unions did.[4] And he emphasized the relationship between monopoly and the tariff: ". . .The trust evils would largely disappear if the 'trusts' were forced into wholesome competition with the world and were deprived of the power they now have to tax the people for their special benefit."[5] He joined Brandeis in promoting legislation for regulated competition.

New blood brought new insights into how things could be done. Faced with the perennial problem of the shortage of money at harvest time, McAdoo shifted government deposits to the South to finance the movement of the cotton crop. And as problems arose an active treasury department improvised solutions.[6]

La Follette could look to the new administration with guarded optimism. Wilson had praised La Follette for his progressive accomplishments and for his thorough preparation for legislative debate. The cabinet had a progressive cast. Still, La Follette was distressed by Wilson's appointments. Until the cabinet was announced La Follette and other progressive

Republicans had been led to believe that Brandeis would be attorney general. His absence from the cabinet list so infuriated La Follette, that he questioned the sincerity of Wilson's progressivism.[7] And, despite Wilson's non-partisan appeals his appointments were partisan. "Indeed, the attitude of the whole Democratic organization towards the Progressive Republicans who assisted directly and indirectly in Wilson's election, is really very exasperating," he wrote Gilbert Roe. "Intense partisanship controls in patronage. Wilson seems very willing to fall in line and appoint machine politicians."[8] Even after he became reconciled to partisan appointments, he remained disappointed in the calibre of the men chosen.[9] The designation of John Skelton Williams as Assistant Secretary of the Treasury after Robert Wooley, an investigator of trusts, had been officially announced for the position, particularly disturbed him, for he considered him to be a Wall Street candidate.[10] And Wilson's appointments to the Interstate Commerce Commission "make those who want to be friendly with his Administration, sick and disgusted."[11] When Wilson overcame opposition to his first ICC appointment La Follette wrote: "What an inspiring spectacle to the millions who voted for Wilson as a true Progressive to see him in one short year triumph over progressive Democrats and progressive Republicans by securing the support of about all that remains of the old Aldrich oligarchy in the United States Senate."[12] Moreover the Democrats were so hungry after a long famine that some new positions were not protected by the merit system, but were open to patronage; La Follette felt this was the most serious attack on the merit system since its establishment in 1883.[13] "And yet," La Follette concluded, "Wilson is a great improvement on Roosevelt and Taft."[14]

La Follette's concern that the President would be hampered by a reactionary congressional caucus gave way to a solicitude for congressional autonomy. Prior to the inauguration La Follette expressed fear that a Democratic caucus, subservient to the money trust, had controlled Congress: "CZAR CANNON is deposed, Boss ALDRICH is gone; but King Caucus now rules."[15] As the new Congress met, under the new administration, the caucus was democratized, even if La

Follette did not think it adequately reformed.[16] But Wilson so dominated the caucus that La Follette refrained from applauding his ability to push progressive legislation through a long recalcitrant body. Even a righteous purpose achieved by wrong methods can hurt, he warned. A rubber stamp Congress could come under the influence of a president controlled by the special interests. Wilson should not have used patronage to dominate the legislature. He should have extended the civil service and provided for election to the rest of the positions.[17]

Nevertheless, La Follette was favorably impressed, upon the whole, with at least the cabinet choices.[18] And he was determined to be a cooperative critic. He called upon progressives in all parties not to play politics for 1916, but to support any worthwhile progressive legislative proposals of the administration.[19]

Wilson began his term as Taft had, with a call for a special congressional session to deal with the tariff. There the similarity ended. Viewing himself as a strong party leader he worked closely with the party's legislative leadership to enact his own comprehensive program. As if to signal his conception of a strengthened and extended Presidential power he appeared before a joint session to deliver his tariff message; not since John Adams had a president taken this step. He reminded Congress that tariffs no longer protected infant industries, as originally conceived; but gave each group of producers what they wanted to maintain an exclusive market and to organize monopolies. Now "nothing is obliged to stand the tests of efficiency and economy." It was necessary to abolish privilege and "put our business men and producers under the stimulation of a constant necessity to be efficient, economical and enterprising, masters of competitive supremacy, better workers and merchants than any in the world." He did not intend changes so drastic as to uproot business but to "adopt freedom in the place of artificial stimulation only so far as it will build, not pull down."[20] The day after he delivered his speech Wilson returned to the capitol for the first of a series of conferences with Democratic leaders.[21]

Nothing in the President's speech was at variance with La

Follette's ideas. Shortly before the opening of the session he had written an editorial opposing the replacement of a protective tariff by one solely for revenue; but he was agreeable to substantial reduction in schedules.[22] La Follette was committed to the concept of a tariff rectifying the difference in the cost of production at home and abroad so that real competition could occur. The test of compatibility would come with the drafting of specific rates.

The Democratic schedule revisions of 1911 nd 1912, vetoed by Taft, had telegraphed their approach to a new tariff. The House bill reduced rates from the 40% of the Payne-Aldrich Act to 29%; the duties were ad valorem with no deceptive provisions to disguise excessive rates; under pressure from Wilson wool was placed on the free list and the sugar duty was limited to three years. To compensate for a decrease in revenue, Cordell Hull drafted an amendment that provided a moderately graduated income tax.[23] The Underwood-Simmons bill was still not satisfactory to La Follette.

La Follette sat as a minority member on the Senate Finance Committee to which the bill was referred; first two amendments to the motion to refer were offered and received his support. Senator Boise Penrose proposed open hearings, though he would not have supported them had the Republicans been in a majority. La Follette pressed a change that would have required that businessmen testifying before the committee answer sixteen questions under oath about their profits, production costs, and wages. While both amendments were defeated, La Follette's sixteen items were included in the questionnaire sent to interested manufacturers. The Democratic members of the committee drafted revisions in secret, intending to impose them on the Democratic senators in caucus without even following the tradition of consulting the minority members of the committee. La Follette responded with an angry attack on "King Caucus" and warned that secret transactions were the first step toward public betrayal.

In the meantime those Democrats who were reluctantly bound by the caucus were heavily pressured, endangering Wilson's narrow majorities on the sugar and wool provisions. To maintain his initiative Wilson denounced lobbyists for special interests. Attempting to embarrass the President, Cummins called for a committee examination of the charge; La Follette converted a political maneuver into a probing investigation by calling upon all senators to disclose property holdings that were affected by the tariff. Neither move could be opposed, and under the glare of the spotlight opposition to free wool and sugar disappeared. For his part, La Follette informed the public that he had a magazine, a farm, and a few shares in a zinc mine; consequently he had abstained from voting on the lead and zinc schedules in 1909.[24]

When the bill was brought before the Senate La Follette listened to days of "standpat" oratory and then called the progressive Republicans into conference; the eleven senators agreed to support wise downward revisions and to try to improve the Democratic measure wherever possible and not follow Republican leadership amendments. As diligent as always, La Follette convinced Wilson to permit him to examine the files of the defunct Tariff Board. Aided by tariff expert William Culbertson and guided by the former chairman of the Tariff Board, Professor Henry Emery of Yale, La Follette drafted substitutes for the proposed schedules on wool, cotton, earthenware, glassware, iron, steel, grain, and sugar. The resulting legislation was not entirely satisfactory to him, but he felt that in many important schedules it was a moderately protective tariff conforming to the principle of the difference in the cost of production — even though the Democrats labeled it competitive tariff rates. The proposal would not injure business, yet it lowered rates sufficiently to permit foreign competition and prevent extortionate prices. Together with Washington's Progressive Senator Miles Poindexter he joined the Democrats in voting for the bill.[25]

La Follette and Joseph Bristow prepared for the income tax amendment with a modification which would have increased the rates above $100,000 from 3% to 10%, while Norris proposed an inheritance tax with a top of 75%. The progressive Republicans were joined in their demands by James Vardaman of Mississippi and James Reed of Missouri. La Follette insisted that the great fortunes had to bear their share of the burden of government. The income and inheritance taxes "will help us to attain that end which our fathers thought they were guaranteeing to us when they provided forever against the law of primogeniture and entail." Extended support for these proposals in the Democratic caucus shook the bill's managers, and the intervention of Bryan and Wilson was necessary to obtain a compromise ceiling of 6% on incomes over $500,000. Progressive Democrats such as Cordell Hull were delighted with the beginning they had made.[26]

One major diversion from the special cession tariff debate was consideration of a joint resolution for the suffragette constitutional amendment. The La Follettes were deeply involved in the women's suffrage movement. As a leading speaker for the group Belle participated in the presentation before the Senate committee. Mary's illness with scarlet fever had prevented her mother from leading the homemakers' section of the pre-inaugural parade, but Robert, Jr., and Philip both marched. Fola carried the banner for the actresses' division in the New York parade, while her husband, the playwright George Middleton, and Gilbert Roe joined the procession up Fifth Avenue. In the capitol rotunda a group of senators and congressmen received state petitions from five hundred and thirty-one women, two from each state and one from each congressional district; Fola presented the Wisconsin document.[27] In offering the Wisconsin petition to the Senate La Follette reaffirmed his belief in "cosuffrage," coeducation, equality of opportunity for men and women. "Democracy is safest where its entire citizenship is most enlightened, most interested, most alert. If the ballot educates men in citizenship and is a source of power and protection to them, surely it is of equal value to women." The heart of this presentation, at a time when vast armies of single and married women were gainfully employed, was on woman as homemaker: "The very basis and foundation of all organized society is the home. . . . Just as it is essential that we should have the cooperation of the women of the country in the development of the home life, so we should have the cooperation of the women of the country in the legislation which underlies the home life and is foundational to all our social relations.''[28] Though she had earned a law degree his own talented wife never practiced, and she wrote the women's column in the magazine. The La Follettes remained active in the movement until the amendment was finally adopted.

During this period there occurred a number of personal events of note. La Follette's eldest son left Washington to become a freshman at the University of Wisconsin, where he was promptly elected class president. Shortly thereafter the family changed residence, as the owner of the Wyoming Avenue house decided to occupy it, and they rented a larger place at 3320 Sixteenth Street where they were to live for the next decade. Finally, La Follette joined his son at the university for a time as he delivered a lecture on Hamlet before he returned to the capital in time to hear the President, in his state of the union address, request a change in the banking and currency legislation and a strengthening of the anti-trust laws.[29]

Where the actions of an earlier Democratic Congress had prepared the way for swift passage of the administration's tariff bill, the activities of the previous Congress created a public climate favorable to progressive objections to the administration's banking bill and forced Wilson to accept revisions along these lines. When it was first announced that a resolution to investigate banking was to be sent to the Pujo Committee on Banking and Currency, La Follette reported that neither he nor the Bryan-Wilson wing of the Democratic party expected a serious probe. But La Follette was soon satisfied that public opinion had forced a real investigation.[30] The Pujo report on the last day of February confirmed progressive charges of growing concentration of corporate control in the hands of investment banking houses (in 1908 La Follette had insisted that a hundred men controlled the nation's credit through interlocking directorates); the share of the twenty largest banks and trust companies in the New York financial resources had grown from 34.97% in 1901 to 42.97% in 1911. Through consolidation, stock purchases in competitive firms, interlocking directorates, voting trusts, and partnerships enormous power was exercised by just four investment banking houses and two banks. J. P.

Morgan and Company, the strongest of the investment houses, with its banking allies, controlled 341 directorships in 112 corporations having aggregate resources of a capitalization of $22,245,000,000. This sum then represented more than the total wealth of the nation west of the Mississippi River and three times that of the eleven states that had once composed the Confederacy.[31]

There was general agreement that the banking system needed revision. It had been established during the Civil War partially to create a market for government bonds, for deposit of these bonds became the basis for the issuance of currency by national banks. The system did not permit needed flexibility; it did not increase currency supply during business expansion or crop movement. Nelson Aldrich's National Monetary Commission offered an essentially European solution to the problem, a banker-controlled National Reserve Association issuing currency based on gold and commercial paper (assets currency) with member-controlled branch banks. While it provided for flexible currency, the plan was anathema to progressives. La Follette emphasized the menace to competition from the concentration of money and credit by those who controlled monopolies. The proposed National Reserve Association put power over the people's money in the hands of the moneyed interests and would permit them to take advantage of the real need for elasticity to prevent competitors of the trusts from obtaining capital.[32]

Carter Glass of Virginia headed a subcommittee entrusted with the responsibility of drafting a Democratic alternative to this plan. Glass offered a privately controlled but decentralized reserve system; Wilson insisted upon a general supervisory board, and it was incorporated into the proposal. When a memorandum containing the provision was leaked to the press, there was a furor among progressive Democrats. The Bryan wing of the party, supported by McAdoo, wanted government control over the system and over the issue of currency. Perplexed, Wilson called upon Brandeis for advice, and Brandeis supported Bryan. Convinced that the Glass plan could not obtain party support, Wilson endorsed government control of the Federal Reserve Bank and the issuance of currency but private control of regional banks. Agrarians balked at this concession to local bankers and objected to the provision for currency based on commercial paper which ignored short term agricultural paper; they insisted upon prohibition of interlocking directorates as well. Wilson promised to proscribe interlocking directorates in a forthcoming anti-trust bill and offered not to interfere with the all but certain House committee addition of short term agricultural paper. After considerable maneuvering the bill passed both houses.[33]

La Follette objected to the new law. It "merely legalized the monopoly control of the credits of the country, which has been builded up by the great financiers."[34] Even though it had a presidentially appointed central board it had banker-controlled district reserve banks, and that is where real power lay. And there was no prohibition of interlocking directorates. In effect, it gave the responsibility for destroying the money power to the money power itself.[35]

Initially La Follette had been favorably impressed by the general outlines of Wilson's anti-trust program, to define proper business practices clearly and to prosecute violators. La Follette had drawn upon the collective experience of a number of progressives in drafting legislation to supplement the Sherman Anti-trust Act in 1911 and 1912, particularly emphasizing the need to define unfair restraint of trade and to undo the damage of the Standard Oil decisions' reference to the rule of reason. With the aid of Brandeis his 1912 proposal was revised and submitted to the Senate again. Through Brandeis, Wilson was informed of the outline of the bill. As Wilson prepared to present his program the stock market began to decline, credit to tighten, and unemployment to grow. La Follette felt that business was creating a panic in order to pressure the President. He was convinced that the fear of growing unemployment had led to the passage of a Federal Reserve Act satisfactory to the money power, to the dropping of the telephone and telegraph anti-trust suits, and to the end of consideration of government ownership of telegraph and telephone. "The Administration announces it has found a way to get cooperation between the big boys who have been doing bad things and the government," he wrote to Rudolph Spreckels. "The bad boys are to stop doing bad things in the *name* of the *'Bad Boy's Combination'* and go on doing the same things under another name."[36] With James McReynolds "fixing things up" with trusts out of court, the trusts were getting on line to be regularized. In addition the administration had tried to Democratize legislation and had failed to consult the progressives, who had an understanding of the question, and the results were "flabby and without teeth."[37]

At about this time La Follette was becoming a little wary of commissions. "Whenever the law is so reconstructed as to provide for the thoroughgoing control of railway rates and services by the commission, then the System will fight to the last ditch to CONTROL THE COMMISSION," he warned. When the interests begin to support a commission they either intend to pass ineffective legislation or obtain "friendly" appointments. More than vigilance was necessary; the electorate should be able to recall commissioners who failed to serve the public interests.[38] He worried when Wilson supported a bill by Sam Rayburn and Louis Brandeis to grant control over financial operations of railroads to the ICC. This would prevent the declining value of securities by government sanction of future issues of securities. Once the government approved the issuance of securities, he feared, it committed itself to increased rates to insure payment for these securities if they went sour. It would "guarantee railroad profits and sterilize corrupt railway finance."[39]

Nor was he comforted by Wilson's appointments to these bodies. He disapproved of the designation of Thomas Jones of the Harvester trust and James P. Warburg of Kuhn, Loeb and Company as members of the Federal Reserve Board; Warburg, at least, was an expert on central banking. Jones withdrew after the Senate Banking Committee balked at confirmation.[40] As ICC vacancies occurred, he was troubled by Wilson's replacements. Henry Clay Hall was a railroad lawyer, he noted, and Winthrop M. Daniels had made such a bad record on the New Jersey Public Utilities Commission that James Martine, the progressive Democrat from New Jersey, was paired against his confirmation. Wilson applied so much pressure to confirm Daniels in executive session that La Follette led a revolt against confirmation of appointees behind closed doors.[41] La Follette's qualms about the new ICC members were confirmed when they both voted for an increase in railroad rates, basing their decision on possible repercussions of the European war; the dissenting minority could find no evidence that increased rates were fair and reasonable. "For the first time in history, the Interstate Commerce Commission has taken unto itself authority to increase rates, without regard to whether the increased rate will produce a reasonable return upon the fair value of the property," he protested. Its ruling was not based on law, precedent or Supreme Court decisions. Thus, the government guaranteed profits of a railroad even if it was mismanaged and fraudulently capitalized. It meant the end of regulation, he predicted, for if the people must foot the bill, they will take charge of the business.[42]

As Brandeis and George Rublee were completing a plan for a strong Federal Trade Commission as the pivot of the administration anti-trust program, La Follette measured Wilson's accomplishments in this area against his platform. He found success only in reducing the tariff. The President had not provided protection against the domination of the money trust as promised. Nor had he enforced criminal laws against trust officials, passed legislation to make private monopoly impossible, or reduced the high cost of living by breaking up criminal conspiracies; and he had compromised with violators of the criminal provisions of the anti-trust laws despite his vows. "Recent events are causing the gravest apprehension for the future of democratic ideals. . . . To his progressive friends in both parties he appears to be rocking the boat."[43]

Despite his intense interest in the anti-trust question La Follette was unable to contribute to the final shaping of either the Federal Trade Commission or the Clayton Anti-trust Act, for in late June, 1914, he became seriously ill. It began with a day of regurgitating bile, and then he noticed a partial loss of feeling on one side and impaired motion on the other so that he walked with a limp. With his strange fascination with poison, he insisted it was a toxic substance and not a stroke. He asserted that he had been informed by his doctors that he was not suffering from hardening of the arteries (some degree of arteriosclerosis would have been normal for a man of his years). The symptoms fit either a cerebral vascular accident or an infectious inflammation of a blood vessel in the brain. In any event, he was limited to writing editorials for his magazine. Belle could not remain at home, because she had contracted to engage in a series of debates on women's suffrage. With eighteen-year-old Robert, Jr., acting as secretary, marketer, and counselor, the senator spent a lonesome and restless summer. "Poor Girl, this has been one awfully gruelling summer," he wrote to Belle who was travelling from one hot Chautauqua tent to another. "How you have stood up under it I don't understand. . . . My but you are a great woman. I love you."[44]

His illness forced him to cancel speaking dates in the vicinity of Washington at a loss of $8000. It became difficult for him to meet the magazine deficits, and his sponsors were reluctant to make up the difference; they were concerned that the magazine had become too much of a strain on him. After exhausting his alternatives, La Follette converted the magazine into a monthly to cut expenses.[45]

It was in his magazine that his sparse comments on Wilson's anti-trust legislation appeared. He was pleased with the provisions to prevent interlocking directorates and to exempt labor from its application. But with good reason he was not optimistic that the Supreme Court would interpret this paragraph to provide labor's exemption; it was uncertain, and labor always paid the price of uncertainty.[46]

In letters to confidants La Follette's summary of Wilson's domestic record to that point coincided with that of Brandeis. Wilson had been disappointing, compromising, but he had done some good things for which the corporate crowd would never forgive him. He was at least "entitled to the credit of having dealt with the subjects that his predecessors allowed the interests to run away with."[47] "I think he has made altogether the best public record that any President has made on progressive policies. In saying this I should add that I have felt he has many times halted just short of doing the right thing in a thoroughgoing way."[48]

By election eve of 1914 the Wilson administration had significant accomplishments in progressive legislation, limited perhaps by Wilson's own hesitation and lack of economic expertise, perhaps by the felt need to reassure the business community in the middle of a growing depression, and perhaps by a concern for the economic dislocations of a European war. Yet the elections were a setback for the progressives. Teddy Roosevelt shocked and divided his own Progressive party by his suggestion that they endorse a conservative Republican for the New York gubernatorial nomination and by his general lack of interest in the coming campaign, one that would be crucial for his fledgling party.[49] The stand of Progressive leaders in favor of striking miners tore the Colorado Progressive party asunder, with national repercussions.[50] And La Follette made his own contribution to the progressive debacle. In Wisconsin the progressives lacked an ongoing organization to resolve conflicting ambitions; except in years in which La Follette ran for reelection, progressives competed for the same constitutency against solid "standpat" opposition. For the first time since the death of Sawyer the conservatives were really ably led, by Emanuel Philipp. And the conservatives had turned their own issues against the progressives. Despite a depression, state residents were faced with rising taxes to meet the costs of growing governmental responsibilities (including a new and expensive highway program) and moderate inflation. The McGovern administration was charged with waste and inefficiency, with undemocratic bureaucratization, and with undue reliance on the university with the result that it was excessively funded. In addition, "fair minded" Democrats, anticipating a close contest, were involved in their own primary, and not swelling the totals of the progressive Republicans. Not the least of the factors leading to progressive defeat was La Follette's vendetta against McGovern for his role in the 1912 convention.[51]

Relations between La Follette and McGovern had always been tenuous. McGovern was not a member of the original coalition formed to fight Sawyer on a state level, a coalition which had come to regard La Follette as its leader. McGovern matured in the Milwaukee reform movement and came as an equal ally with his own power base. In 1908 and 1910 McGovern had refused to enter conferences to select candidates and had advanced his own ambitions. La Follette's caucus was so resentful that they did not want the Senator to endorse him.[52] Governor McGovern built his own political machine and not only ignored La Follette on patronage but even rejected his requests to retain progressive officeholders.[53] Nevertheless, unlike many progressives, La Follette found little fault in McGovern's first term. But one issue that was to become the public basis for his later disapproval brought a comment from him during McGovern's first year in office. "The *supreme test* by which the progressive movement is to stand or fall is that every gain acquired by the instruments of democratic government must be balanced by a substantial practical gain of efficiency in government. In other words, we must make good right along in *results;* otherwise progressive government is no better than reactionary government."[54]

McGovern's role in the 1912 convention ensured his break with La Follette. But this rift was not to occur in 1912, for there was too much danger of a conservative taking advantage of it. "McGovern's foolish performance at Chicago has embittered thousands of progressives against him, and it will require the strongest efforts which I can put forth to save him from defeat," La Follette wrote. "I cannot afford to let his betrayal of my candidacy at Chicago jeopardize our progressive work in Wisconsin."[55] Accordingly La Follette endorsed McGovern strongly and wrote an editorial appeal for his candidacy. He campaigned in Wisconsin and distributed a personal letter calling for the support of the full Republican state ticket.[56]

During his second term McGovern tried to remove insurance commissioner Herman Ekern, one of the senator's closest associates, and vetoed a proposed referendum on women's suffrage, one of the great crusades of the La Follette clan.[57] The two progressive factions became so antagonistic that legislation was stalled for fear the other would get credit.[58] La Follette defended McGovern from complaints against the proliferation of commissions, for commissions justified their expenses by saving the public many times their costs, and disaffection with the University of Wisconsin, reminding his lieutenants that it was necessary to protect the university as a vital part of the state progressive movement.[59] McGovern's real failure was insufficient restraint of excessive appropriations through executive veto and consequent high taxes. Progressives had to increase services through increased revenues, not new taxes.[60]

But in 1914 McGovern was not running for reelection, and the considerations of 1912 no longer applied. He was seeking Stephenson's Senate seat. La Follette was determined to prevent his nomination. Although the La Follette organization issued a campaign document, signed by Houser, accusing McGovern of betraying La Follette and charged him with trying to replace the senator as the power in Wisconsin, Tom Morris, its candidate, lost to McGovern and quiet anti-Catholicism. La Follette would not rest. He was disappointed when no one would run as an independent, but he still opposed McGovern in the general election with a clear conscience because the Democrats had nominated a progressive candidate, Paul Hustings. "It may be that the Lord had ordained that Wisconsin should lead on to a union of the progressives of both parties," he wrote. The defection of La Follette's supporters led to Husting's victory.[61] Nonplussed, McGovern made another attempt at the governor's office in 1916, but was unsuccessful. The La Follette faction remained so wary of McGovern that as late as 1922 it prevented him from heading the new All American Council for fear that he would use this as a springboard for a return to politics and contest La Follette's seat.[62]

While the La Follette camp was concentrating its ire against McGovern a real threat to Wisconsin progressivism arose. Emanuel Philipp had long regretted his support for La Follette in 1900. He had served the conservative cause in lesser capacities as first Charles Pfister and then W. D. Connor mishandled their charge. Philipp came to the fore as progressivism peaked and remained while economic conditions and the advanced program of McGovern caused discontent among the electorate. In 1914 the progressives had neither an incumbent candidate nor an anointed successor; their two most attractive officeholders were locked in combat; and attacks on

McGovern by La Follette and his followers gave currency to conservative charges. Philipp turned the progressive's arguments against them. He touched upon their Jeffersonian belief in economy and efficiency; in place of their fear of corporate domination he substituted concern for a growing impersonal bureaucracy; in place of boss domination he substituted the behind-the-scenes influence of university intellectuals and Charles McCarthy and the reference services. Philipp himself was an intelligent and articulate spokesman of conservatism.

Once again conflicting ambitions produced an excess of progressive aspirants despite the efforts of Alfred Rogers to produce a consensus candidate. La Follette had great faith that the second choice provision would defeat Philipp, but, to his distress, it was not emphasized. Philipp won a plurality, and La Follette could not support his conservative Democratic opponent. When pressured to pursue an independent candidacy he expressed his reluctant willingness, but emphasized his health and Senate seniority. John Blaine attempted the race, and La Follette came to Wisconsin at the end of the contest to speak in his behalf, but he drew few votes, and Philipp won handily.[63]

La Follette's "heart is sad and heavy," Belle wrote to her eldest son. "Of course nothing could ever make your papa believe that Wisconsin or the country is going to be always reactionary. He says one had better die than lose faith. But the time ahead at best looks short to people of our age. It is a great comfort to feel that you children will be ready to do your part."[64] Publicly he showed optimism. Even if some of the statutes comprising "the Wisconsin Idea of Fundamental Democracy" were repealed "NOTHING VITAL WILL BE LOST":

> Every advance movement in history has experienced its checks and reverses from time to time. But nothing can permanently harm a righteous cause. Defeat only strengthens the courage and resolution of a man worthy to fight for human progress.[65]

Privately he was more concerned. Philipp, he realized, was too shrewd to destroy everything in two years and frighten away moderates. He would use "a pretense of economy," and *"a safe and sane business administration"* to render progressive laws innocuous. After reelection he would start dismantling progressivism. Yet, even in private correspondence the senator could not subordinate his perennial optimism, and he pretended to himself and his confidants that 1914 had not been a national progressive disaster. While there was evidence of "standpat victories," he wrote to the faithful Rudolph Spreckels, they were in conservative areas like New Hampshire, Illinois, and Pennsylvania; the fact that Roosevelt carried Illinois and Pennsylvania "in itself is evidence that they were not progressive."[66] He would not admit that progressive influence within the Republican party had been shattered as a result of the creation of the Progressive party and the enormous decline of electoral support for progressive Republicans in states where they had been a powerful minority faction.[67] Despite the 1914 election, national progressive legislation continued to be enacted.

Of all the legislation that La Follette was instrumental in securing, an almost forgotten law was his pride and joy. The only statute to bear La Follette's name, the Seaman's Law was the child of Andrew Furuseth, president of the Seamen's Union. Furuseth, of Norwegian birth, had been a mariner from the age of sixteen; he had sailed the oceans of the world on the decks of ships of every great maritime nation; everywhere sailors were treated as chattel, bound to unseaworthy craft, "hunted down and thrown into the ship's holds in chains" if they tried to escape. Seamen and passengers had been sacrificed to the greed of owners as undermanned vessels, lacking skilled sailors, had sunk, and insufficient lifeboats had been supplied for passengers and crew; those that had been provided had not been manned by able-bodied seafarers speaking the language of their officers.

By December of 1909, when Furuseth, bearing a letter of introduction from Francis Heney, had come to see La Follette, the senator had already earned a reputation as a supporter of labor's causes, although the full extent of his commitment was not to develop for a few years more. As early as 1904 he had rejected the perennial corporate claim that increased prices were the result of increased wages, pointing out that total wages per mile of railroad had not increased as much as earnings.[68] In 1911 he insisted that railroad strikes were unnecessary, for rates were high enough to increase wages, but corporations preferred paying dividends on watered stock.[69] As governor and senator he showed consistent concern for industrial safety and for accident compensation. He even suggested that since the greed of owners was responsible for conditions that led to mine explosions, employers should be tried for murder following disasters.[70] Steelworkers were overworked and underpaid and bore the costs of a heavy accident and death rate. The companies prevented unionization by employing labor spies and by discharging union members, he charged.[71] He approved of the shirtwaist strike, considering it to be an indication of women's demand for a voice in the conduct of business and of an unwillingness to accept exploitation of women and children.[72] He attacked the employers and courts of Paterson, N.J., for denying the rights of strikers to free speech and assemblage although the workers had observed the laws. "The cause of the working men and women of Paterson is the cause of every man and woman of the whole country, whatever their calling or station in life. No community lives to itself alone."[73]

He was particularly disturbed by the use of the judiciary against organized workers; while Congress had not intended the Sherman Act to be applied to labor, its provision for threefold damages had only been applied to labor, never capital; magistrates had seized the savings of workers, but never of capitalists, no matter how ill gotten their gains. The injunction could be a valuable weapon of the court, but it had become a method of abuse against "individuals of small means, and sometimes against the public interest." It fostered "class prejudice, weakens confidence in our courts, and rouses resentment against all law." As applied it did not "contribute to the security of personal and property rights."[74]

He was concerned about laws affecting American labor. He did not stand wholly with those in labor who desired to cut off immigration; he even questioned provisions which required a certificate of good character and absence of non-political imprisonment, for Carl Schurz had been imprisoned for a crime that was not ostensibly political; such legislation permitted another country to decide whom it was willing to send here. And in 1914 he fought to amend a measure requiring a literacy test for prospective immigrants in favor of Russian Jews who were not permitted to obtain an education. Nevertheless, he did not want the importation of skilled labor unless there was a shortage in this country.[75] He was also concerned that immigrants should not be exploited.[76]

La Follette was a vigorous proponent of positive legislative action in this area, pressing for statutory limits on hours of employment.[77] And, taking a stand in favor of unions of government workers, he objected to efforts of the post office to prevent the organization of its employes.[78]

Finally, he endorsed the union position on productivity. Initially, he expressed a positive attitude toward the work of efficiency experts, but he soon found the system vicious in its effects upon workers. And he long had understood the reason that workers reduced output — the maldistribution of wealth caused underconsumption, and they feared they would produce more than could be sold, causing their own unemployment.[79]

Thus, when Andrew Furuseth sat in La Follette's office for the first time, "a great soul speaking through his face, the set purpose of his life shining in his eyes," fervently explaining, in his strong Scandinavian accent, about the treatment of seamen, he found in La Follette a receptive listener and a ready convert. Thereafter, whenever his legislation was being considered, he met every Sunday with the Madisonian in the senator's residence. Although Furuseth, with his monolithic dedication, had obtained legislation in 1895 and 1898 that had improved sailors' conditions and had given Americans the legal right to quit their vessels in ports of the United States, commercial treaties with other nations sanctified the binding of mariners to their ships. Furuseth would only be satisfied when all seafarers had been freed. Legislation introduced in 1910 and 1911 died in committee. But the Titanic disaster spotlighted marine problems, since the loss of life could have been avoided had able-bodied seamen manned sufficient lifeboats. Consequently, a bill introduced by Representative William B. Wilson, working closely with Furuseth, passed the House on August 3, 1912; it was held up in a Senate committee for eight months. La Follette forced its consideration by threatening to delay the appropriations bill. Unfortunately the measure that was finally enacted was so inadequate that he and Furuseth were relieved when Taft vetoed it. During the special session of Congress called by the newly inaugurated Woodrow Wilson, La Follette reintroduced his bill, with added safety provisions. La Follette and Furuseth were disappointed when the Commerce Committee reported favorably on a bill sponsored by Knute Nelson; La Follette considered the measure inadequate and thought Nelson allied to the shipping interests of James Hill. He first objected to laying over the Nelson bill until the regular session and then moved to proceed to consideration of the bill, thus making it unfinished business. Then, when his opponents were absent, he requested that consideration of the Nelson bill begin on October 16 and be voted on not later than October 23. In the interim the Volturno burned and sank. La Follette had Furuseth gather information on the conditions on the ship to be used when he offered his bill as a substitute amendment for the Nelson bill. Giving full credit for his grasp of the technicalities to Furuseth, La Follette outdebated and outmaneuvered his opponents and secured passage of his substitute with perfecting amendments. At its passage Furuseth ran out of the galleries crying, with tears running down his cheeks: "This finishes the work Lincoln began." But the Titanic disaster had sparked an international convention in London (from which Furuseth finally resigned since it was dominated by shipowners). International complications were given as a reason for delay in the House. Despite administration opposition, the bill passed the House on August 27, 1914 and was sent to a conference committee. (President Wilson had initially supported the bill but shifted for fear of violation of treaty commitments.) While the conference committee met, the London convention was finally brought before the Senate; Furuseth had John Sharp Williams introduce an amendment reserving the right of the United States to impose higher standards. The amended convention passed in December of 1914. By the end of February, 1915, the conference report had cleared both houses. The President remained as the final obstacle. Preparing for his appointment with Wilson, La Follette visited Robert Lansing and Bryan at the State Department and found that they were apprehensive concerning treaty commitments. La Follette took Furuseth to plead with the President. Furuseth's passion so moved Wilson (La Follette's eyes welled with tears) that he overcame his own and State Department reservation and signed the bill. At last, the "blot of slavery" on American seamen had been erased.[80]

While the Wilson administration was to guide further progressive legislation through Congress as the election of 1916 approached, after the European conflagration exploded in 1914, its attention was increasingly devoted to foreign affairs.

CHAPTER 9

# "The Blare of Trumpets"

WOODROW Wilson was elected to implement a progressive platform and America's relation to other nations had not been given much consideration by the candidate or the electorate. In international affairs the President sought "to serve our fellow man in quiet counsel, when the blare of trumpets is neither heard nor heeded and where the things are done which make blessed the nations of the world in peace and righteousness and love."[1] Yet he intervened in Santo Domingo, Haiti, Nicaragua, Mexico, Russia, and World War I. Initially a firm advocate of Wilson's foreign policy, La Follette became one of its severest critics.

La Follette had never been an "isolationist." He was concerned with the role of the United States in the world. But he did not confuse internationalism with imperialism, the reality of world power status with the desire to impose one's will. Except for a brief exposition of the party platform during the harmony election of 1900, La Follette had been a persistent foe of imperialism and a consistent exponent of a foreign policy which treated large and small nations with the same respect for their internal sovereignty. One of the primary causes of international involvement during the early years of this century was the export of capital to countries with unstable governments. He did not oppose American economic penetration, but he did insist that businessmen submit to the laws of the country in which they invested; if they wanted to stake their money "on the turn of fortune's wheel in some foreign land, let them take the gambler's chance." If they wanted to make their investments secure, let them risk their own money and their own lives.[2] American businessmen should not be given an unfair advantage. He was disturbed by Taft's "dollar diplomacy." He criticized replacing the treaty right to exclude Japanese laborers with a "gentleman's agreement" in return for an acceptance of American bankers into the Manchurian Railroad consortium. He accused Taft of meddling in Turkish affairs in order to obtain railroad concessions.[3] He was pleased when the Wilson administration seemed to be rejecting "dollar diplomacy." "Humanity is to be placed higher than Property in our international affairs. Patriotism is to be given precedence over Profits. National honor is to count for more than trust aggrandizement."[4] He opposed a bill to "give our exploiters the right to combine in order the better to compete with other foreign exporters"; that would lead to a demand for heavy ship subsidies to carry increased foreign trade, a large navy to protect this commerce, "and thence it is but a short step to absolute imperialism."[5] He commented favorably when McAdoo called a Pan American Conference, and expected an improvement of commercial and political relations as our southern neighbors observed that predators did not represent the United States. He was disturbed by the absence of a credit line and transport despite Wilson's efforts.[6] He seemed unaware that Latin America viewed new Yankee initiatives as domination in a new guise. Yet he was aware of our mistreatment of our one Latin American possession, Puerto Rico. Since the residents were white, he said, we were engaged in the officious man's burden. But rather than improving their conditions, we had granted them fewer governmental rights than had Spain and our tariff laws had led to the wreckage of their coffee industry. Like India, he declared, Puerto Rico was poorer as a result of the officious man's burden. But when the government finally granted the island a legislature, he tried to ensure that the upper class did not add any voting qualifications to those determined by Congress.[7]

Yet he could ignore apparent treaty obligations if it would benefit his larger constituency. He insisted that American goods, carried in American ships in a coastwide trade, should be exempt from paying Panama Canal tolls, for the American public had paid for its construction. The campaign to honor these treaties, he insisted, came from the railroads, who resented rate competition. The British charge d'affaires had not objected to excepting legitimate coastwise trade, and our treaty was with Britain. The repeal of the tolls exemption, he charged, was a surrender to railroads and big business.[8]

Mexico remained Wilson's most persistent problem in Latin America. It had long been ruled by the Porfirio Diaz government, described by La Follette as an autocracy protecting the interests of industrialists. La Follette asked for a careful scrutiny of Diaz's request for extradition so as not to violate his opponents' right of asylum.[9] Francisco Madero's victory over Diaz was well received by most progressives; La Follette was disturbed when Taft massed troops on the border. "What precedent of intervention can he offer as an excuse for meddling in the internal affairs of Mexico at this time?" he asked in anger. He feared intervention without congressional approval and asked reprovingly whether it was for the profits of the interests.[10] He was shocked by Victoriano Huerta's murder of Madero and approved of Wilson's moralistic flouting of the international tradition of extending recognition to effective governments. He was particularly pleased that the President refused to intervene in Mexican affairs to protect private property during the ensuing revolt of Venustiano Carranza's Constitutionalists.[11] But Wilson's reaction to the Tampico incident disturbed him greatly. Tampico was under siege by the insurgents. Rear Admiral Henry Mayo was anchored off Tampico with a small fleet, ready to evacuate American citizens if necessary. When the fleet ran short of gasoline a whaleboat, flying the American flag fore and aft, was dispatched to a warehouse, which happened to be near the Federalists' first line of defense. The crew was arrested; two were taken from the vessel at gunpoint. The local commander returned them to finish loading, and the military governor ordered their release and apologized profusely. Mayo was not satisfied, for a ship flying the flag was sovereign territory. He demanded a formal disavowal, assurance of severe punishment for the offending officer, and a 21-gun salute of the American flag. The governor consulted Huerta, who hoped the incident would arouse nationalistic support for his shaky regime. Wilson seized upon the incident to humiliate Huerta and bring about his collapse. As negotiations broke down, Wilson called a joint session of Congress to approve military action against Huerta. Then faced with information that a German boat was delivering arms (supplied by Remington, from New York via Hamburg), he ordered the occupation of Vera Cruz without authorization while the Senate debated.[12] La Follette was caught in a quandary. He did not want to break with the administration, yet he commented (reflecting the general confusion in Washington): "This order was issued over a disagreement as to whether five or twenty-one blank cartridges should be fired by the Mexicans to accentuate their apology, which had already been voluntarily tendered for the offending act of a subordinate officer." He disliked unilateral action in foreign policy and the dispatch of marines over a petty issue; enormous bloodshed could have resulted if we were involved with a great power "instead of poor, weak, bankrupt, distracted Mexico." "If the President has the power to order the forces of the United States to invade a foreign country, capture a city, and slay its people as in the case of Vera Cruz, he has the absolute power to make war at will." He could not vote to justify the President's action, but once it was taken he found it necessary to hedge, to unite behind Wilson while requesting that the President make it clear that he would never exercise the authority and would leave at the earliest moment consistent with national honor.[13] Mediation by Argentina, Brazil, and Chile provided a face-saving excuse for the United States to withdraw, but the occupation of Vera Cruz thoroughly undermined Huerta so that Carranza came to power, amid an outraged outcry by American investors. The special interests had forced McKinley to go to war with Spain over Cuba, La Follette wrote, and had tried to get Taft to intervene when Madero took over. "And now that a government has been established in Mexico which is manifestly making the interests of the Mexican people its paramount object" they are crying for intervention to protect property interests, which is to be condemned.[14] Wilson resisted, but Pancho Villa's attack across the border precipitated a punitive expedition by General John Pershing. La Follette was worried that the nation was headed towards war but did not want an inopportune break with the administration while he sought reelection — only two years after the conservative triumph.[15]

He was disturbed by the prospect of conflagration: "War is always cruel; . . . war arouses all the fiercest human passions;

that there are always cases of brutality and outrage."[16]

Searching for means to avoid war, he looked to arbitration treaties for peaceful resolution of conflicts. But he made the mistake common to most advocates of arbitration. He was unwilling to submit strongly felt issues, such as exclusion of coolie labor. Yet national reservation of items from consideration would make the treaties inoperative when most needed. And he realized the limitations of peace and arbitration treaties if nations increased the military.[17]

When World War I broke out Philip was in England; in fact, he was a spectator in Parliament when Ramsay MacDonald delivered his tragically accurate prediction of the damage the imminent holocaust would inflict upon European civilization. The senator considered calling his son back but decided that there would be no fighting in England.[18] In contrast to MacDonald he could even pen a flippant note to Phil. Assuming that his presence in England would draw him in that direction, he wrote: "Bob and I just at this time are for the Germans — because everybody is against them and they are so in the minority." While his first sympathy was for France to restore its lost provinces "it was too much for my proclivity to fight with the underdog." He did not want Germany to be carved up by Russia. But he might switch to the new underdog if the Kaiser started to win.[19]

At first he felt fortunate that Wilson, and not the belligerent Roosevelt, had been elected. Americans had confidence in his character and service; but all was subordinate to the fact that "He is keeping us out of the war."[20] Seven months later he was still sanguine, for Wilson had shown firmness and wisdom in guarding American rights and honor and still remaining neutral.[21] A La Follette resolution authorized the President to convey to neutral nations the desire to call an international conference to restore peace among warring countries, an approach still within Wilson's conception of policy. "The neutrality of the United States can not and should not be that of selfish indifference," he insisted. Non-belligerent states should intervene to end the war and to prepare a permanent peace. In the post-war world countries could not tyrannize others or monopolize the world markets; rather progress would be served "by the largest possible development of the national

life of each country." He called for an international tribunal to
discuss vital issues and a federation of neutral nations to
neutralize certain waters and define commercial rights.
Disputes would be settled by arbitration, without resort to
force, but with decisions put into effect through world opinion
and by cutting off intercourse with an offending country. (It is
difficult to understand how he could expect a great power to
submit to imposed isolation without a resort to arms.) But
Wilson did not welcome congressional interference with his
prerogatives, and the resolution died in the Foreign Relations
Committee.

La Follette was disturbed by any actions that threatened
true neutrality. He feared that private enterprise and profit in
munitions encouraged selfish interests to influence legislators
to increase war appropriations and to intrigue in domestic and
foreign affairs to create a war market.[22] Nationalized manu-
facture of munitions would remove private incentive from
military expansion, and government enterprise, at least in
shipyards, produced lower initial costs, better construction,
fewer repairs, and cheaper upkeep. The outcry against the
purchase of interned German merchant ships was not based on
a fear that it would lead to war, "But that the government will
make war on the Shipping trust." Expanded armaments presented a danger in itself. Civilized communities did not permit
men to carry weapons, for that would breed murderers, not
security, peace, and order. "States are but aggregations of
individuals. . . . And nations armed to the teeth quickly resort
to killing as means of settling their differences."[23] His approach
towards armaments was purely defensive. After a negative
initial reaction, he supported increased coastal defenses even
though we had the finest defenses in the world. Our naval
expenditures were already greater than Germany's or Japan's
and more than Great Britain's in peacetime. If Germany could
prevent an invasion with a navy half the size of Britain's should
we attempt to match an English force that we were unlikely to
fight? Naval increases only touched off a competitive upward
spiral, difficult to reverse, benefiting only munitions makers
and saddling the electorate with higher taxes. Would an
attempt to match a navy created by Britain to protect her
possessions lead to a similar policy of aggression towards

foreign governments? An army was needed for defense, he granted, but it seemed excessive to double military expenditures, with annual costs already twice that of the construction of the Panama Canal.[24] He feared the war-breeding tone of the American press. It "persists in giving currency to the malicious invention controlling so much of the European war news" filled with "Ghastly stories of alleged 'German atrocity' (sic)."[25]

By September of 1915 he concluded that these factors had taken their toll. America was no longer neutral in fact as well as name. We were supplying the allies with the munitions and the money to prosecute war.[26]

A break with Wilson on foreign policy was becoming inevitable, despite La Follette's satisfaction with much of the President's domestic record. He was particularly vigorous in his support of Wilson's nomination of his friend Brandeis for the Supreme Court. If he had been nominated ten years earlier, when he was just an able Boston attorney, the senator commented, there would have been no attack on him. But after a decade of work in the public interest, the nomination of Brandeis shook Wall Street.[27] Nevertheless, La Follette could not still his fears about the dangers inherent in Wilson's policies and attitudes.

He challenged Wilson's conception of the presidential role in foreign policy, particularly as outlined in *Congressional Government*. If the President, in the conduct of foreign affairs, can make war inevitable so that "Congress has no alternative but to accept and sanction his course . . . then the President had authority to make war as absolutely as though he were Czar of Russia." Congress had constitutional power to declare war, and it could not rightfully evade its responsibility. Only democratic control of foreign policy could prevent another world catastrophe through autocratic secret diplomacy, he warned.[28] The people "pay the full price." Until they have "the FINAL SAY" they should be able to register their deep convictions with an advisory vote, a referendum on war.[29] Having been forewarned by Wilson's own writings, he was wary lest deceptive executive actions should make conflict unavoidable. And any official violation of strict neutrality might tend in that direction.

The President's reaction to German submarine activity

caused a crisis. The Cunard passenger liner Lusitania was carrying munitions. When the Germans sank it, with considerable loss of civilian life, including 128 Americans, the public was furious. Wilson sent a series of notes and demands to the German government; Bryan thought this correspondence violated America's neutral status and came close to causing a break with Germany. Convinced that the United States had forfeited its opportunity to act as a broker among the warring powers, Bryan tried to sway Wilson and, unavailing, resigned. For a time German notes tried to mollify Wilson, but Germany refused to accept the passage of armed merchant ships carrying contraband. Joining Bryan and a substantial bloc in Congress, La Follette drew a parallel between the right to travel on armed merchant ships and the right to remain in a foreign land torn by revolution. Wilson had ordered American citizens "to abandon their property . . . to avoid the responsibility of protecting them in their rights in Mexico," he reminded the Senate. It was less of a sacrifice "to refrain from travel on armed belligerent ships." And he supported a resolution warning American citizens not to so travel. It was only defeated by the most vigorous administration lobbying.[30]

Just as Wilson laid the foundation for reelection by appropriating the preparedness issue from his opponents while trying to retain his supporters with the slogan "he kept us out of war," La Follette had to provide for his own reelection and for the gubernatorial campaign. As he had feared, Philipp did not present an easy target. He was flexible and inquired beyond his speeches before he acted. After campaigning against the university and the legislative library he reexamined the facts, modified the university supervisory structure and retained the library while drawing upon McCarthy as an advisor. His appointees did not subvert progressive legislation, and he not only refrained from using his office for personal enrichment but taxed his own company. In addition, he blocked a liquor lobby measure and helped prevent a railroad fare increase. Larger revenues and the distribution of former state functions to the counties offset increased costs. A successful progressive counterattack could not be based on the removal of progressive officials and the abandonment of reforestation. And to make matters worse the war in Europe was rapidly replacing domestic affairs in the consciousness of the electorate; Philipp agreed with La Follette on neutrality and preparedness.[31]

Under these circumstances La Follette gathered information, outlined a summer lecture series on local issues, and demanded that the aspirants produce a single candidate. He rejected a quid pro quo for there was "an irreconcilable conflict between the principles for which we stand and organized Privilege for which Philipp and his supporters always stand."[32] Attention was diverted to elect delegates to the national convention, because their loss (with conservatives controlling the state party) could have endangered the whole primary ticket. "I think they *think* THAT I *want* the delegation to the *Nat. Conv.*," he wrote to Belle, "when all I am standing for is to help win the state back which McGovern lost." But McGovern, "that piker whose cold blooded selfish policy made us all this trouble," declared his candidacy before the La Follette progressives had chosen Otto Bosshard and when Bosshard stepped aside for William Hatton, who led in a conference, McGovern refused to accept the result and remained in the contest. In April La Follette had carried fifteen of twenty-six delegates to the national convention with him; but Philipp was the only conservative to be nominated, outpolling his combined progressive opposition; the key office had been lost.[33]

Since 1916 was a presidential year, hard decisions had to be made. The romance with Wilson had long since ended, and the Republican convention resumed its normal importance to La Follette. He had carried only North Dakota and the majority of the Wisconsin delegation and was not a serious contender. While Phil covered the convention as a correspondent, La Follette remained in Washington. Roosevelt, a candidate for nomination, called the Progressive party convention to meet simultaneously with the Republican party. Negotiations foundered. The Progressives wanted only Roosevelt; the Republicans would consider anyone but him. Rejecting leadership restraint, the Progressives chose Roosevelt prematurely. Meantime, the Republicans drafted a conservative platform and nominated a candidate with a progressive reputation, Charles Evans Hughes. Under these circumstances Roosevelt conditionally refused the Progressive nomination; his delegates thought he had conditionally accepted it. When

Hughes took a proper preparedness position, Roosevelt delivered the Progressive nomination to him, completing the destruction of the party he had created. Wilson was easily renominated, as expected.[34]

La Follette condemned the Republican platform but declared Hughes to be "acceptable to the great body of the progressive Republicans . . . able, independent, fearless," probably the only man who could unify Republicans.[35] He soon regretted his words. Hughes ran his campaign on the issue of preparedness, hedged on Mexico, called for higher tariffs, repudiated the Adamson eight-hour law and the Seamen's Act, and, in Wisconsin, sidled up to the only conservative candidate, Philipp. Consequently, La Follette refused to endorse the national ticket; in his own campaign, he took a diametrically opposed view of the issues, and his silence was interpreted as support of Wilson. His Democratic opponent, an able lawyer of German descent, William Wolfe, proceeded to alienate most Germans by attacking La Follette on preparedness, travel on armed merchant ships, and on an arms embargo. Wilson ran in Wisconsin on a single issue — he kept us out of the war. The leading progressive newspaper, the *Wisconsin State Journal*, endorsed Wilson, La Follette, and the Democratic candidate for governor. Burt Williams. Wilson came close to carrying the state, drawing heavily upon progressive districts. La Follette won in a record landslide, almost doubling his opponent's vote and sweeping 69 of 71 counties.[36]

Returning to Washington, he was pleased with Wilson's renewed efforts to mediate an end to the war with a fair peace resulting from a stalemate. In the summer of 1915, after the sinking of the British passenger liner Arabic, the administration had elicited a German pledge not to attack unarmed liners. In February of 1916 Colonel Edward House had negotiated an agreement with Sir Edward Grey: when the Allies decided the time was right, Wilson would call a conference to end the war and prepare a post-war international organization to maintain peace; if Germany refused a reasonable settlement the United States would "probably" enter the war on the Allied side, for Germany had the advantage on the continent and only by American involvement could a compromise peace be achieved. In May, 1916, following the sinking of the Sussex, the Germans renewed the Arabic pledge, conditional upon American insistence that England observe the rules of international law. By the summer of 1916, American pressure on Grey brought the revelation that the Allies had no intention of implementing the House-Grey Agreement as long as there was a chance of military victory and an imposed peace (in fact, they had never taken the agreement seriously). At the same time the British tightened their maritime system and ended freedom of the seas. Coupled with the ruthless suppression of the Irish rebellion, British prestige plummeted. Wilson defended American claims of neutral rights with menacing notes and obtained retaliatory legislation to pressure Britain towards a conference. Realizing that resumption of unrestricted submarine warfare would result in American intervention, the German government called for a peace conference. In an effort not to appear partial toward Germany, the President asked the warring powers to declare their objectives; La Follette hailed this inquiry. Wilson wanted a lasting peace based on equity; Germany and the Allies each wanted a Carthaginian peace and hoped to use America to achieve their aims. Made aware of the impasse, the chief executive delivered an address to the Senate calling for "peace without victory," for only a "peace among equals" could be lasting. La Follette, who had been speaking when Wilson entered, led the applause at the conclusion of the message. Unfortunately, the Germans had already decided that if they could not achieve their minimum goals through negotiations, they had to win the war in 1917 before they exhausted their resources, and they felt they now had enough submarines to knock England out of the war through a total blockade; they calculated that an enraged America could not make a significant contribution in time, even if it declared war. While Wilson might have tolerated submarine warfare against belligerent merchantmen and armed vessels, the resumption of unrestricted submarine activities in the war zone, affecting neutral carriers, resulted in a break in diplomatic relations.[37]

That the United States, alone among neutral nations, broke diplomatic relations with Germany, bitterly disappointed La Follette: "It was hard to sit it out," he wrote about Wilson's report of his decision, "and when it was over I went to my office where I could be alone. I did not want to see anybody." He called upon Bryan, and the two sought a strategy to prevent war. They decided to introduce a resolution to induce discussion until things cooled off. Working desperately they hoped to avoid a precipitate declaration of war similar to the one that followed the sinking of the *Maine*. The atmosphere in Washington became stifling to La Follette: "I feel its deadening pull. Even where something else is the subject of conversation — you feel the weight of something hanging over you." He counted each day without an incident as a gain, as a chance that the crisis would blow over. Germany's action, he felt, was the result of desperation born from unfair treatment. She was not interfering with our neutral rights any more than England; while she threatened to send our ships to the bottom, England was sending them to prize courts. In addition, England was starving German non-combatants. He was probably correct in his opinion that the war would end within sixty days if American ships were prevented from sailing for Europe, but he was not aware of the terms Germany was prepared to impose. "Well sink or swim I will go the way that seems right even if I go alone." Although many senators wanted to resist a resolution supporting the break in diplomatic relations, he found that only five were willing to record their opposition. Ironically, he was out of the chamber gathering documents for a speech when the vote was taken.[38]

His worst fears were not realized, for war was not yet declared. But the announcement of unrestricted submarine warfare brought intense pressure from shipowners for the arming of merchantmen (many of them had kept their ships in port). At the same time delegations from widely diverse groups descended on Washington to lobby for peace. Belle spoke out for peace in Wisconsin, and her husband gathered legal ammunition to resist the demand for war that he was sure would come as soon as the first armed merchantman was sunk. The La Follettes received a foretaste of new wartime divisions as Richard Lloyd Jones, editor of the *Wisconsin State Journal*, wrote a scathing editorial about the meeting Belle had addressed, and Lenroot denounced the peril presented by pacifists before the House. Hearing rumors that Wilson was prepared to seek authority to arm merchant ships, La Follette organized a filibuster to prevent its consideration during that session. In his message Wilson had not made the expected request, but asked for the right to employ other methods to protect American ships and citizens. La Follette feared that this demand was for unlimited authority.[39]

Wilson had resisted pressures to arm merchantmen until the interception of a telegram from the German foreign secretary, Alfred Zimmerman, to the German minister in Mexico City, suggesting an alliance with Mexico in the event of war with the United States; Mexico would be offered her lost territories in the American Southwest. The administration leaked this note to the press just before the debate on the enabling legislation; the electrifying reaction made it all the more difficult to resist the President's requests, but La Follette and his allies remained undaunted. The chairman of the Senate Foreign Relations Committee, William Stone, opposed the bill. Gilbert Hitchcock, the second ranking Democrat, had opposed it in committee but rationalized that the President needed this authority to keep us out of war and sponsored it. On Friday, March 2, Hitchcock moved for unanimous consent to take up the House measure in order to expedite passage. La Follette objected. When Hitchcock repeated his request after midnight Norris, a brilliant parliamentarian, consulted with La Follette, and traded a recess of nine hours for consent. This maneuver ensured the success of the filibuster. During the course of the debate Lodge, Frank Brandegee, and Albert Fall advocated the bill as a step toward war, confirming the charges of its adversaries. Stone, a consistent supporter of the administration, led off for the opposition, insisting that he would not change his earlier advocacy of Wilson's policy of neutrality. When he concluded, four and a half hours later, the leadership realized that the situation was serious, and debate became more heated. Norris pointed out that more proponents than opponents had spoken. La Follette was scheduled to conclude the debate, and as Norris held sway he piled up his materials for his speech; unexpectedly he was informed that the list of speakers had been destroyed. Since the filibuster could not be broken, Robert Owen and Hitchcock intended to follow Norris and frustrate La Follette. He was furious. His son sent him a note counselling restraint: "You cannot afford to get into a physical argument or be arrested by the Sarg't at arms for misconduct. You are notecably (sic) & extremely excited." As La Follette and Hitchcock argued as to who deserved the floor, it appeared that a riot might begin. Harry Lane moved to defend La Follette with a file, suspecting that Ollie James carried a gun. The Senate adjourned in anger but without incident.[40]

Although Wilson could have obtained passage by calling a special session of Congress, he charged: "A little group of willful men, representing no opinion but their own, have rendered the great Government of the United States helpless and contemptible." With the President setting the example, La Follette was subjected to vilification unparalleled even in his controversial career; the Zimmerman note had released national passions that were only to intensify further after American entry into the war. Newspapers attributed "leadership of this ignoble enterprise," his flirting with treason, to "megalomania." College students in Illinois hanged him in effigy. A meeting in Wheeling, W. Va., denounced him as a traitor and cancelled his scheduled address. His last primary opponent called for his internment. A resolution repudiating his stand was introduced in the Wisconsin State Senate, and when its consideration was postponed, almost half the members signed a round robin to express their disapproval. In Washington, La Follette was glared at and even spat upon.[41] For the first time, interventionists had developed real public support; nevertheless, the majority sought peace, even after three merchantmen were sunk with heavy loss of life. While Wilson still hesitated to call for war, it appeared that the Germans were winning their gamble; shipping losses for the Allies approached a million tons a month; their military situation was desperate; and their morale was cracking. After consulting with his cabinet and finding that opposition to our involvement had disappeared, Wilson issued an executive order to arm merchant ships on March 9, and ten days later called a special session for April 2, prepared to ask Congress to declare war.[42]

As the attack on the filibustering senators mounted, as they became increasingly isolated from their colleagues, and as the demand by the metropolitan press for a declaration of war reached a crescendo, the La Follette family wrote to its head and insisted that he publish the speech he had intended to make. He responded in an editorial, reprinted in the

*Congressional Record* at the request of John Nelson, and in an article in *Pearson's Magazine* which appeared after war had been declared. La Follette insisted that congressional leaders had delayed appropriations until the last minute to prevent a real debate on the President's request for "powers which if executed must inevitably bring on war"; the bill to arm merchantmen put war-making powers in executive hands.[43]

Fortuitously, just before Wilson issued his call for a special session, the czarist government of Russia, unacceptable to Americans, was overthrown; this enhanced the credibility of Wilson's rhetoric. Thus when he called upon Congress "to vindicate the principles of peace and justice in the life of the world against selfish and autocratic power," to make the world safe for democracy, Germany included, he was greeted with thunderous applause. Ironically, overlooked in his speech was a passage vindicating the arguments of La Follette and his small "willful" band: "Armed neutrality is ineffectual at best," Wilson admitted, "it is practically certain to draw us into the war without either the rights or effectiveness of belligerents."[44]

La Follette would not let the nation forget the President's tacit admission that he had been right. While he permitted legislation in preparation for war to be considered out of turn, even though war had not yet been declared, he would not allow the resolution to be voted on by unanimous consent. Nor would he stand behind a mistaken President "when the question is one of peace or war, certain to involve the lives and fortunes of many of our people and, it may be, the destiny . . . of the civilized world." Declaring his opposition to war, he angrily protested that Wilson had categorized the spokesmen of a substantial public as willful and then used their arguments to justify war. He chafed at the intolerance created by the press at a time when fairness was particularly necessary and when the anti-war Senate minority represented the American majority. Why not submit the issue to a referendum? In all the polls, people had rejected intervention on this provocation. He refuted Wilson's rationale. It was not a war for democracy: England, Italy, and Japan were still hereditary monarchies, and Germany had better social legislation; we did not make our support conditional on home rule in Ireland, Egypt, and India, but we demanded that the German government be changed to a democracy.

La Follette rejected Wilson's analysis of events, trying to balance Anglophile propaganda with an interpretation that appeared pro-German in the heat of the moment. He contrasted placid relations with Germany against a history of conflict with England. English secret treaties (i.e., with France about Morocco) attempted to expel German enterprise. "England would tolerate no commercial rivalry. Germany would not submit to isolation." Therefore, war became inevitable. Then, England repudiated the London rules of naval warfare, violated the definition of blockade and the laws of contraband, prevented the shipment of food to Germany, mined the North Sea with only three days' notice, and never yielded to American protests. The United States objected to violations by one side and not the other. By not insisting that England respect our neutral rights, he continued, explaining German motivation, we aided in starving German civilians and helped back her to the wall "to fight with what weapons she can lay her hands on to prevent the starving of her women and children, her old men and babes." The German promise not to sink ships without warning was conditional upon British obedience to international law; Britain had not obeyed. Britain had mined her declared war zone; the United States had not protested. Germany had responded by threatening to use mines and submarines to sink ships venturing within a prohibited area. We were being urged to fight Germany for doing the same things Great Britain was doing — sinking ships in a declared war zone. True neutrality would have avoided war, he concluded.

As La Follette sat down, John Sharp Williams rose and responded bitterly: "Mr. President, if immortality could be attained by verbal eternity, the Senator from Wisconsin would have approximate immortality. We have waited and have heard a speech from him which would have better become Herr Bethmann-Hollweg, of the German Parliament, than an American Senator."[45] And the worst was yet to come.

# CHAPTER 10

## *The Diversion of War*

WAR and rumors of war are a "dreadful diversion for peoples demanding juster distribution of wealth. War is the money-changer's opportunity, and the social reformer's doom."[1] La Follette wrote these comments in 1909 when English reform was blighted by competition with the German naval building program; he was unaware that he was describing the fate of the movement that he so ably represented. For more than any other factor the progressive movement fell a victim to World War I. The progressives could have recovered from their own mistakes and internecine strife, but they could not overcome the enhanced image of the businessman, forger of the weapons of victory; nor could they sweep aside the suspicion engendered by proposals of change in the charged patriotic atmosphere of the war and post-war period, particularly with the pervasive challenge of bolshevism to the shared values of progressives and conservatives. And an awareness of sudden death was fixed in the national consciousness by the high battlefield casualties. The shock of mortality, combined with the discrediting of idealistic progressive rhetoric through its misuse to muster support for the war effort, ushered in a decade of self-indulgence and pursuit of material success.

Throughout the war, La Follette seemed isolated and alone (he was joined in opposition only by Norris, Gronna, Vardaman, and Stone). He drew his strength from his close family relations and from numerous communications from ordinary people. "The war clamor and denunciation of the press were as a whisper in his ears compared to the voices which were calling to him throughout the country."[2]

To have been consistent he should have tried to thwart all

those measures furthering an unnecessary conflict. Yet, like many another legislator throughout history, it never occurred to him that he should resist the war effort once the nation was committed. While he felt that of the sixty war measures he had challenged only a few, his own catalogue of opposition was impressive. He resisted the declaration of war, the draft, the espionage bill, the aviation bill as drafted, and many features of food control; he fought for fairer taxation, free speech, and the right of Congress to determine the objects and policies of war.[3]

La Follette found much that was unpleasant as the country geared for war. Without even giving voluntary enlistment a chance (enlistments had sagged earlier, he had written, for there had been little prospect of war), without a referendum on the question, without threat of invasion, a bill he thought unconstitutional, un-American and undemocratic, was rammed through Congress with little debate, a bill that would permit presidential agents to forcefully enter American homes "and violently lay hold of 1,000,000 of our finest and healthiest and strongest boys, and against their will . . . to deport them across the seas . . . to wound and kill other young boys just like themselves." After years of war British possessions, such as Canada, Australia, and Ireland, had no conscription. "The draft is the corollary of militarism and militarism spells death to democracy." He asked that the law be at least tempered with humanity. Conscientious objectors should be exempt from service on their own oath; Germans might not want to kill their kith and kin; besides, soldiers who do not want to fight make poor warriors. And he suggested that a private's pay match that of the police and firemen (as the Canadians had done), so that a soldier's family did not suffer.[4]

The question of conscription had personal ramifications. While he considered the measure unconstitutional, until that question was decided, he advised a correspondent that it was necessary to conform to the law.[5] And his two sons were of draft age. Both boys had been ill recently. Robert, Jr., had had a streptococcus infection in the throat and jaw late in March, 1915, with a temperature of 103. During April and May he experienced swelling of the muscles. In June his tonsils were removed, but this was followed by a severe recurrence of infection in the thighs and groin, and later in the face and throat, complicated by abnormal blood count and a serious weight reduction. Treatment for this often fatal infection was still primitive and Bobbie had a recurrence in 1917 and 1918.[6] His physical condition made service unlikely, but his father recommended enlistment in the National Guard, for rejection would increase the likelihood of rejection by the army. Besides, it was unconstitutional to send the National Guard abroad. The eldest son was exempted, to the relief of all.[7]

While Phil had been operated on in 1916, it did not affect his military eligibility. His mother advised against enlistment but thought it unwise to refuse conscription. She advised that he complete his courses and not leave to work on the farm. For his part, Phil considered it a moral duty to serve voluntarily, for if he disagreed with the war he should not submit to a draft. He felt that he would have wider influence against war if he had served as an officer. But he could not profit from classes at that point. As the fall semester approached, Phil returned to the war-mad university. He registered for conscription, for he had no religious basis for conscientious objection and a farm exemption would be too obviously a way out. He joined ROTC while Furuseth looked into a naval commission, and his father queried about an army commission. Upon his graduation his proud father commented that he had finished "through the earthquake that tore the university from its foundations and threw the faculty into hysterics." In October, as the armistice approached, he received his commission as a second lieutenant.[8]

Conscription was just one war measure that La Follette considered to be misconceived. He approved neither a seven billion dollar bond issue nor a loan to the allies, but he voted for the bill since the military needed materials. A pay-as-you-go tax policy which placed the burden of financing the conflict upon those who profited from it, he insisted, was moral, equitable and discouraged any incentive for combat. In deciding the division between taxes and loans we must remember "always that whatever one citizen loans the Government today other citizens will have to pay in taxes tomorrow, both principal and interest," "mortgaging the masses to the moneylenders." The wealthy, he reminded his colleagues, prefer loans to taxes: loans presented an investment opportunity; taxes had to be paid. The tax-exempt liberty loans returned 3½% to those with earnings below income tax level and returned 5-9% to the wealthy. "Wealth has never yet sacrificed itself on the altar of patriotism in any war. . . ." The wealthy profited from war loans, contracts, and speculation. "Hence wealth is always for war. And when it is successful in bringing on a war it is often powerful enough with war ministers and parliaments and congresses to force war loans to the maximum and by every specious device and argument force taxation to the minimum." Such a policy forces inflation; prices of necessities rise more swiftly than wages, burdening the masses. "How would it injure industry if you were to take 80 percent of the war profits and not touch by your tax, except by the increased tax upon incomes, the enormous profits made prior to the war?" To tax the inordinate profits due to hostilities was "a proposition so obviously just that no sane person would undertake to dispute it."[9] Failure to properly tax large incomes and war profits "furnished the excuse to tax freight rates, passenger rates, postal rates and impose taxes on many other objects," he informed a correspondent.[10]

His conception of equity did not appear obvious to his fellow senators. Under enormous business pressure, the Senate Finance Committee modified the House bill. La Follette produced a minority report with Thomas' and Gore's concurrence. With some good publicity and solid progressive support for his amendments, La Follette overcame efforts to impugn the patriotism of those who wanted higher taxes on the rich. Administration leaders were forced to double the war profits levies and to abandon some direct consumption imposts. Still, the War Revenue Bill was not satisfactory to the senior senator from Wisconsin who joined Borah, Norris, and Gronna in voting against it. He replied to the standard rationale to justify profiteering and tax evasion, — that capital investment should not be discouraged: "Sir, when imposing these taxes upon incomes and war profits we ought to remember that the family that gives up the father and sons at the call of the government gives up all it has, gives up not only its income-producing power, but in giving up the father and the sons it gives up its capital as well as its income-producing power."[11]

His proposals about price control received no better reception than his efforts at equitable taxation. He accepted the Senate version but voted against an unsatisfactory conference report that did not set an adequate minimum price on wheat, removed retail supervision, failed to prohibit the participation of interested parties on contract-making government boards, and gave the president autocratic controls over transportation. While wheat prices were regulated, restraints on cotton, copper, steel, and iron ore had been removed from the bill. Increases could have been tempered had the government enforced anti-trust laws and curbed grain speculation. When a coal shortage loomed he suggested the government control coal at the mine mouth, grant operators the same profit margin, and ensure distribution at a fair charge.[12]

As the nation geared for a war to make the world safe for democracy, La Follette demanded that our aims be clear, that we be disassociated from secret treaties dividing the spoils among the victors, and that hostilities be terminated along the lines of Wilson's peace without victory speech. The nation entered the conflict as an associated power, not an allied power, which left Wilson free to oppose the secret treaties and to negotiate a peace that would prevent future appeals to arms. But as a belligerent Wilson seemed reluctant to restate his goals. The Kerensky government in Russia insisted that it could not convince its soldiers to return to the battlefield unless the allies adhered to the principles of Wilson's January 22 speech. Throughout the allied world conferences of socialists and liberals called for similar statements of allied goals. In the United States many progressives, divided earlier on the events leading to American participation, were reunited on this issue. "We who are opposed to war for territorial aggrandizement, to militarism, to Junkerism and Imperialism," La Follette wrote, insisted on a definition of war aims so that, after bearing the brunt of the fighting for years, we should not be committed to an unjust peace.[13] While the conflict had to be pursued to its end, it was unwise to persist *"to accomplish an undisclosed purpose or to reach an unknown goal."* The German military would be weakened if our declaration of objects reassured them that we sought neither to dictate their form of government nor to reinforce England's naval supremacy.[14] "Congress should assert its constitutional right," he protested, "and declare the

terms upon which this government is willing to make peace."[15]
He offered a resolution rejecting the acquisition of territory or
indemnities and suggested a common belligerent fund to
restore damaged areas; once again, he called for a public
restatement of allied peace terms. For his pains he was widely
denounced as pro-German, even by some old progressive
friends.[16]

Wilson had not abandoned his goals; naively, he had
expected to achieve them through allied economic and military
dependence upon America. He responded to Pope Benedict
XV's appeal for peace by stating that the United States desired
neither the dismemberment of empires nor punitive damages,
but he warned that no enduring peace was possible while
German militarists remained in power. As pressure intensified,
Wilson gathered The Inquiry, a group of experts, to study the
intent of the belligerents and to formulate specific American
objectives. Unfortunately, Colonel House failed to obtain allied
acquiescence in a simple statement of liberal war aims. Then the
new bolshevik government published the secret czarist treaties
and denounced allied unwillingness to adhere to peace
initiatives as an indication of ulterior motives. When the
Austrian foreign minister issued a Christmas Day appeal for
peace, declaring that the central powers desired no forcible
annexation, Wilson felt compelled to respond to allied liberal
and socialist demands with an address to Congress, — the
fourteen points.[17]

La Follette was pleased that Wilson had finally begun to
articulate American purposes. But he raised some questions
about the specific application of these general statements. How
was the wrong to Alsace-Lorraine to be righted? It had
belonged to Germany, Austria, France, and then Germany
again. He suggested polling the populace. Trieste had been
Austrian for 500 years. Should we continue fighting until the
secret treaties with Italy could be enforced? Should we correct
the wrongs done by the Mexican War? or the Boer War? He was
more aware of the difficulties inherent in Wilson's glittering
generalities than were most of his contemporaries.[18]

La Follette had shown similar foresight in voting against the
espionage bill after supporting every amendment limiting the
president's power. It violated freedom of speech, the press, and

assembly. It gave "the Postmaster General power with a stroke of the pen to suppress any newspaper and destroy the property of any publisher before he could have a hearing in a court." He insisted that the anti-war socialist position that American troops should be withdrawn from France should be refuted by arguments, not suppression, and he was appalled by the leftists' treatment.[19] "Law abiding citizens of this country are being terrorized . . . by those sworn to uphold the laws and protect the rights of the people. . . . People are being unlawfully arrested, thrown into jail, held incommunicado for days, only to be eventually discharged without ever having been taken into court, because they have committed no crime. Private residences are being invaded." It was a campaign "to stifle criticism, and suppress discussion." In wartime some rights are relinquished, but not the right of citizens to discuss all matters and control the government lest wartime precedents of arbitrary administrative actions become fixed rules in peacetime. "The people are the rulers in war, no less than peace."[20] Discussion forms an enlightened public opinion to guide elected representatives. "This is . . . the very soul of democracy." Within every country there was a struggle between democracy and autocracy. The war party was the arrogant, despotic, intolerant party of autocracy. "The American Jingo is the twin to the German Junker."[21] And La Follette himself was to become one of the most famous victims of the American Jingo.

After completing his September, 1917, speech on excess profits taxation La Follette received an invitation to address the Non-Partisan League in St. Paul ten days later. He had spoken often in the northwest on the issues that concerned the League, knew their leaders, and found the position of this growing organization on foreign and domestic affairs to be similar to his own. He had taken an interest in its development from its inception. Responding to friends among the leadership, he accepted the engagement. Initially, he had intended to examine the War Revenue Bill, but Borah had already presented a similar analysis. La Follette had been preparing a congressional address on the war aims resolution and decided to shape that for immediate delivery. His sponsors feared the subject was too open to journalistic misrepresentation and might bring further attacks upon their organization. He was prevailed upon to deliver a short extemporaneous speech. His statement caused an even greater furor than his 1912 presentation to the Periodical Publishers Association.[22]

As he began, he explained that the League was necessary since both political parties had failed to render real representative government. He attacked war profiteers who masqueraded as democrats while categorizing anyone who challenged their pillaging of farmers and workers as a traitor. After departing from his notes he reminded his audience of his reasons for opposing American entrance into the war. "I don't mean to say that we hadn't suffered grievances; we had — [ A Voice: 'Yes'] — at the hands of Germany. Serious grievances! [A voice: 'You bet!']" His statements that followed made it clear that he did not consider our grievances to be sufficient provocation for war. "We had a cause for complaint," he continued in a mocking tone. "They had interfered with the right of American citizens to travel upon the high seas — on ships loaded with munitions for Great Britain. [Laughter, cheers and applause.]" While a passenger had a technical right to ride on a munitions-laden vessel, if he does he "takes his life in his own hands just as much as he would if he were on the territory of France and camped in the neighborhood of an arsenal!" While American entrance in the war was legal, the Senator asserted, at the very least it was based on questionable judgment. He then made a statement that became the basis of factual dispute. Bryan, he claimed, had warned Wilson that the Lusitania was carrying explosives, as well as passengers, in violation of a statute, and had appealed to the President to stop the passengers from sailing. Reminding his friendly audience that they had as much right to discuss the prosecution of the war as Henry Clay, Daniel Webster, and Abraham Lincoln had to discuss the Mexican War, he concluded with an extended discussion of taxation and of farmer movements.[23]

The events that followed left an indelible impression upon the La Follette family; decades later over one hundred pages of text in the family biography were devoted to the matter. Despite the availability of three stenographic records of the address, the Associated Press dispatch to the nation's press was seriously in error. While the St. Paul *Pioneer Press* wrote a hostile report, it quoted the speech accurately; its copy supplied to the AP erroneously quoted him as saying "We had no grievance against Germany," whereas he had said we had serious grievances, even if he did poke fun at some of them. Other flaws in the dispatch were all to La Follette's discredit. Those who had hurled epithets at him for his earlier stands now seemed to have a real basis for their charges.

At the secret hearings of the Minnesota Public Safety Commission even the new president of the Non-Partisan League repudiated La Follette's speech; it adopted a resolution charging him with having made a disloyal and seditious speech and petitioned the Senate to expel him. Theodore Roosevelt, in statements filled with invective, echoed their call. Nicholas Murray Butler, president of Columbia University, ignoring academic judiciousness, insisted that Americans might as well serve poison to their soldiers as permit La Follette to speak. Taft called the Senator's conduct detestable. The Wisconsin Republican Central Committee unanimously joined the attack. Richard Lloyd Jones, a former friend and editor of the *Wisconsin State Journal,* which had been created with the Senator's aid, accused La Follette and his supporters of being arch reactionaries for they were helping the Kaiser and autocracy, not democracy. La Follette could not even get his mortgage renewed and only narrowly obtained a new one.

In Madison, where Phil was a student, 400 faculty members signed a round robin accusing their most famous graduate of giving aid and comfort to the enemy; President Charles R. Van Hise, La Follette's intimate friend (who owed his job to his classmate's intercession) added his prestigious endorsement. Phil "never heard the name La Follette spoken in public places without flinching and bracing myself for some epithet." The *Journal* denounced the Beta House, where Phil was living, as a "hotbed of sedition and German propaganda." After an incident at a chapter meeting, following this editorial, Phil and his roommate moved to other quarters. While sharing a Pullman he was greeted icily by John R. Commons, long a family friend; when Commons saw his five dollar gold piece he snapped: "No patriotic citizen would have gold in his possession in time of war." Invited to dinner at the Chi Psi House, the table's occupants angrily left — he remained alone with his host. His father was ousted from the Madison Club and burned in effigy on the university campus. Resolutions calling for the Senator's expulsion or resignation were overwhelmingly passed by the annual conference of the City Superintendents of Wisconsin Schools, the State and County Councils of Defense, and the Wisconsin Alumni Association. After extended and well-publicized debates both houses of the Wisconsin legislature seemed to have decided to adopt loyalty resolutions that did not mention him. Then a friend made an extended, impassioned speech in his defense. Furious, his opponents adopted the Wilcox resolution, specifically condemning the senior senator. La Follette's supporters were victims of the same hysteria. Edwin Gross, formerly a close friend of Lenroot, reported that the junior senator seemed to fear being seen with him. He was threatened with hanging, he thought his phone was tapped by the secret service, and erstwhile friends discussed whether they should ostracize him. It was a difficult period for young Phil and his younger sister; their mother had gone to Washington to be with their father at this crucial moment.[24]

While the nation's press and politicians echoed their Wisconsin counterparts, occasionally the voice of reason asserted itself. The Springfield *Republican* stated that he had done nothing to justify a charge of sedition and that he should be expelled for nothing less. The Topeka *Capital* insisted that expulsion was impractical (and all his political enemies realized this) and said La Follette could be dampened by taking graft and profits out of all war activities.[25] There was considerable support and sympathy for him, but little of it received national attention. Many old friends stood by him: Secretary of the Navy Josephus Daniels sent messages expressing confidence in him and disapproval of the attacks. James Stone accepted La Follette's criticism of the administration and retained contact with him while vigorously pressing for loyalty candidates. After completing the St. Paul speech he still had a commitment in Toledo. Depite threats of mob violence, despite a pervasive vigilante spirit, La Follette insisted upon fulfilling his engagement. For two and a half hours he spoke on war aims to an overflow audience, punctuated by frequent applause and concluded to a rousing ovation. In response to hundreds of letters from supporters, he dispatched a form letter emphasizing his record as an advocate of constitutional government responsive to the will of the people. Aware of the obligation of wartime, he wrote, "I am contending for the constitutional right of free speech, and peaceful assemblage; for the right of the people to discuss the terms of an honorable peace," for Congress to declare war aims, for equitable war taxes on wealth, for constitutional rights "which Webster, Clay, Sumner, Lincoln, and others exercised in time of war."[26] Even in his own defense, La Follette chose an offensive posture.

He did make an attempt to show that the AP dispatch that had caused the furor was in error. During his Toledo speech, his last wartime address out of the confines of the Senate, he informed reporters that the news story had been erroneous. He printed in his magazine both the incorrect reports about his statements and the appropriate selections from the steno-graphic record; but he permitted his following remarks to remain dormant, remarks that might have indicated that the phrase "serious grievances" was delivered tongue in cheek. And he informed Atlee Pomerene, who headed the investigating committee, that his copy was inaccurate. While newspapers carried his corrective statement, and the AP sent it over its wires, no one thought to check out the accuracy of the initial story until eight months later. Yet in his reply to the charges in the Senate, he disdained a detailed defense in favor of a three-hour presentation in favor of free speech during wartime.[27]

A second controversy originated with his contention about Wilson and the Lusitania. Wilson had been alerted by Bryan that the Lusitania was carrying ammunition. After the sinking of the Falaba Bryan had questioned the wisdom of insisting on the right of Americans to travel on belligerent vessels in a war zone, and after the sinking of the Lusitania he had urged Wilson that ships bearing explosives be forbidden to carry passengers, but it is not certain that Bryan asked Wilson to prevent Americans from embarking on the Lusitania. Bryan phoned La Follette to inform him that he would publicly deny La Follette's allegation and then issued a release to the press. La Follette remained confident in his sources. He retained his friend, Gilbert Roe, to prepare his defense. While Roe presented an excellent case, by the time it was delivered conditions had changed so drastically that it was hardly necessary.[28]

During the months that the hearing was delayed, La Follette's ordeal had a nightmarish quality, like a tale by Kafka. "That you or I should have our loyalty to our country questioned," he wrote to James Pierce, "is so grotesque, so monstrous that I have never been able to believe that a sane mind has ever seriously entertained such a thought. . . . My life has been dedicated to the public service." Now those who had attacked autocracy were suspect, he wrote with bitter irony, and those who had undermined the government and robbed the people were "patriots."[29] Heightening this atmosphere was his all-consuming concern for the health of his eldest son, Robert, Jr.

Bobbie, who had been working with his father, had a recurrence of streptococci infection in late January, 1918; his fever rose to 104, his heart was dilated with valve leakage and signs of pleurisy. At its inception the disease travelled more rapidly in five days than it had in five weeks previously. On February 8, he was operated on to drain pus, and for the next five days his life hung in the balance. By the end of the month they knew he would pull through. "There has been a great strain on all of us in Bobbie's severe illness. Now that he is where we can feel more at ease about him, we realize how much of our vitality is gone." The stress on the elder La Follette was particularly great: "Papa has had almost as hard a time as Bobbie. He has been so wrought up over him he will not go to bed nights and hovers about his room." As late as May intense pain still prevented proper rest, despite double doses of morphine. Bobbie's face, eyes, mouth, neck, and shoulders remained badly swollen and he continued to run a high temperature. By the end of May, Belle could report: "Daddy is feeling better since Bobbie is gaining although he is still very apprehensive." Even in the middle of October the wound was not yet healed; he could be lifted to a rocking chair for his meals and could stay as much as three-quarters of an hour before returning to bed; and he no longer needed morphine.[30]

After eight months' absence from the Senate chamber La Follette returned on September 30, 1918, to be greeted by the booming voice of a political opponent, Boise Penrose: "Glad to see you Senator. How's the boy?" The tension that had surrounded La Follette had been eased during the interval.[31]

For the AP had retracted and apologized. Although La Follette had been anxious for the charges to be considered, it was difficult to assemble a quorum of the committee, and the hearings did not begin until May 21, 1918. Roe discussed the petition in detail, pointing out reporting errors. His analysis received much better coverage than anticipated; much to the surprise of Roe and La Follette, Frederick Roy Martin of the AP apologized for the mistake, stating that he had not been previously aware that the initial dispatch might be inaccurate. After this retraction, the committee could only exonerate the Wisconsin senator. Yet he could not be certain of the outcome, and they did not report in his favor until the November elections ended, and the armistice negotiated. La Follette's vote was the key to organizing the Senate. As the Senate debated, La Follette sat in unaccustomed silence, without change of expression; under the advice of Knox, Lodge, and Gronna he did not dignify attacks by noticing them. He was vindicated — 50-21.[32]

One indication of how deeply La Follette was affected by this incident was his uncharacteristic decision to sue some of his detractors, an action that may have caused some to temper their accusations. Through his attorneys, Crownhart, Wylie, and Roe, he initiated an action against the Madison *Democrat* for libel in November of 1917 and followed with a similar suit directed against the *Wisconsin State Journal* and the directors of the Madison Club. Requiring a new political journal, he helped William Evjue raise funds to establish the *Capital Times*. This paper carried the transcript of the preliminary hearings, making apparent the speciousness of all the charges. After the AP retraction, Roe received feelers for an amicable settlement of the case against the *Journal*. The litigation had accomplished its purpose.[33]

The furor over his speech altered La Follette's plans. Before its delivery he had hoped to organize a national campaign against the prosecution of the war on the home front. Afterwards, he was tied to Washington and concentrated on sustaining his forces in Wisconsin. The Wisconsin progressives had been so badly splintered by the war that Walter Goodland, chosen to prepare for the 1918 gubernatorial election, had repudiated La Follette in the interim. Then Senator Husting

died in a hunting accident, precipitating an unanticipated
struggle for a successor.

Despite the super patriots there was still fertile soil for a La
Follette style campaign. Dairy prices had not kept pace with
skyrocketing feed costs. Manufacturers had been permitted to
organize; the offices of milk producers were raided when they
attempted to fix prices and anti-trust proceedings were
instituted. Wisconsin farm cooperatives resented being forced
to buy coal through dealers rather than directly as before.
Farmers demanded profitable prices and an adequate supply of
labor in return for greater production. Farm discontent
focussed on profiteering, mounting costs of manufactured
goods, and attempts to stifle criticism with unwarranted
charges of disloyalty. Normally conservative German Democrats, resenting wartime treatment, were ready to support a
war critic.

James Thompson, the most popular Norwegian-American
politician since Davidson, was convinced that economic issues
would bring victory. But Lenroot, with the support of Philipp,
the "stalwarts," the "loyalists," and even the *Skandinaven,*
succeeded in labeling "Big Jim" as the candidate of La Follette
and disloyalty and narrowly won the nomination. Thompson
carried most of the formerly anti-La Follette German counties
but lost ground in many of the former La Follette strongholds.

Now that he faced Joseph Davies in the special election, — a
man who tried to turn the loyalty issue against him, — Lenroot
modified his stands, appealing to the Thompson vote. The
violence of Democratic attacks on Lenroot's loyalty drew the
warring Republicans together. Victor Berger, the Socialist,
campaigned against the administration's prosecution of the
war. Lenroot won, by a suprisingly close vote, and Berger ran a
strong third, tripling the normal Social Democratic vote.[34]

But the special senatorial election could not have figured in
La Follette's plans. He was concerned with restoring a
progressive to the state house. Events forced a change in
course, for the Wisconsin Society of Equity, a powerful farm
organization, endorsed its president, J. N. Tittemore, as
candidate for governor, and Roy Wilcox, the author of the
anti-La Follette resolution, declared his candidacy and
impugned the governor's loyalty. Faced with a candidate "five

times as vicious as Governor Philipp," after much hesitation they decided to support Tittemore, maintain the appearance of progressive continuity, and draw enough votes to defeat Wilcox. The scenario was properly written: Philipp defeated Wilcox by 500 votes, drawing heavily in the German counties. Economic issues had clearly receded into the background, with the war in the ascendancy, for Lieutenant-Governor Edward Dithmar's vote paralleled that of his old foe.[35]

As the war ended and rumors filtered back about Wilson's difficulty in implementing his fourteen points at the peace table, the pariah began to look like a prophet.

# CHAPTER 11

# *"A Holy Alliance"*

A S the war was coming to a successful conclusion, Woodrow Wilson faced grave internal problems in his efforts to shape the post-war world. He led a minority party and had won his office only after a rupture in the opposition; he had narrowly been reelected with the advantages of incumbency, the peace issue, and the support of many progressive Republicans. To obtain domestic endorsement for his policies he had two choices: He could attempt to forge a bipartisan alliance on foreign policy, at best a doubtful proposition in the American political climate, and particularly difficult since collective security was such a marked departure from traditional attitudes.[1] Or he could promote Democratic candidates for the Senate, hoping to obtain adequate support for his policies. Unfortunately, a president, who is not himself a candidate, is often unable to influence the election of others. In any event a two-thirds Democratic majority was unobtainable, and two-thirds would be required to endorse the forthcoming treaty. This alternative was dangerous. The dislocations of war created a nostalgia for an imagined past, for a return to "normal" conditions, to a prewar world that had been forever destroyed by a holocaust. At that time, the Republican party had been in power. If Wilson failed to retain the support of progressive Republicans, a victory by the party with the largest electoral registration, regardless of its causes, might appear to be repudiation of presidential leadership in foreign affairs, and his victorious opponents might respond to his partisanship by blocking his treaty. He chose the second course with all of its consequences. Given Wilson's temperament and view of his office, it was unthinkable for him to attempt to work with his senatorial opposition. He considered foreign policy to be the province of the president, albeit with popular support, and was confident that the public would force senatorial endorsement. But he forgot to deal with fundamental political reality: his most fervent opponents would not have to seek reelection for years, and they knew that political memory was short.[2]

The result of the 1918 election was unfavorable for Wilson but favorable for La Follette. The new lineup was 49 Republicans to 47 Democrats. With a Democratic Vice-President, La Follette had become the pivotal figure: "Already both sides are indicating quite a mellowness towards a certain much despised member," he wrote home.[3] And with the end of the war his persistent criticism of the administration, particularly on foreign policy, met with much warmer Republican response.

"I have such a feeling of resentment against Wilson that it is not altogether easy to maintain a judicial tone when I write about him," he informed Belle and Bobby.[4] La Follette had no desire to return to the "normal" prewar world, with its unfair distribution of wealth and power. He had hoped that Wilson would lead the country into a more equitable and democratic post-war world, a realization of his rhetoric. Instead, he found him "a skillful performer with words" whose actions contradicted his "New Freedom": he had made the presidency autocratic, suppressed the independence of Congress, and wiped out the constitutional guarantees of free speech. Lacking understanding of railroad problems, he had undermined state commissions, made the ICC the tool of the railroads, and set back government ownership for a generation. Twenty years of democratic gains had been destroyed. In place of "a Government of the people for the benefit of the people," America had a government dominated by wealth to increase its profits, a government inconsiderate of human rights and concerned with property rights. In his first campaign he had promised criminal prosecutions for corporate officials who violated the law, and none had been initiated. He had promised to eliminate private monopolies and criminal conspiracies to raise the cost of living but permitted the interests to use the war to raise prices, and the United States was still "safe" for trusts. By 1919 he had loaded the Industrial Commission with monopoly magnates, permitted Palmer a free hand to violate civil liberties, and undermined the constitution with an undeclared war on Russia. "The real tragedy in Woodrow Wilson's career was the woeful discredit which has come to the great principles he betrayed, the brief espousal of which gave him the presidency and made him the hope of millions."[5]

In his concern for civil liberties La Follette was as harsh with his own party as with the administration. He felt that the espionage and sedition bills, as drafted by the Justice Department,"were the conception of a fifteenth century mind" and he warned his party that if they were to enact them they would go the way of the Federalists after the Alien and Sedition Acts. While the legislative product was better than the original, it was still monstrous. "Unless the impossible should happen," he wrote, "and the Supreme Court have a lucid and courageous hour and by *accident* should happen to *remember* about the *Constitution* and declare the Espionage law *unconstitutional*, it will take a *political earthquake* to *save us*."[6] He did not fear free discussion of ideas, for a "bad idea cannot live in the open air and under the sunlight of free, liberal discussion in the United States." The conservatives promoted Leninism. Bolshevism could be checked by making the government serve the people, and that required free discussion. The blackest blot of "the dark age of suppression" was "the imprisonment of American citizens for daring to express opinions contrary to those held by men in control of the government."[7] For a brief moment he took heart when Scott Nearing, the socialist writer, was acquitted: "The people will repeal the Espionage law in the jury room — if Congress hasn't sense enough to do it by legislation." But the mailing of bombs discouraged him: "With these crazy terrorists — exploding their bombs and the crazy Plutos suppressing free speech it makes the fight for democracy by lawful means of the ballot a pretty slow job these days."[8] And as the "Red Scare" incidents mounted, as Victor Berger was refused his seat in Congress, and five socialists were denied the fruits of election to the New York Assembly, as hundreds of aliens were rounded up to be deported, as a socialist meeting in Madison Square Garden was broken up and the offices of the socialist New York *Call* were invaded, La Follette concluded that the rationale for this behavior was "the old plea that the people are not fit to govern themselves."[9] Through every forum available to him he continued to fight for freedom of speech and for amnesty for incarcerated conscientious objectors and political prisoners.

The post-war fear of the spread of the Bolshevik revolution not only threatened the Bill of Rights, but it was used as an excuse to mount a counterattack against the trade union movement. In return for a no-strike pledge the American Federation of Labor had received tacit aid from the administration and had enjoyed its first successful organizational campaign in a decade. But because of the pledge, wages had lagged behind prices throughout the war. Labor looked toward a better post-war world in fulfillment of Wilson's rhetoric. Instead, price controls, which had deterred large producers, were relaxed, and prices soared. Post-war unemployment tempted manufacturers to return to a ten-hour day, undoing decades of union activity and a considerable wartime achievement, and even to reduce wages in the face of high prices. Efforts to improve labor's standard of living met fierce resistance as employers were determined to destroy unions and return to their conception of the "normal" prewar world, to unilateral decision-making on all matters. The inevitable strike wave was met by court injunctions, strikebreakers, labor spies, private and local police. The "American Plan" — open shops, company unions, and welfare capitalism — was put forth as an alternative to the increasing hazards of unionization.[10] Throughout this onslaught La Follette remained a firm friend to organized labor.

Post-war turmoil was the inevitable result of the "bitterness and class hatred" engendered by wartime inequity, he insisted. Those who profited by war "brazenly flaunt before the public their new made wealth," while inflation brought immeasurable suffering and discontent, leading to the most extensive strikes in our history. He was disturbed that much of the public hoped to deflate prices by reducing wages. Real wages, he showed statistically, had fallen during the war and the post-war period, and in some industries they were too small a percentage of production costs to be much of a factor. On the other hand, profits per dollar had increased. Industry's demand for an open shop, he protested, was a phony battle cry; capital intended to destroy organized labor, eliminate its political power, and end collective bargaining. In this struggle, government was allied with capital. Senators seemed anxious to pass a resolution implying that a proposed mine strike was unlawful, he observed, but they did not protest the illegal coal organization which raised prices; he wanted a complete investigation and laws enforced against operators as well as miners. While the Sherman and Clayton acts had been enacted to protect the people from monopoly and to permit them to organize to defend themselves against combinations, the Justice Department and the courts had misused these measures to their detriment. The deck was stacked against labor. With a strike "the over rich employer" hires gunmen or has troops called out "to shoot them down." Counter-violence was counterproductive, for the employer could summon more gunmen, more soldiers, or fall back on the courts. He vigorously defended the right to strike. "When you force men to work on penalty of imprisonment," differences are not resolved, and the attention of the public is not called "to the dangerous conditions from which the strikers suffer." He warned farmers not to attack labor. Their interests were complementary. Industry was thoroughly organized and controlled prices; only 25% of labor had organized in defense. Farmers should be interested in workers' wages because laboring men were their most important market. The individual cannot stand alone against organized wealth, particularly if backed by the government and the courts. "All labor, all farmers, all consumers everywhere must organize and these organizations must maintain a friendly alliance in common defense for their self preservation," he insisted, and in his last years he tried to forge such a coalition.[11]

Inflation necessitated particular concern for those who did not bargain for their own salaries and working conditions — government employes. He contrasted the ease with which the Senate increased salaries of judges and congressmen with the technicalities unearthed when discussing salaries of government employees. From 1905-15 top officials received increases of 50-80%, lower employees obtained raises of 4-25%; some salaries were only half subsistence level, and such inequity had to be rectified.[12]

His opposition to Wilson's foreign policy followed logically from his stand on American entrance into and prosecution of the war. He had supported clearly delimited war aims. He feared that Tory Republicans, who spoke of unconditional surrender and ravaging Germany, would join Clemenceau in pressing for an imperialist peace. Their attitude had delayed peace for months, while Wilson really wanted a just and democratic peace, without which he would have nothing to show for the sacrifices of the war. When Wilson began to modify the 14 points under pressure of an election, La Follette felt uneasy. He considered Wilson a natural Tory who feared Bolsheviks would triumph if the Junkers collapsed. Yet, when the German revolution came he was disturbed, for it was unclear with whom an armistice could be negotiated. Besides: "We may have the shocking spectacle of the armies that have been fighting to make the world *safe* for democracy being used to *throttle* democracy, under the pretense of 'restoring order' in Germany & elsewhere, as they are now being used in Russia."[13]

The Russian adventure had given ample indication of Wilson's preference for a unilateral exercise of foreign policy, a practice La Follette found clearly unconstitutional. Privately he indicated some sympathy for the Russian experiment, but he was skeptical of his good friend Lincoln Steffens' prophecy that the future was being enacted there.[14] His major concern, though, was with the illegal and unwarranted interference in the internal affairs of another country. Congress had never declared war, yet the President had dispatched an army to Russia, raised for a different purpose, employing funds appropriated for a different use. The world's organized wealth feared Soviet principles. But America's attitude towards the Soviet government was irrelevant. That was a decision for the Russian people. "Disorder and bloodshed have accompanied every revolution of history. We ourselves passed through a period that one of the great historians has devoted a chapter to, entitled 'Anarchy.' From the day of the fall of the Bastille, France was drenched in blood. The bloodier a revolution the stronger the evidence that there preceded it oppression unspeakable. The law of action and reaction is the same, not only in physics but in the affairs of men."[15] He threw Wilson's rhetoric back at him, calling our intervention a crime against "self determination" and the "consent of the governed." He insisted that the Soviet government be recognized; if we recognized the Mannerheim government of Finland despite the killing of 30,000 Red prisoners, we could not claim concern for the execution of 3200 counterrevolutionaries; if we could recognize the Kolchak regime, survivor of the Czar, we could not reject a socialist government, struggling to establish industrial democracy.[16]

Nor did he prefer more indirect methods of coercion. He balked at a bill to supply food for Europe whose purpose was not charity — it excluded Germany — but the prevention of the spread of socialist ideas. Argument and example would prevent socialism, he insisted. To purchase food here and then send it abroad would raise taxes and continue the high cost of living at a time that employers were pressing to reduce wages; it would produce serious domestic disturbances. He contrasted Wilson's treatment of Germany with General Grant's magnanimity. He had fed the defeated Confederates and allowed them to retain their horses and mules.[17]

At least the administration did not attempt a German counterrevolution. Nevertheless, the Versailles negotiations disturbed La Follette. He was not opposed to Wilson's presence at the peace table, but he felt Wilson had conceded too much from the beginning. Britain was amenable to all of Wilson's proposals except those on the freedom of the seas and the limits of German responsibility for war damages, the very principles for which Wilson had entered the war. By agreeing to these reservations in advance the President indicated he would not oppose Britain's imperialist designs for peace but only sought "applause as the one figure in the world." Discouraged as one provision of the fourteen points after another was abandoned or interpreted away, he wrote to his family: "Doesn't it look as though we had been fighting to *enforce those secret treaties?*"[18] The negotiating procedures made the open convenants' phrase "a ghastly joke." With mounting objections to the proposed League of Nations, particularly as a violation of the Monroe Doctrine, he chided Congress for its wartime abnegation of responsibility to declare national war goals. Remembering the sections pledging American abstention from European affairs, he said: "I think the fellows who voted for war raped the Monroe Doctrine themselves." A real League of Peace would abolish enforced military service and prohibit a declaration of war (unless invaded) without a popular vote. People did not seek war; ruling classes did. Disarmament could be achieved if the people made decisions. If any nation possessed an overwhelming army, he warned, it would make a mockery of a League. And a large national navy would render arbitration useless, for a decision to cut off trade with the master of the seas could not be enforced.[19]

In many ways La Follette was even more disturbed by Wilson's autocratic attitude towards foreign policy than by the rest of the negotiations. When the President had refused to call a special executive session to receive the Senate's advice before he broke precedent and sailed to Europe for treaty negotiations, without any senators on the commission, La Follette complained that he had "outgrown the constitutional limitations of his office." (Senators had been peace commissioners after the War of 1812 and the Spanish-American War.) It would be embarrassing if the President negotiated a treaty, without prior consultation, unacceptable to two-thirds of the Senate. Washington had consulted the Senate even on Indian treaties, he pointed out.

La Follette fully understood Wilson's strategy. He intended to complete negotiations without disclosure, and then the Senate would be bound by his commitment. Senators, according to this scenario, would be reluctant to insist upon amendments in order to avoid charges of delaying, and possibly defeating, the treaty; they would hesitate for fear that the President would refuse to transmit any changes to the high contracting parties. But Wilson misread the temper of the Senate. The post-war Congress, dominated by the opposition, would have reasserted itself in any event; Wilson's apparent arrogance intensified his problems.[20]

On March 25, 1919, shortly after Wilson, having failed to generate support for the draft of the League covenant, and having been presented with a round robin, signed by more than one-third of the Senate, declaring the League unacceptable "in the form now proposed," had returned to Paris, La Follette wrote home: "I was moping away up here in my room when there came a faint tap at the door. . . .I opened the door and there *stood Mary — my Mary*!!! Do you know what I did? I just cried! That's what I did. I'm an old man all right . . . Ye Gods but it was good to have my arms around her and hold her

in my lap — my baby." Mary had intended to enter the
university, and Phil had invited her to be his guest for the
junior prom. Then, in a deliberate slight, La Follette was not
invited, despite the custom of requesting the attendance of high
officials. Phil and Mary substituted a few festive evenings in
Chicago. Mary decided not to attend the university, worked in
her father's office, and took night classes at the Corcoran
School of Art.[21]

La Follette was troubled by reports about the informal preliminary conferences: peace terms were being shaped which
determined the future of the world, and the American people
were not being kept informed. La Follette feared Wilson's war
aims would be replaced by "a cold blooded sordid 'peace' treaty
dressed up in a maze of rhetorical flim flam." The Germans had
made an armistice based on the fourteen points; now all that
remained of them could "be covered with a postage stamp."
The German people and a new German government, neither of
whom was responsible for the war, should not be made to suffer.
He thought the synopsis of the treaty was "enough to chill the
heart of the world." Germany was to be stripped of everything
and was to pay enormous reparations.[22] Reading the full treaty
was even more discouraging.

In a front-page editorial headlined "WILSON'S BROKEN
PLEDGES" La Follette trumpeted the objections of the progressive irreconcilables. Wilson had broken relations with
Germany in order to preserve the freedom of the seas, he
reminded his readers, only to surrender it to Great Britain at
the conference table. He advanced principles of self-determ-
ination contrary to the secret pledges and then agreed to a
treaty that embodied the secret spoils agreements in return for
a League compact which enforced by the sword an immoral
treaty to establish an "imperialistic and financial dictatorship
over the world." The treaty endangered American independence; it "surrenders the control of this government to an
armed autocracy and betrays American independence to the
great European powers," he claimed. It was "the death knell of
hope for Ireland, India and Egypt, a crime against China, and a
repudiation of the promises made to the German people."[23] In
future speeches and articles he elaborated his argument, but he
did not change its essence.

One of his greatest concerns was with the ramifications of Article 10, the commitment to collective security. We expected an increased national debt when we entered the war, he told the Senate. We did not expect to relinquish control over our destiny as a nation to a council of nations, in which we had a small voice. We did not expect to place our wealth and lives at the disposal of remote governments to uphold policies "foreign to the purposes and desires of our own people." Through entangling alliances we would become involved in "every political scheme that may be hatched in the capitals of Europe or elsewhere in this world of ours." For, under Article 10, we must preserve the political independence and territorial integrity of all members whether in our interest or not. Nationalist rebels who sought outside aid, as American patriots had, would be considered disturbers of the peace. Asia was awakening, he warned. If the League tried to stifle their aspiration it would lead to a race war in which whites were outnumbered. Under Article 11, he insisted, we were obliged to protect the internal status quo from revolution. Between the two we would be perpetually in a state of war, with a large standing army, and the administration could suppress offensive publications and imprison critics.[24]

The proposed League of Nations was neither a league of peace not a real league of nations, he asserted. It excluded Russia, Germany, Austria, Norway, Sweden, Denmark, Holland, and Spain, while China had declined to sign. Like Metternich's Holy Alliance, a coalition of the victorious governments intended to subjugate and exploit its conquered enemies. The treaty created problems that were bound to lead to another conflagration. The division of the Austrian Emprie left disaffected minorities and nations with unsatisfactory boundaries; central Europe would be afflicted with turmoil and war for years to come. And what should be done about Fiume? Although granted to Yugoslavia, a resurgent Italy, with dreams of Ancient Rome, was occupying it. The economist, John Maynard Keynes, had written that Germany could not meet the economic terms of the treaty, he continued. It removed some of her own administration from German hands and stationed foreign troops on her soil. If enforced, these provisions meant the annihilation of Germany — but it really presaged resumption of hostilities.

Not only was the treaty harsh towards a defeated enemy, it raped and robbed an ally. China's treaty with Germany had specified that rights in the Shantung peninsula were not transferable. When China entered the war against Germany these rights reverted to her. None of the parties to the Treaty of Versailles had any of the rights in Shantung that they conveyed to Japan. China lacked the power to resist. Should the United States participate in "a gigantic theft of valuable rights" from an ally and sister republic "for the benefit of the most despotic Government on earth?" Japan intended to remain: she had staffed the railroad with Japanese employees and had settled between fifty and a hundred thousand subjects on the Shantung peninsula.

The greatest beneficiary of the treaty, La Follette contended with dismay, was Great Britain. With acquisition of the German territories in southwest Africa, clear control over Egypt and the Anglo-Egyptian Sudan, mandates in Palestine and Syria, and protectorates in Afghanistan, Persia, and Tibet, it dominated a territory nine times that of the Roman Empire, with one-fourth of the world's land surface and population, mastered the trade routes of the world, except for the Panama Canal, and had naval and marine supremacy. How trustworthy was England as a mandatory power? It had betrayed its pledge to Egypt in 1882 to withdraw troops as soon as order was restored; now, it had seized Egyptian representatives in Paris and murdered one thousand demonstrators for demanding independence.

La Follette had long opposed English exploitation of India and foresaw future autonomy or independence. And English wartime and post-war policy in the subcontinent aroused his ire.

But of all the English possessions, the Irish drive for freedom was most in the headlines and had the greatest emotional and political impact. Though Ireland was as different from England as Poland was from Germany, Wilson had not even granted Ireland a hearing, La Follette charged, while defending small East European states. In 1921, when the Sinn Fein, clearly the dominant party in southern Ireland, rejected the British offer of a form of Dominion status, he introduced a resolution to recognize Irish independence. "The American doctrine of recognition is merely the practical application of the right of people to alter or abolish any form of government which becomes oppressive." The principles of 1776 rejected the mystique of legitimacy and accepted the will of the people. He spurned secret deals with imperialist powers "to suppress democracy and overthrow self government."

And according to the treaty the League, including the U.S., by supervising arms traffic, would relieve England of the job of preventing supplies from reaching Ireland, India, and Egypt.

Even the labor provisions of the treaty were too vague to have much meaning, he protested. For example, it supervised the trade in women, children, and opium, but did not eliminate it. Discouraged by the conference, Gompers was almost ready to repudiate it; labor standards provided were inadequate and would not benefit American labor. After all, England cast 24 votes at the meeting, the U.S., 4; working conditions in other nations were closer to England's than to our own.

For La Follette the treaty confirmed his initial opposition to the war. "This was a war of Big Business for Bigger Business. It was a war for trade routes, and commercial advantage. It was a war for territory and the right to exploit weaker peoples. It was a mean, sordid, mercenary war."[25]

Presented with an unsatisfactory treaty the question of strategy became paramount. Lodge, as the Republican leader, and Root devised a plan to Republicanize the treaty through reservations, and thus prevent the Democrats from gaining any advantage for 1920. La Follette vigorously rejected this approach. Reservations or amendments would not make it less of a Holy Alliance, professing idealism and peace, while preserving the status quo through "the suppression of nationalities and the prosecution of oppressive warfare."[26] With the other irreconcilables he supported Republican amendments and then joined Democrats in rejecting the amended document. These tactics, with the intractability of Wilson and Lodge, succeeded in defeating the treaty.[27]

Thereafter, La Follette was vigilant lest the United States be brought into the treaty and the League by subterfuge. He opposed sending observers to the supreme council and to the reparations commission, bodies created to carry out the Treaty of Versailles. And he resisted a separate treaty with Germany which attempted to reap the benefits of the treaty without its commitments; by signing this treaty, he insisted, we would assent to the exactions of Versailles, help force Germany to submit to its iniquitous provisions, and involve this country in Europe's quarrels for the next forty years. Instead, he suggested a simple resolution declaring an end to the war. When a Republican administration considered joining the World Court he called it "The League in disguised and diluted form"; the bankers were spearheading the fight to safeguard their almost worthless investments in the bonds of tottering European nations.[28]

La Follette was less critical of wartime management of the railroads than most progressive Republicans, and most progressives were closer to Wilson's solution of the problem than to the Republican leadership. Since the prewar railroads had offered inadequate service despite adequate revenue because of poor management, he endorsed a unified system under government operation to eliminate duplication and reduce rates. (Similarly, he advocated government ownership and operation of express companies, telegraph, and telephone.) In this way monopolies built on transport favoritism would be injured. Stockholders could be compensated by the exchange of low-interest government bonds for railroad securities, properly appraised; the debt could be paid out of earnings.[29]

When Secretary of the Treasury McAdoo recommended a five-year extension of government control of railroads to test its operation under peacetime conditions, La Follette realized that Cummins wanted to return the railroads to normal conditions. He predicted he would be the only member of the Senate Interstate Commission to support the administration request. He feared, incorrectly, that Cummins would convince Norris and Johnson to accept the railroad counterproposal to sugar-coat a return to private management and a modification of the Sherman Act to permit mergers, with enlarged control by the ICC.[30]

Unable to stifle the Cummins bill in committee he attacked it on the Senate floor. Essentially the proposal of the Railway Executives' Committee, it ignored testimony by the directors general of the Railroad Administration, McAdoo and Walter

Hines. Despite tax exemptions, despite monetary grants, despite the gift of an empire in land, the railroads had broken down before the war and would have been in worse shape if the government had not taken over. The bill would return the roads to the same prewar managers under whom they had become largely bankrupt and inadequate. Only McAdoo's supervision of these railroad executives had kept the lines functioning. The proposed legislation would accept bloated corporate book value as the rate base, legitimize watered stock, and formalize inequity and fraud. Under its provisions the government would pay the railroads immediately what it owed them, but railroad reimbursement to the government for improvements during federal operations would be postponed for ten years. Private ownership would require hundreds of millions of dollars of aid and a rate increase of $750,000,000; under continued government control, charges would probably be reduced.

He opposed profit guarantees and the recapture clause, by which half the net income in excess of 6% would be turned over to the ICC to aid roads in financial distress; if the income of a railroad was greater than a fair rate of return it should reduce its rates. Weak roads should be reorganized, not subsidized. The labor provisions prohibited the crucial strike weapon. The same rationale could apply to any industry where a work stoppage could cause hardship. If labor could be subject to dictation, so could farmers, he warned. But his major concern was the return of railroads to private ownership.

He wanted a real test of government operation of the railroads. Two years of wartime government management at a deficit did not ensure continued loss during the experiment. Military service for skilled labor would no longer be a factor. The need to transport military materials, regardless of expense, had negated the profit motive. Maintenance had cost more than ever. If funds were poorly allotted, they were spent under the direction of those who intended to run the lines if returned to private ownership. Albert Cummins, sponsor of the bill, had said that the railroads had overcharged the government $200,000,000 a year for a total of $400,000,000, equivalent to practically the entire deficit. Most important of all, with the end of the war the government had turned the corner. Without an increase in rates, despite strikes in steel and mining, the government had realized substantial surpluses from its operation of the system since July 1, 1919; and it had reduced the accident rate by two-thirds. After years of experience he was convinced that it was "impossible to properly regulate privately owned and controlled railroads. I believe that our Government should own and operate our railroads just as they are owned and successfully operated in many of the leading countries of the world today." Since railroads had been one of his major concerns, he persistently returned to the Esch-Cummins Act. He offered an amendment to prevent guaranty payments unless an investigation found that the company was not overpaying for supplies and was not being mismanaged. In 1923, he protested the railroads' attempts to increase their rate base by ten billion dollars; they tried to claim the estimated cost of reproduction of facilities at war-inflated prices, rather than their original cost as provided for in the Physical Valuation Act.[31] At the end of his career he found he had lost the essence of his longest struggle, to restrain rate increases and to prevent rewarding fraudulent capitalization, at the same time that his initial goal of thorough regulation had been completed.

As the Wilson administration was drawing to a close, its leader disabled during a tour to gather support for the Versailles Treaty but unwilling to withdraw himself from consideration for renomination, the attention of the nation was drawn to the election of 1920. The strongest Democratic candidate, William Gibbs McAdoo, was prevented from mounting an effective campaign for the nomination by his father-in-law's reluctance to disqualify himself. On the Republican side, Hiram Johnson's bid for the prize became bogged down in California as he fought the popular Herbert Hoover for the state delegation and could not pursue an adequate national campaign for delegates.[32]

For his part, La Follette seemed to face a tough campaign to control the Wisconsin delegation. He had only recently been the victim of ultra-nationalist vilification throughout the state, and the end of the war only shifted xenophobic attitudes towards red baiting. His progressive base had been shattered, and some followers wondered whether an adequate organization could be restructured. Governor Philipp and Senator Lenroot joined in opposition with former La Follette supporters William Hatton and Otto Bosshard. But a new La Follette coalition was being forged, and Robert, Jr., his father's secretary after the resignation of John Hannan, ran the campaign. Former supporters who had been driven underground during the war rallied to him. Normally conservative German farmers, victims of wartime anti-German activities, threw their support to their fellow sufferer. The Social Democrats, major targets of anti-war hysteria, allied themselves with him at this time and were to join him in future endeavors. The Non-Partisan League lent him its considerable support. And he had the fervent endorsement of labor, particularly the powerful railroad brotherhoods. The Wisconsin branch of the Committee of 48, remnants of Roosevelt's Progressive crusade, completed the new coalition. La Follette's popular platform condemned the Esch-Cummins Act, the Treaty of Versailles, and the high cost of living; called for the restoration of civil liberties; and included provisions favorable to farmers and workers. Philipp and Lenroot agreed with his criticism of the treaty and offered a platform of loyalty to the Republican party. The senior senator's slate carried 24 of the 26 places, capturing the statewide delegates by a large margin and sweeping both Lenroot's and Philipp's home districts.[33]

Even before the nomination of Warren Harding, Victor Berger, discouraged by socialist dissension, had discussed with La Follette the possibility of gathering radicals into a progressive democratic movement. The Republicans' choice intensified a progressive search for a political alternative. J. A. H. Hopkins, leader of the Committee of 48, had called a convention of progressives, members of the Non-Partisan League, the National Farmers' Council, and other groups, to meet simultaneously with the Labor party convention, with the intention of forming a new progressive party. La Follette was overwhelmingly favored as the candidate. Robert, Jr., and Roe, his representatives at the negotiations, felt that the radicals overestimated their strength and unity. Labor and the Irish were divided; the farmers did not agree on economic issues; and even the Committee of 48 suffered from factionalism. They were not convinced that even the veteran campaigner could weld the disparate elements into an alliance formidable enough to form a

new permanent party. If the Democratic nominee had a good
labor record the alliance could not retain the support of
organized labor. In Chicago that July, during the simultaneous
conventions, Robert Jr., felt somewhat more optimistic though
"We feel as though we were sitting on a mine that might blow
up at any minute." The delegates were practical, not a crowd of
highbrows and uplifters. W. R. Hearst, ready to lend his
support, would not endorse a fizzle. Financing was available,
and they could possibly get on the ballot in thirty-five states.
The junior La Follette knew that he could impose his father's
platform upon both conventions, but he wanted them to reach
the same common ground, for "an unnatural union might not
endure." Then the Labor party, outmaneuvering the
Committee of 48, imposed its platform. La Follette, much to the
surprise of both factions, made it clear that he was not
interested.[34]

The Committee of 48 would not accept this answer as final
and tried to get La Follette to make an independent race. Roe
opposed a candidacy at that time. It would conflict with the
congressional plans of the A.F.L., the railway brotherhoods and
the Non-Partisan League, he argued, and there was still no
agreement on the platform. He suggested an alternative
campaign for a progressive Congress, an idea La Follette was
later to accept. Roe had become convinced that capitalism had
outlived its day, and any successful new party must plan to
replace it gradually, so as not to shock the public. The
necessary educational work might not warrant an immediate
third party. Roe and Crownhart conferred with Hopkins about
an independent candidacy without a uniform platform. Hopkins
was optimistic about getting on the ballot, but La Follette and
his advisers were pessimistic about raising the necessary funds.
La Follette agreed to allow Hopkins two weeks' time to
investigate the situation at his own expense, for the survey
could help in the congressional campaign in any event. Then,
intense pressure to chose George Record as La Follette's
running mate injected the Committee of 48 into too prominent a
position, and Robert, Jr., called Hopkins to tell him his father
had decided to proceed no further. Writing a few days later the
young man insisted that a wonderful opportunity had passed.
"This distinctly is not dad's attitude, however. I think if some

one came along with the money to conduct a campaign he would be a candidate over night."[35]

Wisconsin remained a field of combat as La Follette shifted his focus homeward. After the delegate contest it was apparent to his partisans that the results warranted a campaign for state offices. While they could not hold the entire alliance together, they retained the support of the Non-Partisan League with whom they fielded a joint slate, and a resurgent labor movement. Berger, still smarting from the action of Non-Partisan and progressive legislators' voting to deny him his seat and wary of an extended alliance with bourgeois elements, prevented continued support by the Socialists.

For once, La Follette's supporters had no trouble endorsing a candidate to challenge Lenroot for the Senate, and they were confident that James Thompson would win. Much to their chagrin, prohibition diverted the attention of the electorate from the high cost of living, Lenroot's vote for the Esch-Cummins Act, a freight rate increase and the issue of the League. While prohibition was important to Thompson's fellow Norwegians and he was ready to embrace near beer and light wine, he accepted a strategy of neutrality. Lenroot received prohibitionist support, and Mayor A. C. McHenry of Oshkosh drew enough "wet" votes to cost him the nomination.[36]

When Edward Dithmar insisted upon running for governor despite organized labor's refusal to back a prohibitionist, the La Follette progressives endorsed John Blaine. The conservatives were more seriously divided, for Philipp was so determined to defeat Wilcox that he engineered a conservative convention endorsement of a war veteran, his friend Gilbert Seaman. Blaine won the nomination in a crowded field.[37]

A Republican platform convention withheld endorsement of Blaine and adopted statements unacceptable to La Follette. Citing this meeting, Thompson announced an independent candidacy. La Follette, having recuperated from a gallstone operation at the Mayo clinic, actively campaigned for Blaine and Thompson. With the support of the Hearst press, labor outside of Milwaukee (particularly the International Association of Machinists and the railway brotherhoods), and the rural and German vote, Blaine won easily, while Thompson lost narrowly. Although they did not gain control of the legislature, the La Follette faction had clearly been rejuvenated.[38]

The organization of its forces was still weak. In June, 1921, it began to build its war-shattered structure for the future, even though it anticipated an easy victory for La Follette and Blaine. Although he was encouraged by reports, La Follette decided that he would make a thorough canvass for the primary. Robert, Jr., was sent to Wisconsin for three weeks of full-time organizing and then returned in May, 1922 and pulled the lax reins into his own hands.

In the meantime La Follette raised another issue which alienated conservatives. Infuriated by a court decision overturning a law regulating child labor, disturbed by the appointment of Taft as chief justice less than a decade after the electorate had repudiated him, La Follette delivered a speech to the A.F. of L. convention in Cincinnati, Ohio of June 14, 1922, before he began his campaign for renomination, in which he attacked judicial usurpation of authority. Instead of our forefathers' desire for a government reflecting the will of the people, through gradual encroachment the courts had assumed sovereignty. The law was not what the people enact through Congress; it was something shaped by the constitutional construction of five men on the Supreme Court according to "their peculiar economic and political views." He did not intend to criticize the personnel of the court, he continued, for they were average in ability, wisdom, and character. He was concerned that they exercised "supreme power over the happiness, the rights, and the very lives of the 110,000,000 people of the United States," despite the defeat of a judicial veto power in the Constitutional Convention.

To prevent the continued exercise of "an arbitrary power wholly inconsistent with popular government," he proposed an amendment forbidding federal judges of inferior courts from deciding upon the constitutionality of legislation and granting to Congress the same right to override a judicial veto that it had to override a presidential veto.[39]

This proposal caused a considerable reaction in the press; a particularly vitriolic speech by Columbia University president Nicholas Murray Butler was read into the *Congressional Record* and was followed by bitter tirades from Senator Walter Edge of New Jersey and Senator Frank Kellogg of Minnesota.

His opponents in Wisconsin attempted to capitalize on these attacks but could not arouse the electorate.[40]

Recognizing the importance of the upcoming battle, early in 1921 Lenroot had helped organize a "United Progressive Republican League" composed of "sane" pro-war progressives to defeat all La Follette progressives. He even attempted to expel his old mentor from the party. Their June convention condemned La Follette's war record and fielded a full slate for the primary. Its candidate for Senator was William Ganfield, president of Carroll College.

In the meantime, the Socialist party commended La Follette's wartime stand; it refrained from nominating a candidate to oppose him while specifically stating that it was not endorsing his stand on other issues.

La Follette's first speech of the campaign dealt largely with domestic issues, but, in response to a question, he walked to the edge of the platform, and proudly proclaimed that he would not trade his war record with any man in the United States. Although warned not to discuss the issue, in every section of the state he commented briefly on the events leading to intervention and found uniformly favorable response. The tide had clearly turned against the "super patriots," and his antagonists soon dropped this line of attack.

A shift of strategy by his adversaries became necessary, and they charged him with being a mere voice of protest. Endorsements of his exceptional contributions poured in from major political and intellectual figures of national stature and were read by his supporters at meetings throughout the state. The La Follette men canvassed actively: Robert, Jr., ran the campaign for the entire ticket; Phil spoke in the south; and the senator spent six weeks touring the state. The result was a landslide! He swept 70 of 71 counties, only narrowly losing the one remaining "stalwart" stronghold, and swamped Ganfield 362,445 to 139,327. They had carried all but one congressional seat, the entire state ticket, and a clear majority of the legislature. His vindication was complete.[41]

Although he was confident that the decimated Democratic party was no threat to his reelection, he made it clear that he intended to campaign to solidify his position and to prepare for the future. Belle used the opportunity to speak in favor of efforts to eliminate war. Beginning on October 19, La Follette canvassed for ten days. He went to North Dakota to campaign for Lynn Frazier, who had defeated conservative Senator McCumber in the primary. In Minesota, aiding the independent candidacy of Hendrik Shipstead against an arch-enemy, Senator Kellogg, he took his revenge on the man who had led the fight to drive him from public life and who still attacked his war record. After tracing Kellogg's career of service to the special interests and reading a roll call of his senatorial votes, he made an uncharacteristic, bitter, personal attack on the Minnesotan. Kellogg walked with a pronounced stoop. "God Almighty through nature writes men's characters on their faces and in their forms," he told the overflow crowd in Kellogg's home city of Minneapolis. "Your Senator has bowed obsequiously to wealth and the corporations' orders and to his masters until God Almighty had given him a hump on his back — crouching, cringing, unAmerican, unmanly."[42]

La Follette won by a better than three to one margin, with every county in his column. Robert, Jr., was chosen to the legislature where he skillfully guided his father's adherents. Frazier and Shipstead were among a new group of progressives entering the Senate while the Harding Republicans received a serious setback. Among the casualities were close friends of the President and the supporters of the Fordney-McCumber Tariff. In Congress, the progressives were stronger than at any time since the Taft administration and appeared to hold the balance of power. The Committee for Progressive Political Action had succeeded in electing twelve of sixteen gubernatorial candidates whom they had endorsed. Al Smith became governor of New York in his second try, and Gifford Pinchot emerged as the executive officer in Pennsylvania. It "wasn't a 'Democratic landslide,' but it was a Progressive triumph," commented *Labor*, edited by the progressive Democrat, Edward Keating. "It was gloriously non-partisan. Party lines were smashed and labor displayed its strength in a manner unparalled in the history of the country. . . . La Follette was the outstanding winner and Washington is already talking of him as a most formidable presidential possibility in 1924."[43]

CHAPTER 12

# La Jollette for President

EVEN before Harding's election La Follette had resumed leadership of the progressives in opposition to efforts by the conservative Republican majority to restore prewar "normalcy." The struggle to retain government management of the railroads has been examined previously. From the time the GOP resumed control over Congress, progressives became watchdogs for the integrity and even the very existence of the regulatory commissions that they had fought so hard to create to restrain normal, unbridled corporate control of the economy. Having already challenged some of Wilson's appointees to the Federal Trade Commission and the Interstate Commerce Commission, La Follette played a leading role in the fight to sustain the impartiality of the regulatory commissions during the succeeding administrations.

One of the fondest hopes of the progressives was to create a tariff commission which would scientifically determine the difference in the cost of production at home and abroad, permitting competition from abroad for price fixing monopolies while maintaining American standards for labor. In 1916 Wilson guided legislation through Congress creating such a commission, restricted to an investigatory role, and appointed as members men who had endorsed the progressive view of tariff making. By 1918 the Democratic Congress was already cutting back on appropriations. Chairman Frank Taussig, the leading authority in the field, and former progressive congressman, William Kent, were donating their salaries in order to employ economists while Kent and Commissioner E. P. Costigan lobbied to obtain adequate funds. With a Republican victory the Tariff Commission found itself in greater danger. Quite by accident commissioners found that the

Senate Committee on Appropriations had eliminated its funds, just as the Democrats had eliminated the Taft-appointed Tariff Board years before. La Follette had vigorously supported legislation to create the Tariff Commission. In a three-hour speech he attacked the terminating amendment. He pointed out that the information gathered by the old Tariff Board had been invaluable to him in his analysis of the schedules of the Underwood Tariff. The commission had been hard working and unbiased; it wished to end partisan politics and to consider the tariff as a business question; it had organized and examined all pertinent laws for the past century; and it had investigated the packing trust. He declared "as a Republican that President Wilson has built up a Tariff Commission with which no Republican has any business to find fault if he wants . . . the facts to enable him to legislate properly upon the tariff." When he completed his statement he had won the votes of all but two senators and the Commission was saved.[1]

But this apparent victory was short lived. What could not be accomplished by frontal assault was achieved nevertheless. Although the flexible tariff provisions of the Fordney-McCumber Tariff, enabling the president to raise or lower schedules upon recommendation of the commission, seemed to enhance scientific tariff making, the power of appointment remained in the hands of conservative presidents. The Wilson appointees were gradually replaced by staunch protectionists and rates became largely flexible upwards. (Republican Commissioner William Culbertson, a Wilson appointee, reported that Republican Chairman Thomas Marvin regarded the importation of any goods as ceding a portion of the national domain.) The struggle between the protectionists and the advocates of scientific tariff came to a head in the hearings on the sugar schedule. Commissioner Henry Glassie insisted upon participating in the sugar hearings despite his wife's sizable holdings in a family-owned Louisiana sugar corporation. Edward Costigan's congressional allies inserted a provision into the Independent Office Appropriations Act preventing the payment of salary to a tariff commissioner who participated in cases in which he had a pecuniary interest; Glassie withdrew. Advocates of a reduction in the schedule were now in a majority. To prevent the anticipated report the administration first offered Culbertson a position on the more prestigious FTC and then attempted to postpone any report until after the 1924 elections. To alleviate pressure for delay, Costigan presented La Follette with the history of the sugar investigation. Fearing a campaign issue, the administration stopped trying to influence Culbertson. The focus was shifted to David J. Lewis, then being considered for reappointment — but he remained firm. The majority recommended a reduction. The minority report, based upon a tortured construction of the evidence, opposed the change. Coolidge pocketed both reports and took no action. La Follette concluded that those opposed to quasijudicial, scientific fact finding had taken over the commission.[2]

The FTC suffered a similar fate. When the Republicans regained control of Congress they attempted to cut the commission's appropriations — probably because it was doing good work, La Follette informed his sons. The Senator had found fault with the last appointment of Wilson to this body and the appointments by his successors were uniformly unsatisfactory to progressives. Consequently, George Norris felt compelled to lead the fight, unfortunately unsuccessful, for an investigation of the Aluminum trust (controlled by the family of the Secretary of Treasury, Andrew Mellon); it had ignored an order to cease and desist its illegal practices in 1922; continuing violations were reported to Attorney General Harlan Fiske Stone by the commission; the statute of limitations having expired, Stone ordered a renewed investigation, but the new commission majority would not reveal its findings without Alcoa's consent; with Stone appointed to the Supreme Court, his successor let the matter drop. La Follette was distressed by these developments. While the ICC had declined from a servant of the public to a servant of the railroads, the FTC seemed to be "the one government body which has kept itself clean from the domination and control of the great interests it was designed to curb," he commented. The appointment of William Humphreys had finally given the interests a majority in the last regulatory stronghold, he wrote in disgust.[3]

To La Follette, administrative appointments were one of the clearest manifestations of the pro-business policies of Harding and Coolidge. As Harding began to announce his cabinet appointments La Follette was disturbed that his choices did not indicate a desire to grapple with the trust issue. He grieved over Harding's inaugural address, with its phrases about more business in government and less government in business. He feared that a promise to supervise private investments abroad, ostensibly to promote foreign trade, actually committed the government to collect overseas loans.[4] When Coolidge assumed the reins, La Follette wrote: "President Coolidge's first message to the Congress is an able, concise and frank presentation of the stand-pat reactionary theory of government."[5] Facing a hostile executive, remembering the aggrandizement of Wilson, he was particularly incensed with Harding for appearing before Congress, participating in debate, and writing letters to be read in Congress to influence legislation. He found the first session under Harding particularly frustrating. The old guard, he complained, had a large majority and was "arrogant and relentless" in putting over its program. He found his progressive correspondents "discouraged and sullen." Although he was unable to carry out his promise to make Harding good, he kept busy trying.[6]

When the administration decided to return to a highly protective tariff, La Follette spearheaded the resistance as he had more than a decade earlier. "Suppose a majority of the present Congress was bent on serving the interests of the whole people and not special interests, how long do you think the Fordney-McCumber tariff bill would be considered by the Senate?" he asked a Milwaukee audience. The worst tariff bill in history would not get ten votes on its merits. Yet it was going to pass. While conditions had changed, proper adjustments would lead to rate reductions, not the increases provided, for the existing schedules encompassed more than the differences in the cost of production.[7]

That the Harding administration should so favor business at the expense of consumers, while La Follette's farm constituents were doing so badly, was particularly mortifying. During the war and the immediate post-war period, American agricultural output had increased substantially to meet the demands of a war-torn Europe. Recovery of European production coincided with one of the most severe international depressions in history. While the effects of this recession in the United States were short lived, farmers were faced with reduced per capita consumption of grain; life styles had changed; the immigration that had long provided a constantly expanding domestic market for produce had been cut off. La Follette attempted to find a solution for the exclusion of farmers from the prosperity of the twenties. They were thrifty, hardworking, intelligent, scientific producers with unrivalled soil and climate and abundant harvests, he told the Senate in 1922. That agriculture lay prostrate despite the absence of natural calamities was "an indictment against the justice and integrity of the National Government." "Those who are nominally in control of the political government dare not make a move without first consulting those who rule the economic world." Trusts, through special interest legislation, had created an unparalleled inequality in the distribution of wealth. Their surplus profits, whether invested at home or abroad, created more products than could be profitably consumed. Industry could only be sustained through inflation, which leads to deflation. Monopolists profited by both. During inflation they earned interest by issuing high mortgages. During deflation the mortgage became a larger percentage of the value of the farm; agrarians borrowed half bushel dollars and paid back in full bushel dollars. Deflation was deliberately caused, he charged. Monopolists convinced the Federal Reserve Board to curtail advances based on liberty bonds and then acquired the bonds at deflated prices. Banks were calling farmers' loans and refusing renewals. Agrarian problems were intensified by the Esch-Cummins Act; freight rates became too high to market produce profitably. Agricultural income was falling; the packing monopoly was deliberately restraining prices. Credit was short. Country banks were permitted to collapse while New York banks were saved no matter how badly managed. Efforts by farmers to obtain a larger share of the retail price through marketing cooperatives were undercut as grain gamblers tried to destroy these enterprises, the FTC had reported.

Excessive business overhead expenses — high executive salaries, interest charges on watered stocks and bonds — with production at half capacity, had heightened the industrial depression. If the overcapitalized trusts were deflated, monopoly practices were ended, and fixed overhead expenses based on

illegal activities were reduced, the problems created by the
depression could be met.

By 1924 he was able to offer some solutions for the farm
problem, beyond attacking trusts. He wanted a marketing
system free of control by the interests, for the Danish farmer
received 80¢ of each consumer dollar, his American counterpart
only 40¢. Since bread was expensive while wheat was cheap, he
asked that bread prices be reduced to increase the domestic
market. He was particularly impressed by the solutions offered
by the Norris-Sinclair and McNary-Haugen bills, that the
government help the farmers to market their product, only he
wished the bills amended to ensure that the benefits accrued to
the farmers, not middlemen. Through the use of a farmer controlled marketing cooperative, sponsored by the government,
the producers could obtain what they were entitled to, the
actual cost of production plus a reasonable profit.[8]

La Follette was particularly affronted by Harding's
favoritism towards business when the administration intervened to prevent passage of veterans' adjusted compensation.
The former soldiers reacted so strongly to the anti-war
senator's forceful advocacy of their cause that his secretary
could write: "We are a regular junior Veterans' Bureau." He
contrasted the munificence towards business with stinginess
towards veterans. $25,000,000 had been given to Colombia to
help American oil companies. Enormous subsidies had been
granted to the shipping interests. The Senate had voted large
outlays for the military while retrenchment had been mandated
for hospitals for the disabled. If income was inadequate, he
queried, why was the administration urging repeal of the excess
profits tax with its annual revenue of $450,000,000.

He could not accept tax benefits for the rich while needed
services were neglected. He protested Mellon's suggested
reduction of imposts above $66,000 and the loophole that
permitted the wealthy to invest in tax-exempt government
securities. He insisted that income tax publicity was basic to
democracy, for otherwise the affluent would just lie about their
income, just as the Wisconsin railroads had prevaricated under
the license tax and the rich had been evading the assessment on
inheritance. And he rejected reliance on a levy on sales as a
revenue measure. He complained that administration proposals

would "exempt wealth from even so much of the tax as we have been able to impose upon it to help pay the expenses of the war." He sought time to draft a graduated inheritance tax to pay the interest on the war debt and to retire the principle in twenty to thirty years, but was busy resisting "many schemes designed to rob the people." He was impressed with the suggestion of a correspondent that a constitutional amendment be passed to allow the citizens to tax wealth in the event of war, for that "would do more to prevent war than all the disarmament conferences that are likely to assemble in the near future."[9]

Similarly, Harding's concept of a normal merchant marine ran counter to his own inclinations. By 1915 he had decided that since a private merchant fleet had "closed the highway to market for American products, it is the duty of the government to open that highway." Faced with an urgent wartime transport shortage, Wilson had built and converted vessels; with a national fleet a progressive dream could be effectuated. But even before a long-run shipping policy had been reached, La Follette had found serious fault with the Shipping Board. Wages were already inadequate. Private firms, supported by the board, attempted to impose a 25% wage cut, to eliminate overtime, and to reduce allowances for room and subsistence. Though profitable, the companies wanted to destroy the union, he charged. The were driving sailors to other jobs, and, though the board did not understand, a merchant marine could not be properly developed unless manned by American seamen and officers (as the union demanded). Board policies, in effect, favored the development of the British merchant fleet. American concerns, responsible for the operation of the board's ships, had worked out profitable arrangements with British shippers that injured national interests. La Follette was quick to speak out against Harding's decision to sell $3,000,000,000 worth of vessels for about $200,000,000, to lend the purchasers $125,000,000 in order to recondition them, and then to pay them $750,000,000 in operational subsidies over a period of ten years. Federal craft should be honestly and efficiently run to serve the interests of American businesses and shippers. The bill was contrary to the will of the American people, he asserted. It had vigorous farmer opposition, had appeared on neither the

Republican nor the Democratic platform and was the program
of an administration repudiated in the congressional elections.
He denied that such legislation would save money; even then, it
was worth $25,000,000 to maintain a great merchant fleet in
peacetime commerce. Board members were not shipping
experts; they had promoted subsidies rather than trying to
increase trade; they had withdrawn government  service
whenever private competitors saw a chance for a profit.
Nevertheless, the deficit had been decreased from $16,000,000 a
month to $4,000,000; it was incurred, not on federally
operated vessels, he asserted, but on freighters run under
contracts devised to lose money. The board had refused
Congress information on the identity of the unprofitable craft.
The bill permitted the board to decide to whom the steamers
should be sold, without competitive bidding; it gave subsidies
to American boats even if the owner possessed more British
than American bottoms; and the subsidized companies would
not be prevented from overcharging the public.[10]

Throughout the early 1920's he persisted in his fight against
monopoly, government for the interests, and the corruption
that inevitably followed. The new industries of the 1920's
became the center of heated controversy, and La Follette was a
natural participant in the debates about water power (although
Norris took the leading role), radio, and electric appliances.
"Several of us are trying to stop the passage of the Oil and Coal
bill and the water power grab," he wrote to his son in 1919.[11] La
Follette was aware of the importance of water power at an early
stage in its development. In 1910 he had called for state control
of water power so that its development benefited all citizens,
not just monopolistic millionaires, who already sought political
control "to prevent the enactment of laws which would
safeguard that great storehouse of energy for the benefit of the
people."[12] And as private development of power advanced he
pointed out that rates in Ontario were lower than the United
Stages — although the provincial companies paid taxes. Unlike
the United States, charges were set close to cost, and residents
paid no higher taxes than businesses. He was happy that
Samuel Untermeyer was doing a good job of investigating the
young giant, General Electric, and offered him help if he wanted
to work with Congress, for he was not getting any play outside

New York. As radio became a more important factor, he charged that such monopoly interests as G.E., Westinghouse, United Fruit and A.T.&T. had organized the Radio Corporation of America to control the industry. He supported legislation offered by Norris' junior colleague, Senator R. B. Howell, to limit the licenses of radio stations to two years.[13] But the headline-making struggle was over the naval oil reserves.

La Follette saw the potential for venality in the oil reserves before the Harding election, but his initial interest covered a wider field. He was concerned that the public, and not just private entrepreneurs, benefit from federally owned natural resources. Consequently, he wanted reasonable prices established for all the oil and coal produced from government fields. On the other hand, he insisted that the naval oil reserve be exempted from leasing and commended Secretary of the Navy Josephus Daniels for his courage in protecting the navy against pilferage by private interests. (Daniels had locked horns with Secretary of the Interior Franklin Lane who insisted that individuals who had filed claims prior to the creation of the reserve should be permitted to obtain a lease.) He predicted that the Elk Hills reserve could be preserved from loss for a thousand years. Even at this time he recognized Edward Doheny's ambitions for the California reserves, the realization of which was later to be so damaging to the presidential aspirations of McAdoo. Ironically, Senator Thomas Walsh of Montana quoted Doheny's testimony that the reserves could be drained by adjacent drilling, and his statement was instrumental in securing passage of legislation authorizing the President to lease the reserves. In 1920 Daniels attempted to protect the oil reserves by having them shifted to the naval department, under his jurisdiction.[14]

Initially, when Harding was elected, many conservationists felt secure. Gifford Pinchot, their acknowledged leader, had conferred with the candidate and endorsed his views on the subject. Harry Slattery, "a prosaic if likeable" Washington lawyer from South Carolina, previously secretary to Pinchot and the National Conservation Association, had written Harding's conservation speech. But Harding's cabinet appointments were inauspicious.

Edwin Denby, Secretary of the Navy, an automobile

manufacturer, was a former congressman, undistinguished except that he had been a member of the committee that had cleared Ballinger. Albert Fall, the new Secretary of the Interior, seemed a clear danger to Pinchot, who disliked the Interior Department in any event, and to La Follette, who knew his record in Congress. A resident of New Mexico, he was one of a breed of ambitious westerners for whom the public domain was a source of personal enrichment. A Democrat, he sought political advantage by switching parties as statehood approached. His wealth was drawn from mine holdings in Mexico and New Mexico, from banking investments, from his law practice, and from ranching. As early as 1910 Fall had been apprehended by Pinchot's forest rangers grazing three times as many sheep on the public domain as he was entitled to. An erect, confident man, who wore a wide-brimmed stetson, Fall had become a legend in Washington for his reckless encounters with gunmen and gamblers, and it was in the Senate that he joined Harding's poker table.

Soon after Fall assumed his office Slattery and Pinchot checked persistent rumors that the west coast oil reserves and the Alaska timberlands were being transferred to Interior. Pinchot led a concerted attack on the transfer of the forests, with the vigorous support of Secretary of Agriculture Henry C. Wallace, and by March of 1922 he felt confident enough of victory to divert his attention to his race for governor of Pennsylvania. The focus shifted to oil, and Slattery took the initiative.

The transfer of the naval oil reserves had already been completed when Slattery became aware of the change. He went to Theodore Roosevelt, Jr., Assistant Secretary of the Navy, to obtain his support, only to be shown the door when he predicted that Fall would offer the reserves to private interests. He then sought the elder statesman of the progressives — Robert La Follette — with whom he had worked to protect these reserves in 1919.

After an unsuccessful attempt to offer the lead to the less controversial Borah and Johnson, La Follette contacted Daniels to discuss the transfer of the oil reserves and expressed surprise that there was no adverse comment from naval officers. He started gathering information by asking for copies of the President's order of transfer from Secretary of State Hughes who forwarded the request to Fall. Finally acquiring a copy of the order he decided that it was illegal. To follow up his inquiries he put Slattery in contact with Daniels, Daniels' Washington correspondent, Edward Britton, former Attorney General Thomas Gregory, and retired Admiral Robert Griffin, former Chief of the Naval Bureau of Engineering (promising discretion), and he obtained a list of names of key naval personnel to contact for information (Commanders J. O. Richardson, N. W. Wright, H. A. Stuart, and Captain D. F. Boyd). Continuing his probe, he sent a letter to Edward Finney of Interior, inquiring about the legal basis for the transfers and leases, and to Denby, calling for the official orders and transcripts involved in the transmission. To combat Fall's claim that Teapot Dome would be drained by adjacent drilling if not leased, he sought contrary information from F. G. Bonfils, publisher of the Denver *Post*, Governor Robert Carey of Wyoming, Wyoming state engineer, G. B. Morgan, and Mayor W. A. Blackmore of Casper, Wyoming, the location of Teapot Dome. William Randolph Hearst was enlisted with a request to look up the legal side of the case, possibly to enjoin the administration. On April 21, a week after published news of the Teapot Dome lease, La Follette introduced a resolution, largely drafted by Slattery, detailing all the information the Senate required from the government on the oil leases. On April 28 La Follette made a bitter speech calling for an investigation by the Public Lands and Surveys Committee, chosen by him because of its favorable membership, indicating the possibility of corruption. The next afternoon he returned to the attack, and the resolution was passed unanimously. La Follette had spearheaded an investigation of the greatest scandal of the 1920's, helped convince Walsh to lead it, fed him information, and, whenever the investigation lagged, Slattery returned to him for aid and comfort. He aroused public interest by reviving the Committee on Manufactures inquest into rising gasoline prices while crude prices were declining. And he continued to prod the inquisitors in his speeches and his magazine. He pointed out that the Naval officials who had earlier helped Daniels transfer the fields to the Department of Navy had been reassigned out of the country. The Department of Justice, he insisted, must take civil action to recover the plunder and punish the plunderers. Denby should resign, for La Follette was not sure he could be impeached. He had nothing but praise for Walsh, Slattery, and the courageous naval officers who had defended the reserves. Subsequently it was revealed that Fall received about $400,000 in bribes from Doheny and Sinclair, and he became the first cabinet member to be jailed for corruption; the courts nullified the ill-gotten leases.[15]

His fight to protect naval oil reserves and favorable association with some naval officers did not result in an endorsement of naval expansion. He was against large appropriations for surface vessels; by the time they were constructed they would become obsolete and would need to be replaced by submarines and aircraft. With unparalleled coastal defenses and the second largest navy, the United States was already impregnable from attack; it was expending more on the military than any other nation ever had before the war to end war; 85.8% of the 1923 budget was for past and future wars. Preparedness, Germany had learned, did not prevent war. But the purpose of this fleet, he feared, was imperialism. He welcomed the Washington Conference, but was careful to point out that its naval provisions only created a naval holiday, restored each nation to the same state of preparedness as in 1914, and in itself "is a poor insurance against another war." It did give time for the common people to demand the use of national funds for reconstruction, not naval building. But he was disturbed by secret conferences. As the disarmament conference concluded he charged that it had been a cloak to hatch the Four Power Treaty, which was not to obtain peace but to maintain a Pacific status quo; it was a secret alliance which morally bound the country to fight to protect the "rights" of the "high contracting parties" in violation of traditional American policy, and it was a surrender of our national security and independence. In a controversy we would submit to an adjustment decided upon by a conference of imperialistic powers. It tied us to British and Japanese interests in the Far East and to Japan's atrocities in Korea, China, and Russia. It arrayed America against China, India, Russia, and Germany and might create a countervailing alliance. Since our concepts of liberty and equality were obnoxious to Japan, he predicted that our involvement would lead either to conflict or the surrender of our principles. And, as always, he saw the hand of capital: J. P. Morgan and other bankers held an enormous British debt, and the alliance with the United States was to help the imperialist powers to exploit the riches of Asia to repay it. "The Four Power Treaty," he insisted, "is an imperialistic treaty pregnant with the destruction of democracy at home and the destruction of whatever remnant of liberties are left for the people of Asia."[16]

He saw investments by American bankers as a crucial factor in American relations with other nations and he was not pleased by the effects of capital outflow. He opposed a provision of the revenue bill of 1921 that exempted American investments abroad from domestic taxation. It enabled capitalists to obtain inordinate profits abroad, exempted them from the financial burdens of the war from which they had profited, while the nation searched for new revenue sources to pay the debt. We had imposed prohibitive tariffs to encourage domestic capital investment in undeveloped water power and mines, to create jobs, and now we were to give incentives to overseas investments. Export of capital would reduce domestic output and increase prices.[17]

He questioned the wisdom and equity in American policy on intergovernmental debts and wondered about the influence of international bankers in forming this policy. In 1921 he complained that Harding was not collecting overdue interest and was permitting foreign debtors to pay the principle at their convenience while the United States was hard pressed to liquidate domestic obligations twice as large as its overseas loans. Although the terms for the loans had been set at the same rate as it cost the United States to raise funds, Harding wanted the right to make any deal that he pleased. In a debate in 1923 he protested the creation of the Dawes Commission, with its long-term funding of debts of European governments to the United States. In order to ensure repayment, America would have to preserve British and French imperialism for the next two generations. To be free of entanglement it would almost pay to cancel the obligations except that it would give imperialist nations fresh credit to build a larger military with which to enslave the world, and cancellation "would be an outrage upon American taxpayers," who had been assured the associated powers would pay on the same terms as the Liberty bonds. Only if a nation proved it was too poor to pay should a variance from the original terms be permitted. While it was true that British subjects were heavily taxed, Britain made lavish expenditures on the military to oppress colonials and to monopolize the world's oil. If England wants an extension she should declare assets that included territories acquired during the war, an area larger than Europe with a population of 51,725,000, and investments abroad two to three times what she owes us. Why did she charge Commonwealth countries 5% while insisting that she could only afford 3½% interest on her American liabilities? And of what importance was J. P. Morgan's desire to be reimbursed $400,000,000 in British overdrafts?[18]

He constantly saw the hand of capitalists in our overseas policy. When Mexico passed legislation to regain control over its natural resources he approved of their action and opposed intervention for the sake of American investors. And when insurgents rebelled against the radical Obregon government he supported Obregon but rejected American shipment of arms, for "in this case our war material is to be furnished to the right side. . . . Another time our war material may be furnished to the wrong side." It was a precedent that could be used by American oil companies to force concessions. If the people of Mexico wanted to overthrow a wise and liberal government it was their choice to make. Washington's concept of neutrality would be violated if we interfered in the internal affairs of another country.[19]

As Americans became more and more aware of the importance of foreign affairs, La Follette began to consider his first trip to Europe. Phil had preceded him just prior to the war, and he was aware of the personal value of such a voyage. As he contemplated an independent race for president, a tour of the continent could not injure his credibility as a candidate. (Burton K. Wheeler felt that the leader of the Progressives should have first-hand experience of the European situation.) W. T. Rawleigh, an importer and manufacturer of health products, long a financial benefactor and a factor in the survival of *La Follette's*, had suggested spending two months abroad just before the election of 1920. In July of 1923 the La Follettes began to plan a trip with the Basil Manlys (he was a close adviser of La Follette in planning the 1924 campaign). In August they boarded the SS Washington; they encountered wind, rain, and fog but no high seas; nevertheless the elderly passenger felt physical discomfort for a time. Arriving in London they went sightseeing and visited Norman Angell and John Maynard Keynes whose writings had impressed La Follette. They discussed American and European problems with members of the Labour party and suggested regular correspondence between progressives and Labourites. While touring the English countryside, they were impressed by conversations with the board of directors of the Cooperative Wholesale Society, and the senator determined to concentrate some of his energies on promoting the cooperative movement in the United States. In their tour of the continent they stopped in Trieste, Venice, Moscow, Vienna, Warsaw, Frankfurt, Berlin, Munich, Nuremberg, and Paris. In Germany they met with Prime Minister Gustav Stresemann, members of the Reichstag, labor and business leaders, and, guided by the Denver progressive banker, James Causey, investigated the effects of the Versailles Treaty and French occupation of the Ruhr. Joining with Steffens and the sculptor Jo Davidson they proceeded to Russia. There, La Follette was impressed by improvements in working and living conditions and with the establishment of day care centers for working mothers, but, despite access to all the ministers he requested to see, including acting Premier Alexei Rykov, he was disturbed by the refusal to tolerate criticism or opposition. In Italy he was impressed by Benito Mussolini's skill as an actor; in an interview Il Duce wanted to talk about how the trains ran on time; the Wisconsin lawyer wanted to discuss freedom of speech and the press. Chest pains and heart trouble forced him to shorten his tour. When he met Davidson again in Paris he sadly summed up his impressions of Europe: "it is a crime to have waited so many years to see all this beauty." Although he had returned early upon advice of his doctor, he continued to suffer from pain that did not yield readily to treatment.[20]

In a series of articles the Wisconsin elder statesman commented upon "What I saw in Europe." The Europeans, he

reported, were wearied by ten years of war and disillusioned by
betrayal of high war aims. He feared that, having seen treaties
and rights violated by government, they were prey for tyrants.
And American financial imperialism had decreased European
respect for the United States. Both the French and German
governments were controlled by interests, he asserted, which
prevented peaceful solution to problems. In the Ruhr the
German workers had just walked out when the French soldiers
walked in; the occupation was a violation of the treaty, and the
army was arbitrary. The French wanted to separate the
Rhineland from Germany and to create a new Napoleonic era.
He felt the United States should use its moral influence to
modify the terms of peace to help the development of a
democratic Germany. In editorials and a speech in the Senate
he described conditions in Germany — profiteering, dislocated
transport, shortages of provisions, bread lines, food riots, nine
million on charity, starvation in Essen. "Hunger is the
firebrand of revolution," he warned. As he had in 1919, he called
upon Americans to put aside the passions and the prejudices of
the war and offer immediate relief. Delay meant revolution and
chaos — the advent of communism or the restoration of the
monarchy.[21]

In his discussion of Russia he emphasized the spirit of hope
of the workers, the reverence in which Lenin was held, the
ability and dedication of the Soviet officials, and the fact that
despite the severe handicap of a lack of raw materials, the
Russian factories functioned well, with better working
conditions than under the Czar. Russia was no democracy, but
he had assured Russian officials that he would not try to force
democracy on other nations, except by example. His personal
observations clearly reinforced his earlier commitment towards
recognition of the USSR and the establishment of normal
relations between the two nations.[22]

Having established his first-hand knowledge of Europe and
personal contact with European leaders, La Follette was a more
convincing candidate for president of a world power. He was
considered to be the leader of the progressive bloc and, as such,
to command more certain votes than anyone in the Senate.
And, through seniority, he and members of his faction chaired
key committees. His followers controlled the state government,

and his eldest son was distinguishing himself as a skillful legislative leader. La Follette looked the role. John Owens called him the most impeccably dressed man in the upper House. "A reproduction of his shoes and brown spats would serve excellently to illustrate an advertisement. His black morning coat and his gray trousers are the ultimate in cut and texture. As the late winter wanes, he appoints himself a harbinger of spring, changing the black and gray for something fawn-colored of equal merit. And always the Piccadilly collar and the cravat convey a subdued elegance. Crowning the heavy head is the mass of upstanding hair, the famous pompadour, plainly the object of affectionate, even vain attention." He had survived the opprobrium of the war years and was at the pinnacle of his career.[23] And he had been preparing for an independent race since the aborted attempt in 1920.

In 1921 he had informed a correspondent that a new party was necessary, but he was not certain that the time was ripe for a new political alignment. If they could coordinate an effort to increase the liberal congressional delegation, then they could organize political constituencies for the presidential contest two years later.[24] A firm proponent of an educated electorate, La Follette sponsored the People's Legislative Service, under the direction of Basil Manly. Like most of his ventures it was perenially short of funds, and, during the 1920's, when the coffers were empty he called upon W. T. Rawleigh. The service issued the People's Pamphlets, which Manly saw as potential campaign documents. La Follette wrote the first publication on the sugar trust, insisting that the monopoly had raised prices despite a decline in the unit cost of production. Reiterating his lifelong theme he stated that the people could not find protection in the government or law for "The PRIVATE MONOPOLY SYSTEM is the government. *Private Monopoly makes* and administers the law." The majority of the people had to unite to destroy "the political control which insures the economic control of Private Monopoly over their lives and homes."[25] It was transparent that a new party was in the forefront of his thoughts.

Three conferences were held in 1922 in preparation for the presidential election, and they exemplified the nature of the available support, the problems involved, and the approaches that were to be adopted. The first meeting of the Conference for Progressive Political Action (a name devised by the New York Socialist lawyer, Morris Hillquit) was initiated by the Railroad Brotherhoods for February 21, 1922. The chairman, William H. Johnston of the International Association of Machinists, became a mainstay of La Follette's presidential campaign. The assembly attracted representatives of fifty international labor unions, the Non-Partisan League, the Committee of Forty Eight, who were the official custodians of the Progressive party label, the Socialist party, the Farmer Labor party, and religious social service groups. The participants were well aware that a similar coalition of trade unions, progressives, and socialists had formed the British Labour party, and, in the post-war world, had replaced the Liberal party as the second major party in England. After some organizational work they called a second meeting for December. The second gathering was preceded by a well-publicized caucus called by La Follette, as chairman of the People's Legislative Servicce, to discuss the cooperation of progressives in Congress and the country. At the first of its sessions thirteen senators and thirty-seven congressmen either attended or wired their support. Not all were willing to support an independent candidacy, and La Follette remained solicitous that the progressive caucus should not be endangered. An open meeting and a dinner held the following day attracted progressives of national stature including the venerable Samuel Gompers. Observers reported that they all supported La Follette and indicated that all were optimistic as a result of the elections. The assemblage of the CPPA later that month reached two important decisions. They would not accept credentials from members of the Communist party, fearing a repetition of the unfortunate experience of the Farmer Labor party with their disciplined infiltrating tactics. And they decided to defer consideration of a third party; the diverse gathering adopted a six-point platform and adjourned.[26]

While La Follette's supporters continued to push ahead towards an independent candidacy, they retained their hope that a progressive could emerge from a major party convention. Manly commented that more open primaries were necessary for, with the exception of McAdoo, no progressive could be nominated by any other route. And once McAdoo was brushed with Doheny's oil stain, he lost the inside track. Since the Republicans were sure to choose Coolidge, an independent candidacy looked more promising. If the Democrats bypassed McAdoo, La Follette was assured Brotherhood support. Still he refused to commit himself. Publicly, he concentrated on increasing progressive effectiveness in the new, more promising Congress that was to meet in December of 1923. Rather than spread their influence by seeking prestigious chairmanships, they should converge on important economic committees — interstate, commerce, and finance, he suggested. If the Republicans would not accede to their demands they should offer the Democrats the majority and the chairmanships in return for all vacant seats on these committees. He felt that this was the only way to enact sound legislation.[27]

Although La Follette was repeatedly ill in 1923 and early 1924, before during and after his European trip, he carefully formulated his strategy. First, he did not want to compromise the reelection of progressive legislators. Consequently, he decided to run as an independent candidate, without a full slate, reserving the possibility of forming a new party until after the election. This fitted in well with organized labor's tradition of non-partisan support of friendly candidates, a policy formulated largely to meet the building trade unions' need to forge alliances with the dominant political party in each area to maintain favorable building codes and to ensure awards to union contractors. Their policy did not always guarantee united support for progressives; in politically effervescent Colorado a dispute erupted concerning the progressive Democratic ticket of William Sweet and Alva Adams; in the end two state tickets were entered; both supported the same La Follette electors. Second, although in Wisconsin La Follette delegates ran for the Republican National Convention, he withdrew his name in other states and refrained from entering the fray. Third, while he accepted Socialist support, he did not want them to push themselves into the forefront where they were strong, and he would accept assistance neither from Communists nor from organizations in which they played an important role. No progressive convention that joined hands with Bolsheviks could be trusted, he wrote to his son-in-law. "Communism is just as hostile to progressive democracy as the control of government by the tyranny of the monopoly of organized wealth." They wanted to divide progressives, and, by creating chaos, to bring about the dictatorship of the proletariat. Finally he hoped for an election so close that it would be decided in Congress; consequently, it was crucial to elect enough progressives, regardless of party label, to control the balance of power.[28]

In January of 1924 La Follette finally committed himself to the race and Manly drafted the secret plan. A central committee of five would be established to sponsor the first move. Phil was not to be on the committee, but he was in charge of drafting his father and of the main office in Madison. By mid-April they would need to create a five-man committee in each state and a three-man committee in each county to circulate petitions, place electors on the ballot, and conduct the active campaign.[29]

Phil had done his work well. By the canvassing activities of thousands of volunteers, petitions containing a quarter of a million signatures were delivered to the La Follette for President Committee during the Democratic convention, requesting that La Follette seek the highest office, and thousands more were being delivered each day. W. T. Rawleigh, as chairman of the committee, presented them to the senator on July 3. Distressed that an announcement before the end of the Democratic convention would injure his pose as a reluctant candidate drafted to run for lack of a progressive alternative, La Follette replied: "The two old parties have betrayed the people. . . . I see nothing in either of their platforms on which to build a hope for tomorrow . . . they have ignored the supreme issue, involving all others: the encroachment of the powerful few upon the rights of the many." He announced his candidacy as an independent before the convention of the CPPA in the same Cleveland auditorium in which Coolidge had been designated. The delegates were young, there was no band, and the enthusiasm was not staged but spontaneous. Yet, as one commentator observed, he was endorsed, rather than nominated, and was openly left the choice of a running mate. The Socialist party convention added their approval on July 7.[30]

When the Democratic convention completed its work, La Follette felt that the nomination of John Davis was as good as could be expected, for he would be the lone progressive running against two conservatives. Belle mocked his chance of success: "When Davis was nominated I admitted that the White House seemed nearer than ever before which was in the nature of attending the Congregational church oftener than any other."[31] The emergence of Davis clarified the question of a running mate. La Follette had hoped that Brandeis would accept, but Gilson Gardner was unsuccessful in his mission. When Burton K. Wheeler denounced his party's choice of a Wall Street lawyer and endorsed La Follette he became the logical mate. A New Englander by birth, the junior senator from Montana was a close associate of Tom Walsh, enemy of Anaconda and chief senatorial investigator of Teapot Dome. During the war, as United States District Attorney, Wheeler had been more interested in fighting graft than in breaking strikes by supposedly pro-German and seditious workers. In 1920 the Non-Partisan League had sponsored his unsuccessful Democratic campaign for governor. Elected to the Senate in 1922, at the age of 40, he led the successful fight against Cummins as chairman of the ICC (upon which La Follette had placed a high priority), and his investigation of the Justice Department eventuated in Daugherty's resignation and a retaliatory federal indictment of Wheeler.[32]

La Follette's platform projected a number of issues; he would cleanse the executive departments; he would recover the naval oil reserves and change the laws to prevent alienation of the public domain; he would repeal the Esch-Cummins Act and establish public ownership of railroads; he denounced the Mellon tax, called for economy, military retrenchment, inheritance and excess profits taxes, and income tax publicity; he pressed for a constitutional amendment to permit Congress to override a judicial veto; to help farmers he offered to lower the tariff, exercise more direct control over the FRB, reduce railroad rates, and promote cooperatives; he would protect the rights of workers to organize and bargain collectively, end injunctive abuses in labor disputes, and eliminate child labor; veterans would receive a bonus; he proposed a St. Lawrence seaway and public ownership of water power; he suggested more direct government — direct nomination and election of the president, popular referendum on war, unless invaded, and

federal provisions for legislative initiative and referendum; and
he would revise the Treaty of Versailles to initiate the terminal
phase of imperialism. The contemporary issue of prohibition did
not interest him. While the KKK was not mentioned in his
platform he was the first candidate to attack the Klan.[33] La
Follette had never concentrated on issues central to blacks,
though he had shown greater concern than most of his
contemporaries. As a congressman he had fought against
streetcar segregation in the capital. When the Wilson administration instituted a policy of racial discrimination in
government he had personally objected to Wilson and had
called the department heads. In his Labor Day radio address he
insisted "that every man and woman under the American flag
who lives by useful and creative work of the hand or brain is
entitled to an equal chance in life, to equal protection of the
laws, and equal participation in the control of government." "I
have always stood without reservation against any discrimination between races, classes and creeds," he wrote to Robert
Scripps. Yet, in 1922, the year of the Dyer Anti-lynching bill,
the only reference to the struggle in his journal was the
publication of statistics on lynching. Consequently, Oswald
Garrison Villard noticed only one black delegate at the
convention, and there is little evidence that he altered the
Republican character of the black vote.[34]

La Follette returned to the platform topics during the
campaign, even adding a few issues, such as tariff reduction
and reorganization of regulatory commissions. He devoted
entire speeches to foreign policy, tracing a history of neutrality
which had been broken by imperialist policies serving the
House of Morgan and summing up a lifetime of anti-imperialist
and anti-war arguments. Nevertheless, he declared in his
announcement of candidacy: "to break the combined power of
the private monopoly system over the political and economic
life of the American people is the one paramount issue of the
1924 campaign," and he never shifted his emphasis. Peace and
disarmament were impossible with monopoly domination.
Monopoly oppressed labor; it robbed the consumer; and it was
reducing farmers to the level of European peasants.[35]

La Follette's campaign suffered from many handicaps. He
drew support from a number of disparate groups, each of which

was jealous of its own independence, and proper coordination became an impossible task. A unified effort was made more difficult by three central offices, John Nelson's for the west and Manly's and Roe's for the east, causing unnecessary duplication. This problem was complicated by intractable state election laws that prevented the acquisition of a new line on the ballot; consequently, in those states, La Follette was obliged to run as the candidate of an established party — Socialist, Farm Labor, Non-Partisan — , and other members of the coalition were obliged to vote for him under an unpalatable party label. In Colorado the Progressives had one slate of electors with two tickets; in New York and elsewhere they had two slates of electors. They were disappointed in promises of cooperation, particularly from the labor movement, and adequate funds were never donated. They budgeted $3,000,000 for the campaign and raised a total of $460,000, half of which was expended through national headquarters. The AFL provided but $25,000; the whole labor movement $50,000. The Republican national head-quarters spent $4,270,469 alone, and estimates of the total Coolidge election fund ran as high as $15,000,000. Faced with a financial crisis the Progressives charged admission to rallies, took up collections at meetings, hawked campaign medals, and sold certificates of progressive faith in denominations of $1 to $1000. Imagination could not replace wealthy backers. W. T. Rawleigh, the national treasurer, raised contributions largely from himself, donating $28,000. On his western trip La Follette could not plan ahead, for he could not be certain that he could pay the railroad. Without funds he could not make effective use of radio, a medium which he felt held great promise both to give people a first-hand knowledge of political debate and to minimize press misrepresentation. "They are tragically short of help and the finances are harassing everyone," Belle wrote in despair to her son.[36]

One of the ironies of the La Follette campaign was that while his greatest emphasis was the crusade against monopoly, two key elements in his entourage were not particularly anti-monopoly. The socialists saw monopoly as a natural development of capitalism and expected socialized relations of production to lead to socialized ownership of the means of production. Trade unions often found it easier to reach agreement with large corporations than with marginal small firms. Gompers felt that the future lay with the trusts, approved of Herbert Hoover's promotion of business associations, and only wanted a voice for labor, in accordance with the "B & O plan."[37] While Gompers agreed with many of La Follette's programs, the two men diverged on central philosophy.

The La Follette Progressives were vigorously attacked. The Senator's opponents resurrected and broadcast all the wartime charges against his patriotism. They stopped at nothing in an effort to label him a radical. A venomous article in *Forum* compared him to Marat; in the *Saturday Evening Post* they called him a paternalistic demagogue, his platform a catch-all for discontent, and his campaign infiltrated by Communists; numerous Republican speakers charged that he was financed by a Soviet slush fund. The most serious ideological attack was on his provision for reform of the Supreme Court, and it was repeatedly stressed as proof of radicalism. When early polls showed La Follette ahead of Davis, the Democrats were dismissed as a factor, and Republican orators insisted that the choice was between "Coolidge and Chaos" — chaos was a white-haired old Wisconsin gentleman. Overzealous partisans intimidated Progressives. Permits for meetings were denied. Vigilantes, aided and abetted by local law enforcement agencies, terrorized his campaigners. Workers were threatened with the loss of their jobs if La Follette was elected.[38]

Such tactics proved superfluous for the election was a Coolidge landslide. La Follette had little money and little media support. Sympathetic treatment by the *Nation* and *New Republic* and articles entitled "Why I Shall Vote for La Follette" by Felix Frankfurter, Zona Gale, Jane Addams, John R. Commons, Norman Hapgood, and Herbert Croly could not hope to stem the tide of anti-La Follette literature. The austere Coolidge was able to still the Teapot Dome issue and to remove tainted officials with such personal decency and consummate skill that it hardly caused a ripple. While La Follette had been given a chance of carrying California, his party could not get on the ballot in the Golden State, and he was forced to run on the Socialist ticket, which ended his chances. He had counted on some of the midwestern states, but a partial failure of the

Canadian wheat crop restored farm prosperity and the Republican agrarian vote. With a fifty percent turnout La Follette received only Wisconsin's electoral vote; he ran ahead of Davis in eleven other states, particularly in the west, and in a number of cities, building strength among the new immigrants. In the absence of complete slates it was impossible for the Progressives to elect a large number of officials, without which a new political party could not flourish. But his candidacy was one stepping stone for urban voters out of the Republican party and into a later New Deal coalition.[39]

La Follette reacted defiantly to the election returns. Publicly, at least, he dismissed the decision of the Republican Senate caucus to strip him of his seniority. He refused to concede that the electorate had endorsed the Harding-Coolidge administrations. He insisted that the "interests" had applied economic thumbscrews to ensure the election of Coolidge and to prevent progressive success; they had threatened voters' jobs and mortgages. They had distorted the facts and twisted the truth with their control of public opinion through the press, motion pictures, and radio. They had inspired financial panic before; now, they had just created a political panic. But he would not yield up free institutions because of one battle. Almost before the election returns were in he was laying plans for the next campaign and for the creation of a new party. He hoped to use Wisconsin as a springboard by capturing the other Senate seat and the congressional delegation in 1926. In other states he would establish a party organization. If it had gained enough strength by 1926 it would run independent candidates. If not, it would back progressives on the old party lines until sufficient support had developed. Problems arose immediately. The railroad brotherhoods opposed any conference that tied them to a third party; they hoped for a Democratic nomination of McAdoo in 1928. Other groups wanted a coalition of organizations like the British Labour party. "I am not for a class party — or a party composed of organized labor & organized farmers & organized socialists," he wrote to his sister. The citizen ought to be the unit of political organization; otherwise there would be "organized strife for class or group control." The party should be formed on principles appealing to all Americans who believe "in a government of *the people by and for the people.*" "I believe in democracy — It is a religion with me. I don't say that we can win the next election on these principles. But I do say that it will win in the end."[40]

"If I live you will see the Progressive movement make *strides* as never before within the next two to four years." La Follette's commitment to a third party had come too late. In December he reported to Rawleigh that Belle was to be operated on as soon as she was strong enough and that he himself was ill. On May 9 he suffered another bronchial attack. Sunday evening, May 17, La Follette retired early with chills. As the next morning broke he was awakened by a heart attack. Confined to bed he watched his immediate family gather as he slowly declined. On June 18 his heart stopped, and the great voice was stilled. No one in the family wore black as the procession returned with the simple grey casket to his Madison home. In the railroad yards, at waysides, wherever the train rolled, workers and farmers bared and bowed their heads in tribute to the fallen warrior. The highways to Madison were choked with traffic; tens of thousands, moving slowly, made the pilgrimmage to his bier in the two days that he lay in state in the rotunda of the capitol. Just before his illness he had penned these lines: "I would be remembered as one who in the world's darkest hour kept a clean conscience and stood to the end for the ideals of American democracy."[41]

# Notes and References

## Preface

1. William Hard, "Fighting Bob — Elder statesman," *Colliers* 72 (September 8, 1923), 12.

2. Gordon Hostetter, "The Public Speaking of Robert M. La Follette," Loren Reed, ed., *American Public Address*, 111-32; Carroll P. Lahman, "Robert M. La Follette as Public Speaker and Political Leader, 1855-1905," 1075-1104; William Kittle, "Robert M. La Follette, A Statesman after the Order of Lincoln," *Arena* 35 (1906), 571-76; *Current Literature* 42 (1907), 270-71; 51 (1911), 496-500.

## Chapter One

1. Belle Case La Follette and Fola La Follette, *Robert M. La Follette*, pp. 1-25; David Paul Thelen, *The Early Life of Robert M. La Follette, 1855-1884*, pp. 1-20; Louis A. Warren, "The Lincoln and La Follette Families in Pioneer Drama," *Wisconsin Magazine of History* 12 (1919), 359-75 Fred Greenbaum, "The Social Origins of Wisconsin Progressives," *QCC Scholar* 2 (1968), 35-43.

2. B & F La Follette, *La Follette*, pp. 13-27; Thelen, *La Follette*, pp. 11-27.

3. Robert M. La Follette, *La Follette's Autobiography*, pp. 11-12.

4. Fola La Follette, "Robert M. La Follette, My Father," *Twentieth Century Magazine* 5 (1912), 515-19; La Follette, *Autobiography*, pp. 79, 134-35; B & F La Follette, *La Follette*, pp. 5, 32-33, 37-41; Thelen, *La Follette*, pp. 41-42.

5. Pamphlet, "Opinions of the Press," May 7, 1879, R. M. La Follette MSS, Wisconsin State Historical Society (RML MSS WSHS); Pauline Grahame, "La Follette Wins," *Palimpset* 12 (1931), 179-89; B & F La Follette, *La Follette*, pp. 28-36; Thelen, *La Follette*, pp. 27-40.

6. Rasmus B. Anderson with A. O. Barton, *The Life Story of Rasmus B. Anderson*, pp. 608-26; B & F La Follette, *La Follette*, pp. 28-36; Thelen, *La Follette*, pp. 27-36, 42-45.

7. R. M. La Follette, *Autobiography,* pp. 3-4; B & F La Follette, *La Follette,* pp. 42-47; Thelen, *La Follette,* pp. 51-54; Lahman, *La Follette,* pp. 142-74.

## Chapter Two

1. R. M. La Follette, *Autobiography,* pp. 5-7; Thelen, *La Follette,* pp. 51-57; Richard W. Hantke, "Elisha W. Keyes, the Bismarck of Western Politics," *Wisconsin Magazine of History* 31 (1947), 29-41; Dorothy Fowler, *John Coit Spooner, Defender of Presidents,* pp. 45-64; E. Bruce Thompson, *Matthew Hale Carpenter, Webster of the West,* pp. 255-63; Richard Current, *Pine Logs and Politics, A Life of Philetus Sawyer, 1816-1900,* pp. 352-75; Sam Ross, *The Empty Sleeve, A Biography of Lucius Fairchild,* pp. 62-120.

2. Thelen uses Willet Main's diary as proof that Keyes did not oppose La Follette. But Main emphasized national, not local affairs, and one would hardly know he was engaged in a bitter battle for sheriff. If, after Main's defeat, the Madison *Democrat* could still depict the Republican ticket as written by Keyes, it was because a political boss was a good target. Willet S. Main Diary, 1880, entries August 9, 19, September 8, 14, 15, 16, 17, 18, 22, 29, October 4, 7, 11, November 4, WSHS; *Wisconsin State Journal,* September 15, 16, 22, 1880; R. M. La Follette, *Autobiography,* pp. 5-7; B & F La Follette, *La Follette,* pp. 46-48; Thelen, *La Follette,* pp. 56-59.

3. R. M. La Follette, *Autobiography,* pp. 5-7; B & F La Follette, *La Follette,* pp. 46-48; David Thelen, "Robert M. La Follette, Public Prosecutor," and "La Follette and the Temperance Crusade," *Wisconsin Magazine of History* 47 (1964), 214-23, 291-300.

4. B & F La Follette, *La Follette,* pp. 49-56; R. M. La Follette (RML) to Belle La Follette (BCL), August 17, 1883, R. M. La Follette MSS, Library of Congress (RML MSS LC).

5. Current, *Sawyer,* pp. 352-75; Thelen, *La Follette,* pp. 66-72.

6. Main Diary, August 11, 12, 14, 18, 19, 20, 27, 1884 WSHS: J. B. Treat to Elisha Keyes, August 24, 1884, Elisha Keyes MSS WSHS; Thelen, *La Follette,* pp. 66-72; R. M. La Follette, *Autobiography;* B & F La Follette, *La Follette,* pp. 58-60; Russel N. Baird, "Robert M. La Follette and the Press, 1880-1905," pp. 1-36; Ross, *Fairchild,* pp. 186-200; Resolution of Dane County Delegates; RML to Thomas Nelson, August 11, 1884; Nelson to RML (ca. August, 1884); RML to John Johnson, August 11, 1884; Sam Harper to RML, August 6, 7, 15, 19, 21, 1884, September 5, 1884; Harry C. Martin to RML, August 7, 29, 1884; Eli Pedersen to RML, August 1, 7, 1884. Some Dane county Norwegians were supporting Keyes candidate, J. B. Treat, but elected Henry Taylor without knowing of his support for La Follette, Henry

Taylor to RML, August 1, 6, 8, 24, 1884, RML MSS LC; *Wisconsin State Journal*, August 15, 19, 28, 29, September 10, 1884.

7. B & F La Follette, *La Follette*, pp. 58-60; Thelen, *La Follette*, pp. 70-72; R. M. La Follette, *Autobiography*, pp. 19-22; *Wisconsin State Journal*, September 10, 12, 17, 25, 1884, October 24, 1884. There is no indication that Keyes' faction attempted to undercut La Follette in the *Journal*, Main's diary, or Keyes' correspondence.

8. Henry Casson to RML, December 21, 1884, RML MSS LC; Ross, *Fairchild*, pp. 186-200; Fowler, *Spooner*, pp. 64-70.

9. R. M. La Follette, *Autobiography*, pp. 23-27; B & F La Follette, *La Follette*, pp. 61-72.

10. R. M. La Follette, *Autobiography*, p. 29; Baird, *Press*, pp. 39-41; U.S. *Congressional Record*, 49 Cong., 1 Sess., 3746-48, 4045, 4243-44; cf., 49 Cong., 2 Sess., 18 (1887), 1057.

11. U.S. *Congressional Record*, 49 Cong., 1 Sess., 17 (1886), Appendix, 223-26; 49 Cong., 2 Sess., 18 (1887), Appendix, 146-47; 50 Cong., 1 Sess., 19 (1888), 6513; Baird, *Press*, pp. 39-50.

12. Milwaukee *Sentinel*, July 18, 1888, as quoted in Baird, *Press*, pp. 60, 62; R. M. La Follette, *Autobiography*, pp. 44-50; B & F La Follette, *La Follette*, pp. 76-81; U.S. *Congressional Record*, 50 Cong., 1 Sess., 19 (1888), 6307-11; cf. 51 Cong., 1 Sess., 21 (1890), 4473-84, 4668-70 for his argument in favor of the McKinley Bill. "The cost of labor in every product is practically the cost of the product," he argued. "If we repeal the protective duties we must contest for the markets with labor paid less and living poorer."

13. Fowler, *Spooner*, pp. 32-75; Ross, *Fairchild*, pp. 120, 186-210; Current, *Sawyer*, pp. 214-19.

14. R. M. La Follette, *Autobiography*, pp. 31-37; B & F La Follette, *La Follette*, pp. 64-65, 81-84; U.S. *Congressional Record*, 50 Cong., 1 Sess., 19 (1888), 1934-36, 2033,2038; 50 Cong., 2 Sess., 20 (1889), 1586; 59 Cong., 1 Sess., 40 (1906), 6048, 8261-62.

15. RML to. W. D. Hoard, (ca. 1888), marked confidential; July 20, 1889; RML to Lucius Fairchild, April 16, 1889; RML to President William Harrison, April 10, 1889; RML to James Freeman, April 18, 1889; RML to Lourie Bell, April 18, 1889, RML MSS LC; George W. Rankin, *William Dempster Hoard*, p. 25.

16. A. H. Long to RML, October 24, 1884; H. E. Ticknor to Sam Harper, February 16, 1888; Harper to Dear Friend, February 29, 1888; cf., W. A. Johnson to Harper, October 15, 1888; C. H. Baxter to Harper, October 20, 1888; C. T. Osborn to Harper, November 2, 1888; Charles Harper to Sam Harper, October 16, 1894, RML MSS WSHS.

17. In 1888 J. B. Treat withdrew after tentative inquiries and in 1890 was accused of undercutting La Follette. Theodore Golden to Sam Harper, January 28, 1888; T. M. Randall to Harper, May 3, 1888;

James Taylor to Harper, October 23, 1890; George B. Clementson to Fred Zimmerman, July 4, 1896, RML MSS WSHS.

18. B & F La Follette, *La Follette*, p. 89.

19. B & F La Follette, *La Follette*, pp. 87-90; Rankin, *Hoard*, p. 91; Roger E. Wyman, "Voting Behavior in the Progressive Era: Wisconsin as a Case Study," pp. 70-114; T. N. Hubbell to Sam Harper, September 25, 1890; L. P. Reptiek to Harper, October 17, 1890; J. Long Botham to Harper, October 18, 1890; E.I. Ridd to Harper, October 22, 1890; Theodore Goldin to Harper, October 23, 1890; James Taylor to Harper, October 23, 1890; Phil Allen, Jr., to Harper, October 24, 1890; Charles Harper to Sam Harper, October 27, 1890, RML MSS WSHS.

## Chapter Three

1. Deposition by R. B. Ogilvie, ca. October, 1891, RML MSS WSHS.

2. The logic of the evidence and the events that followed lend credence to La Follette's version of the incident. Current, *Sawyer,* pp. 258-69; La Follette, *Autobiography,* pp. 63-71; statement by La Follette of his interview with Sawyer, dictated October 14, 1891, RML MSS LC; Sawyer to RML, September 14, 1891, RML MSS WSHS.

3. Incomplete and unsigned deposition, probably by George Weeks, October 21, 1891; George Weeks to RML, October 30, 1891, RML MSS WSHS.

4. B & F La Follette, *La Follette*, pp. 95-99; R. M. La Follette, *Autobiography*, pp. 63-71; Current, *Sawyer*, pp. 258-69. A deposition signed by Henry Adams, George Bryant, Robert Ogilvie, Sam Harper, Herbert Chynoweth, Ralph Vernon, Romanzo Bunn, and William Hoard testified that his letter detailing the interview with Sawyer was the same as the account he told them immediately after the event, RML MSS WSHS.

5. Sympathizer to RML, October 30, 1891, RML MSS WSHS.

6. W. H. Nennett to RML, October 30, 1891, RML MSS WSHS.

7. Current, *Sawyer,* pp. 158-69; Lahman, *La Follette,* pp. 317-28; B & F La Follette, *La Follette,* pp. 95-99; R. M. La Follette, *Autobiography,* pp. 63-71; The Madison *Democrat,* somewhat wishfully, thought La Follette was finished as a political factor. Even those Republican journals which initially tried to be neutral ended by attacking him. His only real support came from the Democratic Milwaukee *Journal,* Baird, *Press,* pp. 74-108.

8. B & F La Follette, *La Follette,* pp. 103-105; R. M. La Follette, *Autobiography,* pp. 21, 77-82.

9. Nils P. Haugen, *Pioneer and Political Reminiscences,* pp. 1-108; Stuart Brandes, "Nils P. Haugen and the Wisconsin Progressive

Movement," pp. 1-67; Robert S. Maxwell, *La Follette and the Rise of Progressives in Wisconsin,* pp. 7-8; Albert O. Barton, *La Follette's Winning of Wisconsin,* pp. 40-55.

10. Rankin, *Hoard,* pp., 1-95.

11. R. M. La Follette, *Autobiography,* p. 92; B & F La Follette, *La Follette,* pp. 102-103; Kenneth Acrea, "The Wisconsin Reform Coalition, 1892 to 1900: La Follette's Rise to Power," *Wisconsin Magazine of History* 52 (1968), 132-58.

12. Nils Haugen to RML, February 23, 1894; RML to Haugen, undated telegram (ca., July, 1894); Haugen to RML, July 13, 15, 16, 17, 1894; RML to Ole Barton, May 26, 1894; Barton to RML, July 6, 1894; RML to William Blades, July 14, 1894; Sam Harper to RML, July 19, 1894, RML MSS LC; Nils Holm to Sam Harper, June 4, 1894; Nieven Gieosan to Harper, May 6, 1894; Haugen to Harper, June 15, 1894; June 17, 1894; W. A. Pradt to Harper, June 15, 1894, RML MSS WSHS: RML to Haugen, April 12, 1894; June 2, 1894; BCL to Haugen, June 1, 1894; H. S. Comstock to Haugen, June 1, 1894, Nils Haugen MSS WSHS; R. M. La Follette, *Autobiography,* pp. 77-81; B & F La Follette, *La Follette,* pp. 106-109; Acrea, "Reform Coalition"; Herbert F. Margulies, *The Decline of the Progressive Movement in Wisconsin, 1890-1920,* pp. 22-30; Haugen, *Reminiscences,* pp. 109-20; Brandes, *Press,* pp. 35-70; Lahman, *La Follette,* pp. 328-68.

13. B & F La Follette, *La Follette,* pp. 109-11.

14. R. M. La Follette, *Autobiography,* pp. 82-83; B & F La Follette, *La Follette,* pp. 112-13; Acrea, "Reform Coalition."

15. Form letter, Sam Harper to Stewart Reed, October 16, 1894, RML MSS WSHS.

16. RML to Dr. R. D. Rood, July 4, 1896; Nils Haugen to Walter Hidden, June 4, 1896; Lahman, *La Follette,* pp. 368-95; Acrea, "Reform Coalition"; Haugen, *Reminiscences,* pp. 112-20; R. M. La Follette, *Autobiography,* pp. 82-84; B & F La Follette, *La Follette,* pp. 116-17; Elihu Coleman to RML, June 19, 1896; RML to Charles Otto, May 9, 1896; A. L. Fontaine to RML, June 20, 1896; B. J. Castle to RML, June 20, 1896; A. R. Hall to RML, July 2, 1896, RML to Earl Rogers, July 6, 1896, RML MSS WSHS.

17. John Whitehead argued that no money was ever offered: Whitehead to Ralph Gabriel, April 22, 1914, John Whitehead MSS WSHS. But the evidence indicates it was: George P. Rossman to RML, March 8, 1897; George Cooper to RML, August 9, 1896; M. A. Hoyt to Gilbert Roe, August 15, 1896; RML to A. Beckwith, August 17, 1896. La Follette asked James O. Davidson to help Hall because he felt an ugly fight was being waged against him; RML to Davidson, September 18, 1896; RML to A. R. Hall, September 18, 1896, RML MSS WSHS; Lahman, *La Follette,* pp. 34-55, 368-95; Acrea, "Reform

Coalition"; R. M. La Follette, *Autobiography*, pp. 84-85; B & F La Follette, *La Follette*, pp. 116-24.

18. B & F La Follette, *La Follette*, pp. 118-21; Barton, *Winning Wisconsin*, pp. 71, 80-87; Margulies, *Progressive Decline*, pp. 33-35; Sam Harper to Nils Haugen, December 5, 1896, Haugen MSS; RML to BCL, July 18, 1897, RML MSS LC; C. D. Denke to RML, January 6, 1897; RML to Julius Roehr, January 8, 1897; RML to J. S. Van Duzer, January 8, 1897; Haugen to Harper, January 2, 1898; Harper to Haugen, February 5, 1897; RML to Vivian Harvey, January 8, 1897; Theodore Fillmer to RML, July 6, 1897; H. E. Ticknor to RML, July 8, 1897; George Cooper to RML, July 19, 1897, RML MSS WSHS.

19. David Thelen, *The New Citizenship;* cf. Allen F. Davis, *Spearheads for Reform*, pp. 8-25. By showing that reform leadership and issues varied from town to town and did not include the business elite, who controlled the urban political parties, Thelen challenges Samuel Hays, "The Politics of Reform in Municipal Government in the Progressive Era," *Pacific Northwest Quarterly* 55 (1964), 157-69. For Denver cf. Fred Greenbaum, *Fighting Progressive, Edward Prentiss Costigan.*

20. Allan O. Lovejoy, *La Follette and the Direct Primary in Wisconsin*, pp. 3-40; B & F La Follette, *La Follette*, 119-20; R. M. La Follette, *Autobiography*, p. 85; RML to George Cooper, September 7, 1896, RML MSS WSHS. In 1890 La Follette had supported an election reform bill making false registration, buying and selling votes, intimidation and violence against campaign workers a federal offense: U.S. *Congressional Record*, 51 Cong., 1 Sess., 21 (1890), Appendix, 467-69. David Thelen insists La Follette led a coalition of "out" politicians until converted to progressive issues by urban reformers and the 1897 legislative session: Thelen, *New Citizenship*, pp. 290-312. The reform legislative leaders, A. R. Hall and James O. Davidson, were members of the "out" coalition and it was a decade after Milwaukee reformers joined his coalition that their program was enacted. Cf., Kenneth Acrea, "Wisconsin Progressivism: Legislative Response to Social Change, 1891 to 1909," 345.

21. R. M. La Follette, *Autobiography*, pp. 86-90; Lahman, *La Follette*, pp. 56-94; Lovejoy, *Primary*, pp. 3-40; Chicago *Times-Herald*, February 23, 1897; Harper to Samuel Shaw, March 7, 1894; E. W. Chafin to RML, February 24, 1897; Harper to A. J. Myrland, March 5, 1897. R. M. Easley raised the danger of scattering support while the machine concentrated on one candidate unless there was a primary caucus, R. M. Easley to RML, February 23, 1897, RML MSS WSHS.

22. Barabor *News*, August 26, 1897.

23. R. M. La Follette, *Autobiography*, pp. 85-89; B & F La Follette, *La Follette*, pp. 119-24; Barton, *Winning Wisconsin*, pp. 71, 80-87; Margulies, *Progressive Decline*, pp. 33-42; Chicago *Record*, August 28, 1897; Monroe *Times*, September 4, 1897; RML to BCL, July 18, 1897; September 22, 23, 30, 1897, RML MSS LC; H. W. Burmeister to RML, July 19, 1897; D. C. Hayes to RML, August 7, 1897, RML MSS WSHS.

24. Gilbert Roe to Gwyneth King, July, 1898; RML to Isaac Stephenson, January 17, 1905, September 11, 1905, RML MSS LC; R. M. La Follette, *Autobiography*, pp. 94-97; B & F La Follette, *La Follette*, 124-29; Margulies, *Progressive Decline*, pp. 40-43; Barton, *Winning Wisconsin*, pp. 90-125; Acrea, "Reform Coalition"; Lahman, *La Follette*, pp. 395-440; Robert C. Twombly, "The Reformer as Politician, Robert M. La Follette in the Election of 1900," pp. 1-56; RML to Percy H. Heath, July 14, 1898; RML to W. G. Evans, April 15, 1898; L. H. Barnett to RML, August 18, 1898; C. R. Marks to RML, August 18, 1898; S. Clayton Goff to RML, July 26, 1898, RML MSS WSHS.

25. B & F La Follette, *La Follette*, p. 129; Philip La Follette, *Adventures in Politics*, pp. 6-7.

26. Isaac Stephenson, *Recollections of a Long Life, 1829-1915;* RML to Stephenson, January 17, 1905, September 11, 1905, RML MSS LC; Margulies, *Progressive Decline*, p. 45.

27. Twombly, "La Follette," pp. 31-56; Barton, *Winning Wisconsin*, pp. 120-50; R. M. La Follette, *Autobiography*, p. 99; Joseph Babcock to RML, May 17, 1900; RML to Babcock, May 31, 1900, RML MSS LC.

28. RML to Thomas Gill, May 12, 1900, quoted in R. M. La Follette, *Autobiography*, pp. 99-103; Margulies, *Progressive Decline*, p. 47.

29. RML to Gilbert Roe, May 7, 1900, Gilbert Roe MSS LC.

30. RML to My Dear Sir, July 18, 1898, May 15, 1900; RML to James Stone, undated (ca. June, July, 1900); RML to James Frear, May 28, 1900, July 10, 1900, RML MSS LC; Twombly, "La Follette," 121-72; Alfred Rogers to Gilbert Roe, July 6, 1900, Roe MSS; John Whitehead wrote that Philipp spent money in Waukesha for La Follette. Whitehead to Ralph Gabriel, April 22, 1914, Whitehead MSS WSHS.

31. La Follette was so concerned with harmony that Stephenson had to dissuade him from appointing Philipp as state chairman. Lahman, *La Follette*, pp. 441-85; Twombly, "La Follette," pp. 173-207; Acrea, "Reform Coalition"; Robert S. Maxwell, "La Follette and the Election of 1900," *Wisconsin Magazine of History* 35 (1951), 23-29; Padraic Kennedy, "La Follette's Imperialist Flirtation,"

*Pacific Historical Review* 29 (1960), 131-44; George Bryant to Gilbert Roe, November 1, 1900, Roe MSS LC; cf., Jorgun Weibull, "The Wisconsin Progressives, 1900-1914," *Mid America* 47 (1965), 191-221 for a statistical analysis.

## Chapter Four

1. B & F La Follette, *La Follette*, pp. 109-11, 136-37; Gwyneth King Roe, "Two Views of the La Follettes, Madison, 1890's," *Wisconsin Magazine of History* 42 (1958), 102-108; P. F. La Follette, *Adventures in Politics*, pp. 6-10.

2. Lahman, *La Follette*, pp. 507, 511-16.

3. Inaugural Address of Robert M. La Follette, Regular Session, 1901 in Lahman, *La Follette*, pp. 516-66; Baird, *Press*, pp. 115-58.

4. Emanuel Philipp, assisted by Edgar T. Wheelock, *Political Reform in Wisconsin*, p. 31. John Whitehead insisted La Follette's merciless use of the executive power precipitated senate resistance, otherwise he could have obtained most of the legislation he wanted. Whitehead to Ralph Gabriel, April 22, 1914, Whitehead MSS.

5. R. M. La Follette, *Autobiography*, pp. 105-19; Fowler, *Spooner*, pp. 154-58; Alfred Zimmerman to Gilbert Roe, Dec. 12, 1900, Gilbert Roe MSS; Philipp, *Reform*, p. 31; Lovejoy, *Primary*; Lahman, *La Follette*, pp. 516-604; Maxwell, *La Follette*, pp. 28-35; Barton, *Wisconsin*, p. 263; Henry W. Wilbur, "A Coming Man," *Gunton's Magazine* 23 (1902), 250-53; T. S. Adams, "The Drama of Wisconsin Politics," *Independent* 54 (1902), 1824-26; Amos Wilder, "Governor La Follette and What He Stands For," *Outlook* 70 (1902) 631-34; E. Ray Stevens, "The La Follette-Spooner Campaign," World's Work 4 (1902), 2677-80; Ellen Torelle, ed., *The Political Philosophy of Robert M. La Follette*, pp. 64-68; *Outlook* 68 (1901), 199-201.

6. R. M. La Follette, *Autobiography*, pp. 105-19, 166; cf., Haugen, *Reminiscences;* Stephenson, *Recollections*.

7. Margulies, *Progressive Decline*, pp. 60-67; H. A. Taylor to E. W. Keyes, April 15, 1901, April 19, 1901, August 8, 1901; John Hicks to Keyes, August 17, 1901, Keyes MSS; RML to James L. Frear, December 11, 1901, RML MSS LC, "Things have been going from bad to worse in the stalwart camp, and it is going to be plain sailing," Alfred Rogers to Gil Roe, April 21, 1902, RML MSS LC.

8. John Morton Blum, *The Republican Roosevelt*, pp. 37-54. La Follette's efforts to neutralize the Roosevelt administration were unsuccessful. RML to Theodore Roosevelt, February 21, 1901; Alfred Rogers to James Frear, February 26, 1902; RML to General (Bryant?), October 12, 1902, RML MSS LC.

9. Alfred Rogers to James Frear, February 26, 1902; Rogers to Gilbert Roe, April 21, 1902; RML to Rogers, September 2, 1902; RML

to O. J. Schuster, May 29, 1902, RML MSS LC; B & F La Follette, *La Follette,* pp. 145-57; Margulies, *Progressive Decline,* pp. 60-67.

10. Governor Robert M. La Follette, Message to the Legislature, January 15, 1903; Emanuel Philipp, *The Truth About Wisconsin Freight Rates;* Maxwell, *La Follette,* pp. 48-55.

11. RML to Charlie (Dow?) (ca. 1902), RML MSS LC; Lahman, *La Follette,* pp. 729-77; Maxwell, *La Follette,* pp. 48-55; R. M. La Follette, *Autobiography,* pp. 120-28; B & F La Follette, *La Follette,* pp. 156-61; RML to John Thomas, February 10, 1904; Thomas to RML, April 9, 1904, Lincoln Steffens MSS Columbia University.

12. Emil Baensch to John Miller, April 18, 1905, RML MSS WSHS.

13. John Strange to Alfred Rogers, April 18, 1904, RML MSS WSHS. In Portage there were threats not to develop marl beds if La Follette were elected. William Culver to H. W. Chynoweth, April 23, 1904, RML MSS WSHS.

14. John Strange to Alfred Rogers, April 18, 1904; Silas Doubleday to Rogers, April 20, 1904; Roy Smelker to H. W. Chynoweth, April 25, 1904, RML MSS WSHS.

15. John Strange to Alfred Rogers, April 18, 1904, RML MSS WSHS.

16. Edward Browne to J. K. Parish, April 23, 1904; Roy Smelker to H. W. Chynoweth, April 25, 1904; Gerhard Dahl to Chynoweth, April 24, 1904; R. E. Smith to Chynoweth, May 11, 1904, RML MSS WSHS.

17. RML to Levi Ankeny, April 6, 1907, RML MSS LC.

18. R. M. La Follette, *Autobiography,* pp. 137-38; Margulies, *Progressive Decline,* pp. 72-73; Lahman, *La Follette,* pp. 731-839; Lovejoy, *Primary;* Jere Murphy to John Hannan, July 27, 1903; RML to Hannan, November 1, 1903; Nils Haugen to James Frear, January 23, 1904; RML to Frear, February 2, 1904; unsigned to Hannan, February 18, 1904, RML MSS LC.

19. Lahman, *La Follette,* pp. 838-39; Lovejoy, *Primary.*

20. R. M. La Follette, *Autobiography,* pp. 137-46; B & F La Follette, *La Follette,* pp. 165-86; Maxwell, *La Follette,* pp. 66-73; Margulies, *Decline,* pp. 72-81; Barton, *Winning Wisconsin;* 410-37; Philipp & Wheelock, *Reform,* pp. 62-103: W. D. Connor to John Hannan, July 1, 1904; H. S. Comstock to Hannan, July 14, 1904, RML MSS LC; H. A. Taylor to E. W. Keyes, May 16, 1904, Keyes MSS WSHS.

21. R. M. La Follette, *Autobiography,* pp. 140-41; W. D. Connor to John Hannan, July 1, 1904, RML MSS LC.

22. Margulies, *Progressive Decline,* pp. 76-78; H. S. Comstock to John Hannan, July 14, 1904, RML MSS LC; Theodore Roosevelt to Henry Cabot Lodge, July 22, 1904; Roosevelt to George Courtelyou,

October 5, 1904, October 6, 1904, in Elting Morison, *Letters of Theodore Roosevelt,* Vol. 4, 863-64, 971-74.

23. RML to Gilbert Roe, July 27, 1904; BCL to Roe, August 15, 1904, Gilbert Roe MSS LC; Roe to Lincoln Steffens, August 3, 1904; BCL to Roe, August 14, 1904, Steffens MSS U Colu; Lincoln Steffens, "Enemies of the Republic. Wisconsin: A State where the People have restored Representative Government. The Story of Governor La Follette", *McClure's* 23 (1904), 563-79.

24. Margulies, *Progressive Decline,* pp. 78-82; Jorgen Weibull, "Wisconsin Progressives."

25. Robert M. La Follette, Gubernatorial Message, January 12, 1905.

26. Isaac Stephenson to RML, January 13, 1905, RML MSS LC.

27. RML to Isaac Stephenson, January 17, 1905, RML MSS LC.

28. Stephenson, *Recollections,* pp. 220-34; RML to Isaac Stephenson, September 11, 1905, RML MSS LC; Alfred Rogers to Gilbert Roe, January 18, 1905, Roe MSS LC; B & F La Follette, *La Follette,* pp. 188-89; Lahman, *La Follette,* pp. 950-60, 1002-29; cf. BCL to Lincoln Steffens, July 30, 1904, Steffens MSS in which Belle urged that Stephenson be given proper credit for his importance as a La Follette adviser and for the pressures he withstood to remain loyal to the progressive cause.

29. Lahman, *La Follette,* pp. 970-1029; B & F La Follette, *La Follette,* pp. 187-92.

30. La Follette, *Adventures in Politics,* pp. 12-13.

31. R. M. La Follette, *Autobiography,* pp. 149-58; Fred L. Holmes, *Regulation of Railroads and Public Utilities in Wisconsin;* John R. Commons, "The La Follette Railroad Law in Wisconsin," *Review of Reviews* 32 (1905), 76-79. U.S. *Congressional Record,* 49 Cong., 2 Sess., 18 (1887), Appendix, 184-88, Torelle, *La Follette,* p. 186.

32. R. M. La Follette, *Autobiography,* pp. 149-58; Holmes, *Railroad Regulation.*

33. La Follette's acceptance of the nomination for governor, 1902, quoted in Torelle, *La Follette,* pp. 58-90.

34. Fred Greenbaum, "Progressivism: A Complex Phenomenon," *New Politics* 6 (1967), 85-90.

35. John R. Commons, "Robert M. La Follette," *North American Review* 187 (1908), 672-77; Nils P. Haugen, *Reminiscences;* Edward A. Fitzpatrick, *McCarthy of Wisconsin;* R. M. La Follette, *Autobiograpy.*

## Chapter Five

1. Walter Wellman, "The Rise of La Follette," *Review of Reviews* 31 (1905), 299-305.

2. Theodore Roosevelt to Nicholas Murray Butler, May 21, 1904; Roosevelt to Henry Cabot Lodge, July 22, 1904, in Morrison, *Roosevelt Letters*, IV, 802, 863-64.

3. R. M. La Follette, *Autobiography*, pp. 115-16, 205-208; James Peterson to RML, February 27, 1905; RML to Theodore Roosevelt, February 19, 1907, RML MSS LC.

4. B & F La Follette, *La Follette*, pp. 199-202; La Follette thought Spooner was nervous that he might want to present himself, RML to Alfred Rogers, January 7, 1906; John Spooner to E. A. Hitchcock, June 30, 1906, RML MSS LC.

5. R. M. La Follette, *Autobiography*, pp. 161-162.

6. U.S. *Congressional Record*, 59 Cong., 1 Sess., 40 (1906), 3059, 3207-64, 5684-97, 6505, 6622, 6627, 6774, 6811-12, 7083-84, 7993, 9090-96, 9259, 9269, 9364-66, 9683-85; BCL to Fola La Follette, April 24, 1906; RML to Theodore Roosevelt, January 30, 1907; RML to S. C. Baker, April 23, 1907, RML MSS LC; R. M. La Follette, *Autobiography*, pp. 174-80; B & F La Follette, *La Follette*, pp. 203-209. Gabriel Kolko, in *The Triumph of Conservatism, A Reinterpretation of American History, 1900-1916* and *Railroads and Regulation, 1877-1916*, develops a thesis that progressives sought the political rationalization of business and offered conservative solutions to new industrial problems; he uses the Hepburn Act as an example. The evidence does not sustain his argument. Cf., Fred Greenbaum, "The Progressive World of Gabriel Kolko," *Social Studies* 55 (1969), 224-28.

7. R. M. La Follette, *Autobiography*, pp. 162-67; B & F La Follette, *La Follette*, pp. 209-11; RML to T. Roosevelt, January 28, 1907, March 9, 1907, RML MSS LC.

8. T. Roosevelt to RML, January 23, 1907, February 5, 1907; RML to Roosevelt, January 28, 1907, RML MSS LC; R. M. La Follette, *Autobiography*, pp. 162-67; B & F La Follette, *La Follette*, pp. 209-11; U.S. *Congressional Record*, 59 Cong., 1 Sess., 40 (1906), 3059.

9. RML to BCL, January 7, 1907; RML to Judson Welliver, July 9, 1910; RML to Jonathan Bourne, July 11, 1910, RML MSS LC; U.S. *Congressional Record*, 61 Cong., 2 Sess., 45 (1910), 5563-66; 62 Cong., 1 Sess., 47 (1911), 4186; *La Follette's* 1 (January 30, 1909), 3; 1 (February 6, 1909), 5; 1 (March 13, 1909), 3; 2 (May 7, 1909), 4.

10. Alfred Rogers warned La Follette that many supporters would not canvass unless he campaigned personally. Rogers to RML, February 8, 26, 1906, June 5, 1906, RML MSS LC; Henry Johnson to RML, November 20, 1905; RML to John Blaine, May 30, 1906; W. H. Dick to RML, June 18, 1906; RML to Isaac Stephenson, June 23, 1906; E. E. Browne to RML, July 16, 1906, RML MSS WSHS; J. D.

Stuart to James O. Davidson, November 14, 1905; Davidson to John G. Gaveney, January 19, 1906; W. A. Jones to Davidson, January 24, 1906, March 9, 1906; O. W. Arnquist to Davidson, May 9, 1906; A. H. Reid to Davidson, May 17, 1906; Davidson to W. D. Connor, June 22, 1906, Davidson MSS WSHS; Herman Ekern to Nicolay Grevstad, December 17, 1905; Ekern to RML, February 17, 1906; Ekern to Irvine Lenroot, February 17, 1906, Ekern MSS WSHS; Edwin Gross, "A Political Grab Bag," manuscript, Gross MSS WSHS; Padraic Kennedy, "Lenroot, La Follette and the Campaign of 1906," *Wisconsin Magazine of History* 42 (1959), 163-74; Herbert Margulies, "Political Weakness in Wisconsin Progressivism, 1905-1908," *Mid America* 41 (1959), 154-72; Stephenson, *Recollections.*

11. Stephenson, *Recollections*, 235; RML to Herman Ekern, May 15, 1907; E. W. Wing to Ekern, May 15, 1907; W. S. McElroy to Ekern, July 25, 1907, Ekern MSS WSHS; Margulies, *Progressive Decline*, pp. 96-104; B & F La Follette, *La Follette*, pp. 259-61; Maxwell, *La Follette*, pp. 175-77; cf. John Hannan to RML, November 21, 1906; Irvine Lenroot to Alfred Rogers, December 6, 1906; Rogers to Lenroot, December 4, 1906, RML MSS LC. La Follette argued that he did not injure the primary law for Stephenson had been accused of violating corrupt practices laws. *La Follette's* 1 (February 6, 1909), 3; 1 (February 20, 1909), 3. Elisha Keyes gloated at La Follette's defeat. E. W. Keyes to John Gaveney, September 23, 1908, Keyes' Letterbooks, WSHS.

12. U.S. *Congressional Record*, 60 Cong., 1 Sess., 42 (1908), 3434-53, 3566-78, 3793-805, 3962, 4018-21, 7161-99, 7221-26; R. M. La Follette, *Autobiography*, pp. 195-203; B & F La Follette, *La Follette*, pp. 238-56 has an excellent account of Aldrich's parliamentary maneuvers; RML to the family, June 1, 1908, RML MSS LC.

13. *Everybody's Magazine* 18 (1908), 736; Brandes, *Haugen*, pp. 198-200; Haugen, *Reminiscences*, pp. 140-51; Stephenson, *Recollections*, pp. 235-56; Gilbert E. Roe, "Senator La Follette and Representative Government," *Independent* 64 (1908), 717-25; James A. Frear to Fred Sims, May 13, 1907; John Hannan to RML, May 26, 1907; Irvine Lenroot to RML, April 25, 1908, RML MSS LC.

14. B & F La Follette, *La Follette*, pp. 257-59.

15. RML to W. H. Taft, June 18, 1908, October 12, 1908; Taft to RML, July 19, 1908; RML to H. Stroud, November 28, 1908; RML MSS LC; B & F La Follette, *La Follette*, pp. 261-63.

16. Lincoln Steffens to Tom Johnson, October 16, 1908, RML MSS LC.

*Chapter Six*

1. B & F La Follette, *La Follette,* pp. 266-67.

2. *La Follette's* 1 (January 9, 1909), 1 (January 16, 1909), 2. Before commencing publication preliminary subscriptions were solicited, Alfred Rogers to Herman Ekern, July 24, 1908, RML MSS WSHS.

3. B & F La Follette, *La Follette,* pp. 267-70; U.S. *Congressional Record,* 60 Cong., 2 Sess., 43 (1909), 2374, 2549-58.

4. *La Follette's* 1 (January 9, 1909), 12; 1 (March 13, 1909), 3.

5. William Manners, *TR and Will,* pp. 3-28.

6. *La Follette's* 1 (January 9, 1909), 4; 1 (February 20, 1909), 4; 1 (February 27, 1909), 3-4; 1 (March 6, 1909), 3.

7. George W. Norris, *Fighting Liberal,* pp. 121-32; Blair Bolles, *Tyrant from Illinois,* pp. 169-224; Kenneth Hechler, *Insurgency,* pp. 27-82; *La Follette's* 2 (March 26, 1910), 3; (April 2, 1910), 3.

8. R. M. La Follette, *Autobiography,* pp. 183-93; B & F La Follette, *La Follette,* pp. 272-78; Henry Pringle, *William Howard Taft,* pp. 418-41; Hechler, *Insurgency,* pp. 92-145; "The Senator for the Ultimate Consumer. How Robert M. La Follette contended for an Honest Tariff," *Harpers Weekly* 53 (July 24, 1909), 7-8; Boston *Transcript,* May 5, 1909, quoted in George E. Mowry, *Theodore Roosevelt and the Progressive Movement,* pp. 49-65; *La Follette's* 1 (May 3, 1909), 3; 1 (July 3, 1909), 3; U.S. *Congressional Record* 61 Cong., 1 Sess., 44 (1909), 724, 2351-52, 2527-35, 2694-701, 2727-52; BCL to Josephine Siebecker, July 4, 1909; RML to W. H. Taft, July 13, 1909; like most other progressives La Follette had at least one schedule he wanted raised — in his case, barley, RML to Harvey Wemdt, April 22, 1909, RML MSS LC.

9. B & F La Follette, *La Follette,* pp. 279-81.

10. George W. Norris, "The Insurgents and the Party," *Metropolitan Magazine* 32 (1910), 656-62.

11. Mowry, *Roosevelt and Progressives* pp. 70-71; B & F La Follette, *La Follette,* pp. 281-82.

12. *La Follette's* 1 (August 21, 1909), 3-4.

13. James Penick, Jr., *Progressive Politics and Conservation, the Ballinger-Pinchot Affair;* Manners, *TR and Will,* pp. 104-38; Mowry, *Roosevelt and Progressives,* pp. 66-87.

14. *La Follette's* 1 (August 21, 1909), 3; 3 (September 2, 1911), 1; 4 (February 17, 1912), 3-4; U.S. *Congressional Record,* 62 Cong., 1 Sess., 47 (1911), 4262-67.

15. *La Follette's* 2 (January 22, 1910), 3; 2 (June 11, 1910), 3, 12; U.S. *Congressional Record,* 61 Cong., 2 Sess., 45 (1910), 4549-64, 5564, 6586, 6882-905, 7139-44; B & F La Follette, *La Follette,* pp. 295-98; RML to Gilbert Roe, April 27, 1910, RML MSS LC. In a letter to Taft

during the campaign La Follette had urged Taft not to repudiate
Roosevelt's recommendation for physical valuation. The administration moved in the opposite direction, trying to sanctify previous
capitalization, even if excessive. RML to W. H. Taft, July 17, 1908,
RML MSS LC.

16. B & F La Follette, *La Follette*, p. 298; *La Follette's* 1 (January
16, 1909), 4.

17. B & F La Follette, *La Follette*, pp. 305-12; Margulies,
*Progressive Decline*, pp. 103-07; Richard Lloyd Jones, "Among La
Follette's People," *Colliers* 45 (September 3, 1910), 17-18; RML to
Louis Brandeis, June 20, 1910; John Hannan to Charles Crownhart,
June 30, 1910; RML to Judson Welliver, July 9, 1910, RML to W. C.
Hewett, July 15, 1910; Hannan to Gilbert Roe, July 21, 1910; Hannan
to Francis Heney, July 27, 1910; Hannan to Moses Clapp, July 28,
1910; Hannan to Victor Murdock, August 1, 1910; RML to M.
Syverson, August 12, 1910; RML to Samuel Gompers, August 20,
1910; RML to William Cary, August 25, 1910; RML to Fremont
Older, September 14, 1910, RML MSS LC. The La Follette
progressives were careful to distinguish their procedures from the
"stalwarts" and did not hold any convention. But they did get
together informally to select a ticket and prevent defeat through
competing ambitions. Theodore Kronshage to Thomas Morris, May
21, 1910; Crownhart to A. S. Sanborn, May 26, 1910, RML MSS
WSHS.

*Chapter Seven*

1. R. M. La Follette, *Autobiography*, pp. 211-13; B & F La
Follette, *La Follette*, pp. 313-15, RML to Louis Brandeis, December
30, 1910; RML to Clarence Jones, December 30, 1910; RML to George
Loftus, January 17, 1911; RML MSS LC.

2. Mowry, *Roosevelt and Progressives*, pp. 132-56; Gifford
Pinchot to Theodore Roosevelt, August 18, 1910, Gifford Pinchot
MSS LC; RML to Judson Welliver, July 9, 1910, RML MSS LC.

3. RML to Jonathan Bourne, July 11, 1910, RML MSS LC.

4. RML to Judson Welliver, July 9, 1910, RML MSS LC.

5. RML to Louis Brandeis, December 30, 1910; RML to Irvine
Lenroot, December 29, 1912, RML MSS LC.

6. Theodore Roosevelt to RML, January 3, 1911, RML MSS LC.

7. RML to T. Roosevelt, January 19, 1911, RML MSS LC.

8. W. A. White to RML, January 4, 1911, RML MSS LC.

9. Irvine Lenroot to RML, April 25, 1908; Henry Cooper to RML,
October 6, 1910, RML MSS LC.

10. RML to Fremont Older, April 18, 1911, RML MSS LC.

11. RML to Merle Vincent, May 3, 1911, RML MSS LC.

12. RML to Fremont Older, April 18, 1911, July 3, 1911, RML MSS LC.

13. *La Follette's* 3 (February 4, 1911), 7-9; 12.

14. W. H. Houser to RML, June 17, 1911, RML MSS LC.

15. B & F La Follette, *La Follette*, pp. 322-27; U.S. *Congressional Record*, 61 Cong., 3 Sess., 46 (1911), 3759-60; 62 Cong., 1 Sess., 47 (1911), 184; *La Follette's* 3 (March 11, 1910), 3.

16. *La Follette's* 3 (May 27, 1911), 3; 3 (June 3, 1911), 3: 3 (September 16, 1911), 4-6; 3 (September 23, 1911), 4-6, 15; 3 (September 30, 1911), 5; U.S. *Congressional Record*, 62 Cong., 1 Sess., 47 (1911), 1673, 4184-90. Louis Brandeis expressed his support of the La Follette bill and a variation of this position was adopted by Wilson through the influence of Brandeis.

17. U.S. *Congressional Record.* 62 Cong., 1 Sess., 47 (1911), 2398, 3139-53; Mowry, *Roosevelt and Progressives*, pp. 160-68.

18. *La Follette's* 3 (August 26, 1911), 3; 3 (November 25, 1911), 4.

19. RML to Benjamin Hampton, March 9, 1911; RML to Gilbert Roe, June 4, 8, 23, 28, 1911, July 8, 11, 1911, January 12, 1912; RML to Nils Haugen, August 29, 1911, September 24, 1911; Haugen to RML, August 28, 29, 1911; RML to Dwight Parker, October 28, 1911; John Nelson to RML, October 11, 1911, RML MSS LC.

20. R. M. La Follette, *Autobiography.* The book was to be published by Doubleday, Page, but after threats of libel suits the publishers decided upon a small first edition. La Follette balked, and the two parties agreed that he would publish it himself, with Doubleday's plates and printing. About 40,000 copies were sold. B & F La Follette, *La Follette*, pp. 466-72.

21. George Record to RML, October 4, 1911; Alfred Rogers to RML, April 9, 1911, RML MSS LC.

22. Amos Pinchot to James Garfield, October 3, 1911, James R. Garfield MSS LC.

23. J. R. Garfield to Gifford Pinchot, March 7, 1911, Gifford Pinchot MSS LC.

24. James R. Garfield Diaries, entries October 9, 10, 1911, Garfield MSS LC.

25. James R. Garfield Diaries, October 15, 17, 1911, Garfield MSS LC; Garfield to RML, October 17, 1911; RML to Garfield, October 23, 1911, RML MSS LC.

26. B & F La Follette, *La Follette*, pp. 350-54.

27. W. H. Houser to RML, tgm., October 16, 1911; Amos Pinchot to RML, October 20, 1911, RML MSS LC.

28. Garfield Diary, entries, November 10, 1911 - January 5, 1912, James Garfield MSS; W. H. Houser to John Hannan, December 1, 2,

1911, National Progressive Republican League Papers, LC; Alfred Rogers to RML, undated, RML MSS LC; B & F La Follette, *La Follette,* pp. 350-75; Garfield to Amos Pinchot, September 28, 1911; Garfield to Gifford Pinchot, November 16, 28, 1911; Theodore Roosevelt to Garfield, December 2, 1911. Roosevelt congratulated Garfield: "That seems to me to have been a very satisfactory outcome." Roosevelt to Garfield, January 4, 1912, Garfield MSS LC.

29. Gifford Pinchot, Diary, entries November 12, 1911 - January 29, 1912, Pinchot MSS; B & F La Follette, *La Follette,* pp. 350-93.

30. W. A. Woodworth to J. S. Temple, February 4, 1912; Woodworth to E. P. Costigan, March 11, 1912; William Raine to Costigan, October 4, 1912, Edward P. Costigan MSS UColo.

31. Unsigned to D. F. Carpenter, December 7, 1911; E. S. Burnstead to J. S. Temple, January 12, 1912; E. P. Costigan to W. L. Houser, November 1, 1911, Costigan MSS; *Rocky Mountain News,* January 17, 1912; cf. Fred Greenbaum, *Fighting Progressive,* pp. 32-41.

32. Gifford Pinchot Diaries, January 19, 1912 - January 22, 1912 Pinchot MSS LC; B & F La Follette, *La Follette,* pp. 384-95.

33. B & F La Follette, *La Follette,* pp. 350-99; RML to A. A. Boyden, January 9, 1912; RML to Gilbert Roe, January 12, 1912, RML MSS LC.

34. Robert S. Maxwell, "A Document on the Progressive Campaign of 1912," *Mississippi Valley Historical Review* 36 (1949), 113-15; B & F La Follette, *La Follette,* pp. 398-405; *Literary Digest* 44 (1912), 318-19; *Independent* 72 (1912), 369-71; *Current Literature* 52 (1912), 246-48; *La Follette's* 4 (March 23, 1912), 7-9, 13, 15; The question of press censorship had long concerned La Follette: "In Russia the autocratic government officials decide what may be printed in the press. In this country we have a censorship quite as effective, though perhaps not so sweeping. It is the censorship of Business." *La Follette's* 2 (May 21, 1910), 3.

35. Gifford Pinchot to RML, February 17, 1912; RML to Hiram Johnson, tgm., January 30, 1912; Gilson Gardner to RML, February 17, 1912; Benjamin Lindsay to RML, February 8, 1912; Irvine Lenroot to RML, April 6, 1912; RML to Gilbert Roe February 6, 21, 1912; RML to Rudolph Spreckels, April 7, 1912, RML MSS LC; E.P. Costigan to J. C. Harper, February 22, 1912, Costigan MSS U Colo; B & F La Follette, *La Follette,* pp. 408-22.

36. RML to Gilbert Roe, February 6, 1912, RML MSS LC.

37. *La Follette's* 4 (March 2, 1912), 1.

38. *Literary Digest* 44 (1912), 318-19; B & F La Follette, *La Follette,* pp. 408-22; RML to Rudolph Spreckels, April 7, 1912; RML to Alfred Rogers, February 13, 1912, RML MSS LC.

39. Mowry, *Roosevelt and Progressives,* pp. 220-31; B & F La Follette, *La Follette,* pp. 424-28.

40. RML to Frederick Howe, March 24, 1912, RML MSS LC.

41. RML to Ray Stannard Baker, (ca. March, 1912), RML MSS LC.

42. RML to Ray Stannard Baker (ca. March, 1912), RML MSS LC; Mowry, *Roosevelt and Progressives,* pp. 231-36.

43. *La Follette's* 4 (March 16, 1912), 3-4; 4 (June 29, 1912), 3: RML to George Middleton, March 6, 1912; RML to Kenesaw Mountain Landis, January 29, 1912, RML MSS LC.

44. RML to Alfred Rogers, June 9, 1912, RML MSS LC.

45. *La Follette's* 4 (July 20, 1912), 7-8; 4 (July 27, 1912), 8-9, 14; 4 (August 3, 1912), 7-9, 15; RML to Gilbert Roe, July 8, 1912, RML MSS LC.

46. *La Follette's* 4 (July 20, 1912), 7-8; 4 (July 27, 1912), 8-9, 14; 4 (August 3, 1912), 7-9, 15; RML to Gilbert Roe, July 8, 1912, RML MSS LC.

47. RML to John Hannan, tgm., June 22, 1912, RML MSS LC.

48. Mowry, *Roosevelt and Progressives;* R. M. La Follette, *Autobiography,* pp. 275-79; B & F La Follette, *La Follette,* pp. 435-39; New York *Times,* June 19, 20, 1912; Herbert Margulies, "The Background of the La Follette-McGovern Schism," *Wisconsin Magazine of History* 40 (1956), 21-29; Oscar W. Schoongarth to James Stone (ca. 1912); Records of Meetings of the Wisconsin Delegation to the National Convention of the Republican Party, Chicago, June 17, 18, 1912, James Stone MSS WSHS.

49. Amos Pinchot, *History of the Progressive Party, 1912-1916,* edited by Helene Maxwell Hooker, p. 165.

50. Mowry, *Roosevelt and Progressives,* pp. 247-55.

51. RML to Rudolph Spreckels, July 12, 1912; RML to Charles Crane, August 21, 1912, RML MSS LC; *La Follette's* 4 (August 10, 1912), 3.

52. *La Follette's* 4 (August 17, 1912), 4-5; 4 (August 24, 1912), 7; 4 (October 5, 1912), 9-15; 4 (October 12, 1912), 6-8, 9-16; 4 (October 19, 1912), 9-17; 4 (October 26, 1912), 9-18; 4 (November 2, 1912), 9-16.

53. BCL to Charles La Follette, July 27, 1912, RML MSS LC.

54. *La Follette's* 3 (February 18, 1911), 3; 3(April 22, 1911), 3-4; 4 (February 24, 1912), 4-5; 4 (July 13, 1912), 3; 4 (July 27, 1912), 3-4; 4 (August 17, 1912), 3-4.

55. RML to Gilbert Roe, July 8, 1912; RML to Rudolph Spreckels, July 12, 1912, RML MSS LC.

56. *La Follette's* 4 (November 19, 1912), 3; 5 (March 8, 1913), 3.

57. B & F La Follette, *La Follette,* pp. 453-57; U.S. *Congressional Record* 62 Cong., 3 Sess., 49 (1913), 3779, 3795-801.

## Chapter Eight

1. Albert Bushnell Hart, ed., *Selected Addresses and Public Papers of Woodrow Wilson*, pp. 1-5.

2. Arthur S. Link, *Woodrow Wilson and the Progressive Era*, pp. 25-32; John Morton Blum, *Woodrow Wilson and the Politics of Morality*, pp. 65-68.

3. William Gibbs McAdoo, speech at the Press Club, New York City, January 21, 1911; speech at the Advertising Convention, Boston, Massachusetts, August 4, 1911, William Gibbs McAdoo MSS LC.

4. W. G. McAdoo to Byron Newton, June 7, 1911, McAdoo MSS LC.

5. William Gibbs McAdoo, *Public Service Corporations and the Public*, pp. 14-15.

6. New York *Times*, April 8, 22, 1913; August 1, 2, 1913; August 3, 8, 26, 1914; October 7, 1914.

7. B & F La Follette, *La Follette*, pp. 458-63.

8. RML to Gilbert Roe, August 28, 1913, RML MSS LC.

9. RM. to W. T. Rawleigh, February 2, 1914, RML MSS LC.

10. *La Follette's* 5 (April 12, 1913), 1.

11. RML to Rudolph Spreckels, February 16, 1914, RML MSS LC; cf. *La Follette's* 5 (December 6, 1913), 1.

12. *La Follette's* 6 (April 18, 1914), 1.

13. *La Follette's* 5 (October 25, 1913), 1,3; cf. RML to Rudolph Spreckels, October 12, 1913, RML MSS LC.

14. RML to Spreckels, February 16, 1914, RML MSS LC.

15. *La Follette's* 4 (March 9, 1912), 5; 4 (September 21, 1912), 4-5.

16. *La Follette's* 5 (April 19, 1913), 1, 3.

17. *La Follette's* 7 (January, 1915), 3.

18. *La Follette's* 5 (March 15, 1913), 1.

19. *La Follette's* 5 (April 5, 1913), 1.

20. Hart, *Wilson*, pp. 6-8.

21. Link, *Wilson and Progressives*, pp. 34-36.

22. *La Follette's* 5 (March 22, 1913), 1.

23. Link, *Wilson and Progressives*, pp. 36-39. La Follette had supported a bill to decrease the metal schedule as consistent with the difference in the cost of production concept. *La Follette's* 4 (March 2, 1912), 4-5.

24. Link, *Wilson and Progressives*, pp. 39-43; B & F La Follette, *La Follette*, pp. 472-74; *La Follette's* 5 (May 24, 1913), 1, 3; 5 (June 28, 1914), 4; 5 (June 28, 1914), 4; 5 (July 5, 1913), 1, 3.

25. B & F La Follette, *La Follette*, pp. 476, 479-83; La Follette's (September 20, 1913), 1, 4; cf., *La Follette's* 5 (September 13, 1913), 1;

5 (November 22, 1913), 11.

26. B & F La Follette, *La Follette*, p. 481; Link, *Wilson and Progressives*, p. 39; U.S. *Congressional Record*, 63 Cong., 1 Sess., 50 (1913), 3819-21. While Norris was much more enthusiastic about an inheritance tax than an income tax, La Follette thought great income was more a menace in the hands of its creator than its inheritor.

27. B & F La Follette, *La Follette*, pp. 476-79.

28. U.S. *Congressional Record*, 63 Cong., 1 Sess., 50 (1913), 2951.

29. B & F La Follette, *La Follette*, pp. 484-85.

30. *La Follette's* 4 (March 9, 1912), 4-5; 4 (May 11, 1912), 4.

31. House Report #1593, 62 Cong., 3 Sess., 86-97; reproduced in Donald R. McCoy and Raymond G. O'Connor, *Readings in Twentieth Century American History*, pp. 84-85; B & F La Follette, *La Follette*, p. 486.

32. *La Follette's* 4 (February 17, 1912), 3.

33. Link, *Wilson and Progressives*, pp. 44-53; Robert H. Wiebe, "Business Disunity and the Progressive Movement, 1901-14," *Mississippi Valley Historical Review* 44 (1958), 664-85.

34. RML to D. L. Braucher, June 10, 1914, RML MSS LC.

35. *La Follette's* 5 (December 27, 1913), 1; 6 (January 3, 1914), 1. La Follette pointed out that most progressive Republican congressmen voted for the bill: *La Follette's* 5 (September 27, 1913), 1; 9.

36. RML to Rudolph Spreckels, December 26, 1913, RML MSS LC; *La Follette's* 6 (January 10, 1914), 1; B & F La Follette, *La Follette*, pp. 475, 487.

37. RML to Spreckels, February 16, 1914, RML MSS LC; *La Follette's* 6 (January 3, 1914), 1; B & F La Follette, *La Follette*, pp. 487-88.

38. *La Follette's* 5 (April 26, 1913), 1.

39. *La Follette's* 6 (January 31, 1914), 1-3; 6 (February 7, 1914), 1-2; Link, *Wilson and Progressives*, p. 68.

40. *La Follette's* 6 (July 18, 1914), 3; Link, *Wilson and Progressives*, p. 77.

41. B & F La Follette, *La Follette*, pp. 488-91; *La Follette's* 5 (December 6, 1913), 1; 6 (April 18, 1914), 1; RML to Rudolph Spreckels, February 16, 1914, RML MSS LC.

42. *La Follette's* 7 (January, 1915), 1, 2. For an opposite view of the validity of the rate increase cf., Robert W. Harbeson, "Railroads and Regulation, 1877-1916," *Journal of Economic History* 27 (1967), 230-42.

43. *La Follette's* 6 (April 25, 1914), 2.

44. RML to BCL, April 9, 1914, quoted in B & F La Follette, *La Follette*, pp. 498-99. He lost ten pounds during this illness. RML to

Josephine Sibecker, August 12, 1914, RML MSS LC.

45. B & F La Follette, *La Follette*, pp. 500, 510-11; Alfred Rogers to Irvine Lenroot, December 5, 1914, RML MSS LC.

46. B & F La Follette, *La Follette*, 501; La Follette's 7 (February, 1915), 5. The paragraph was written so that labor was not wholly immune from the bill's provisions, and it was retained in this form despite all Gompers' efforts and threats, Link, *Wilson and Progressives*, pp. 55-56, 69-70, 73-74. William E. Borah, who opposed exempting labor from the anti-trust laws on the grounds that it would be special interest legislation, did not think that the labor provisions of the Clayton Act changed labor's legal rights in any way. U.S. *Congressional Record*, 63 Cong., 2 Sess., 51 (1914), 13918-24.

James Weinstein in *The Corporate Ideal in the Liberal State, 1900-1918* uses the FTC to prove that a minority of sophisticated corporation leaders in the National Civic Federation formulated the ideal of a liberal corporate order, using the FTC to replace the dangerous Sherman Act. The FTC was closer to progressive intent than to the NFC sponsored bill and it continued to meet progressive expectations even after war induced changes in executive attitudes. Robert Wiebe, *Businessmen and Reform*, shows business divisions, failures, and partial successes in legislation; corporate leaders bent undesirable laws after public vigilance relaxed.

47. RML to Rudolph Spreckels, January 7, 1915, RML MSS LC; B & F La Follette, *La Follette*, pp. 497-98.

48. RML to Whitley P. McCou, October 23, 1915, RML MSS LC.

49. Mowry, *Roosevelt and Progressives*, pp. 299-307.

50. Fred Greenbaum, *Fighting Progressive*, pp. 58-73.

51. The best analyses of the La Follette-McGovern split and the victory of Philipp are Margulies, *Progressive Decline*, pp. 99-158; Herbert F. Margulies, "The Background of the La Follette-McGovern Schism," *Wisconsin Magaine of History* 4 (1956), 21-29; Maxwell, *Philipp*, pp. 58-95. For the constant problem of organizing to choose candidates cf. A. W. Sanborn to Herman Ekern, October 24, 1908; Minutes of a Meeting Held at the Third Floor of the Woman's Building, Madison, June, 1909, Ekern MSS WSHS; James Stone to O. G. Rewey, June 2, 1909; Stone to Chris Munson, June 11, 1909; Stone to John Hannan, October 27, 1909; Hannan to Stone, November 1, 1909, James Stone MSS WSHS.

52. RML to Thomas Davidson, July 8, 1910; W. J. McElroy to John Hannan, August 17, 1910, RML MSS LC; Margulies, "La Follette-McGovern Schism"; cf., Herman Ekern to Irvine Lenroot, April 28, 1908; Charles Crownhart to Lenroot, May 27, 1910, RML MSS WSHS; Edwin Gross to Ekern, July 20, 1907, Ekern MSS WSHS.

53. RML to Francis McGovern, December 19, 1910; RML to Alfred Rogers, January 2, 1911; RML to Jennie Nelson, January 2, 1911; RML to P. F. Leuch, January 18, 1911; RML to William MacAllester, January 18, 1911; RML to A. D. Helgeson, January 21, 1911; Alan Conover to RML, February 3, 1911; McGovern to RML, February 6, 1911; RML to McGovern, September 11, 1911, RML MSS LC: cf. O. G. Munson to James Davidson, January 21, 1911, Davidson MSS WSHS. Munson felt McGovern gave every job to the faithful, ignoring efficient progressive officeholders.

54. RML to Richard Jones, September 4, 1911, RML MSS LC.

55. RML to Rudolph Spreckels, August 20, 1912, RML MSS LC.

56. *La Follette's* 4 (October 12, 1912), 3; 4 (October 26, 1912), 3; N. H. Dunn to W. B. Cutler, October 14, 1912; Dunn to Frank Nimocki, October 12, 1912; RML to Dear Friend, October 29, 1912, RML MSS LC. La Follette doubted his ability to deliver his faction to McGovern: "I hope you can hold our fellows together but doubt it as I have been suspicious of that bunch for a long time. Never mind there is *another day*." RML to Walter Owens, June 18, 1912, Herman Ekern MSS WSHS.

57. *La Follette's* 5 (January 18, 1913), 3; 5 (June 22, 1913), 1, 3; RML to Herman Ekern, April 24, 1913, RML MSS LC.

58. Alfred Rogers to RML, July 11, 1913, RML MSS LC.

59. RML to Herman Ekern, April 14, 1913; RML to Alfred Rogers, April 25, 1913; RML to D. C. Reynolds, January 24, 1914, RML MSS LC.

60. *La Follette's* 6 (July 25, 1914), 1.

61. RML to Alfred Rogers, September 4, 1914, October 8, 1914; RML to BCL, October 15, 1914, RML MSS LC.

62. John Hannan to RML, April 11, 1922, RML MSS LC.

63. Margulies, *Progressive Decline*, pp. 115-63; La Follette's 6 (July 18, 1914), 3; 6 (August 22, 1914), 1; 6 (September 12, 1914), 3; 6 (October 17, 1914), 2; 6 (October 24, 1914), 1; "We have not had a *man* in the governor's office for eight years," RML to Alfred Rogers, June 25, 1913; RML to Herbert Bigelow, January 16, 1912; RML to Phil La Follette (PFL), August 22, 1914; RML to Rogers, September 10, 1914; RML to CFF, tgm, November 1, 1914, RML MSS LC; cf. H. S. Comstock to Rogers, January 12, 1914; W. L. Houser to Rogers, January 12, 1914; Ed LeRoy to Rogers, January 30, 1914, Rogers MSS LC.

64. BCL to RML, Jr., November 5, 1914, RML MSS LC.

65. La Follette's 6 (November, 1914), 2.

66. RML to Alfred Rogers, September 10, 1914; January 18, 1915; RML to Rudolph Spreckels, January 7, 1915, RML MSS LC.

67. Cf., Greenbaum, *Fighting Progressive*, pp. 55-87.

68. Message to the Wisconsin Legislature on Railroad Regulation, quoted in Torrelle, *La Follette,* p. 93.

69. RML to William J. Tierney, November 24, 1911, RML MSS LC.

70. La Follette's 1 (February 13, 1909), 4; 1 (July 17, 1909), cf. RML message to the Wisconsin legislature, January 15, 1903, as quoted in Torrelle, *La Follette,* p. 130; U. S. *Congressional Record,* 59 Cong., 1 Sess., 40 (1906), 7659.

71. *La Follette's* 4 (February 24, 1912), 3-4.

72. *La Follette's* 2 (April 23, 1910), 3.

73. *La Follette's* 5 (June 28, 1913), 1.

74. *La Follette's* 4 (January 13, 1912), 4; form letter on injunctions, May 20, 1908, RML MSS LC.

75. U.S. *Congressional Record,* 62 Cong., 3 Sess., 49 (1913), 1771-78; RML to John Hannan, April 13, 1914; RML to N. I. Stone, December 22, 1914, RML MSS LC.

76. *La Follette's* 1 (June 5, 1909), 4.

77. Cf. U.S. *Congressional Record,* 63 Cong., 3 Sess., 49 (1913), 4208-209; 64 Cong., 1 Sess., 53 (1916), 9760, 9764-70, 13651-52; *La Follette's* 2 (April 23, 1910), 3; 2 (April 30, 1910), 3; 5 (July 9, 1913), 1-3; 8 (September, 1916), 1, 2.

78. U.S. *Congressional Record,* 62 Cong., 2 Sess., 48 (1912), 10728-29, 10799, 10800.

79. La Follette's 1 (August 21, 1909), 4-5; 3 (March 25, 1911) 4; 8 (October, 1916), 4.

80. B & F La Follette, *La Follette,* pp. 521-36; *La Follette's* 2 (November 12, 1910), 4; 5 (March 29, 1913), 3, 4, 14; 5 (April 5, 1913), 5, 13; 5 (August 30, 1913), 1; 6 (March 28, 1914), 1, 3; 7 (March, 1915), 1, 2; 7 (November, 1915), 1; U.S. *Congressional Record,* 62 Cong., 3 Sess., 49 (1913), 4409-11, 4423-25, 4581-85; 63 Cong., 1 Sess., 50 (1913), 5776-85; RML to BCL, October 24, 1913, August 26, 1914, RML MSS LC; Link, *Wilson and Progressives,* pp. 61-63.

### Chapter Nine

1. Address at Gettysburg, July 4, 1913, Hart, *Wilson,* p. 13.

2. *La Follette's* 8 (August, 1916), 2.

3. *La Follette's* 3 (March 4, 1911), 3.

4. *La Follette's* 4 (March 29, 1913), 1.

5. RML to family, January 21, 1917, RML MSS LC.

6. *La Follette's* 7 (June, 1915), 1, 2.

7. *La Follette's* 1 (April 10, 1909), 5; U.S. *Congressional Record,* 64 Cong., 2 Sess., 54 (1917), 3477-79.

8. *La Follette's* 4 (May 11, 1912), 1; 6 (June 27, 1914), 1-2; RML to Fred MacKenzie, June 22, 1914, RML MSS LC.

9. *La Follette's* 1 (May 1, 1909), 3-4.

10. *La Follette's* 3 (March 18, 1911), 3.

11. *La Follette's* 5 (May 1, 1913), 3; 5 (August 16, 1913), 1, 3.

12. Robert Quirk, *An Affair of Honor.*

13. *La Follette's* 6 (May 2, 1914), 1; RML to BCL April 24, 1914, RML MSS LC; U.S. *Congressional Record,* 64 Cong., 1 Sess., 53 (1916), 3886-90.

14. *La Follette's* 8 (January, 1916), 1.

15. BCL to the family, June 26, 1916, RML MSS LC.

16. *La Follette's* 6 (October 17, 1914), 1.

17. RML to Frank Gilmore, December 7, 1911, RML MSS LC; *La Follette's* 6 (October 3, 1914), 1, 2.

18. RML to BCL August 5, 1914, RML MSS LC.

19. RML to PFL, August 28, 1914, RML MSS LC.

20. *La Follette's* 6 (October 3, 1914), 1-2.

21. RML to Henry Lockney, May 17, 1915, RML MSS LC.

22. U.S. *Congressional Record,* 63 Cong., 3 Sess., 52 (1915), 3631-33; B & F La Follette, *La Follette,* pp. 518-19.

23. U.S. *Congressional Record,* 63 Cong., 2 Sess., 51 (1914), 9458-59; *La Follette's* 7 (February, 1915), 1-2.

24. U.S. *Congressional Record,* 64 Cong., 1 Sess., 53 (1916), 6369, 11330-47; Torrelle, *La Follette,* pp. 190-202; *La Follette's* 8 (September, 1916), 2.

25. *La Follette's* 6 (October 17, 1914), 1.

26. *La Follette's* 7 (September, 1915), 1.

27. *La Follette's* 8 (February, 1916), 1, 2; 8 (April, 1916), 1, 2.

28. *La Follette's* 8 (March, 1916), 1, 2.

29. *La Follette's* 8 (May, 1916), 1.

30. U.S. *Congressional Record,* 64 Cong., 1 Sess., 53 (1916), 3886-90; B & F La Follette, *La Follette,* pp. 537-59; Walter A. Sutton, "Progressive Republican Senators and the Submarine Crisis, 1915-16," *Mid America* 47 (1965), 75-88.

31. Margulies, *Progressive Decline,* pp. 164-78; RML to Josephine Siebecker, October 15, 1915. La Follette informed his family that the new generation was unaware of progressive savings through corporate taxes and preventing increased freight, gas, electric, and insurance rates. Philipp had reduced direct taxes by reducing services and by increasing indirect taxes by a larger amount. Unfortunately it would be hard to convince the electorate. RML to the family, November 12, 19, 1915, RML MSS LC.

32. RML to Dunbar Lyceum Bureau, October 23, 1915; RML to A. W. Sanborn, December 19, 1915; RML to Ralph Smith, October 5, 1915; RML to John Hannan, October 9, 1915, RML MSS LC.

33. RML to BCL, January 5, 1916; BCL to family, March 13, 1916. La Follette opposed the conference as undermining the primary and

returning to the caucus. "The direct primary is the essential democratic thing we have done." RML to Charles Crownhart, May 12, 1916; July 8, 20, 1916; John Hannan to RML, September 2, 1916, RML MSS LC; C. C. Gittings to James Stone, January 28, 1916, Stone MSS WSHS; Margulies, *Progressive Decline*, pp. 177-89; B & F La Follette, *La Follette*, pp. 562-81.

34. B & F La Follette, *La Follette*, pp. 562-72; Mowry, *Roosevelt and Progressives*, pp. 327-62; Greenbaum, *Fighting Progressive*, pp. 75-87.

35. *La Follette's* 8 (June, 1916), 1, 2.

36. B & F La Follette, *La Follette*, pp. 572-85; *La Follette's* 8 (November, 1916), 1; Charles Crownhart to J. W. Pryor, October 24, 1916; John Hannan to E. G. Beinhard, November 7, 1916; Hannan to Louis Brandeis, November 10, 1916, RML MSS LC.

37. Link, *Wilson and Progressives*, pp. 252-68; Link, *Wilson, the Diplomatist*, pp. xii-xvi, 31-81; B & F La Follette, *La Follette*, pp. 586-97; Samuel Flagg Bemis, *A Diplomatic History of the United States*, pp. 590-616.

38. B & F La Follette, *La Follette*, pp. 586-97; RML to family, February 2, 3, 4, 6, 7, 8, 15, 1917, RML MSS LC.

39. B & F La Follette, *La Follette*, pp. 595-602; Link, *Wilson and Progressives*, pp. 268-74.

40. B & F La Follette, *La Follette*, pp. 603-25; undated note from RML, Jr., to RML (March 4, 1917); RML to BCL, tgm., March 5, 1917; RML to BCL, March 6, 1917, RML MSS LC.

41. Dallas *Morning News*, March 6, 1917; Philadelphia *Public Ledger*, March 6, 1917; RML to BCL, March 6, 1917; RML MSS LC; B & F La Follette, *La Follette*, pp. 626-34.

42. Link, *Wilson and Progressives*, pp. 275-82.

43. B & F La Follette, *La Follette*, pp. 626-44; *La Follette's* 9 (March, 1917), 1-4; BCL to RML, March 10, 1917, RML MSS LC.

44. Hart, *Wilson*, pp. 188-97; Link, *Wilson and Progressives*, pp. 272-82; B & F La Follette, *La Follette*, pp. 640-49.

45. U.S. *Congressional Record*, 65 Cong., 1 Sess., 55 (1917), 223-35; *La Follette's* 9 (April, 1917), 1-3.
Sess., 95 (1924), 6019; *La Follette's* 16 (1924), 21, Murray, *Harding*, pp. 378-80.

## Chapter Ten

1. *La Follette's* 1 (April 24, 1909), 4.

2. B & F La Follette, *La Follette*, pp. 651-53; Phil wrote to his father: "Oh, dear Daddy, I love you for your courage, for your

bravery, but most for fortitude which gives you the courage and strength to do as you see without making you bitter. Oh I pray to God that I may in some small way be worthy of you. . . ."

"Just as the newspapers belie you, and call you traitor, so will the people of a few years hence idalize (sic) you and call you the bravest man that America has ever produced!" PFL to RML, March 10, 1917, RML MSS LC.

3. RML to E. U. Wing, November 18, 1917; RML to J. W. Cotter, December 10, 1917, RML MSS LC.

4. U.S. *Congressional Record,* 65 Cong., 1 Sess., 55 (1917), 1354-64, 1476-78, 1619-20, 6856; *La Follette's* 8 (October, 1917), 1; 9 (May, 1917), 2-5; B & F La Follette, *La Follette,* pp. 731-37.

5. RML to Marvin H. Witte, July 25, 1917, RML MSS LC.

6. BCL to RML, June 3, 1915, July 25, 1915; BCL to Mary La Follette, July 11, 1915, August 28, 1915; BCL to Josephine Siebecker, April 30, 1915, September 7, 21, 1915; BCL to Fola La Follette, October 15, 1915; RML to William and Charles Mayo, August 24, 1915; N. H. Dunn to E. C. Lachner, September 6, 1915; BCL to RML, February 10, 1917, RML MSS LC.

7. RML, Jr., to BCL, May 31, 1917; RML to BCL, June 1, 2, 1917; RML to RML, Jr., (1917); PFL to RML, August 25, 1917, RML MSS LC.

8. RML to PFL, January 30, 1916; May 23, 26, 1918; June 13, 1918; RML to BCL, February 22, 24, 25, 26, 1916; June 20, 1917; October 18, 1918; BCL to PFL, April 11, 16, 20, 23, 1917, PFL to BCL, April 14, 1917; PFL to RML, August 25, 1917; May 19, 23, 1917, RML MSS LC.

9. U.S. *Congressional Record,* 64 Cong., 2 Sess., 54 (1917), 4489-501, 4510-13; 65 Cong., 1 Sess., 55 (1917), 6201-10, 6503-19; 65 Cong., 3 Sess., 57 (1918), 818-32, 4738-54. Cf. *La Follette's* 9 (September, 1917), 1-3; 9 (December, 1917), 1; 10 (February, 1918), 1; 10 (May, 1918), 1-2; 10 (June, 1918), 1-3.

10. RML to John Linton, December 26, 1917, RML MSS LC.

11. U.S. *Congressional Record,* 65 Cong., 3 Sess., 57 (1918), 818-32, 4738-54; B & F La Follette, *La Follette,* pp. 740-47; *La Follette's* 11 (1919), 2-3, 9-12.

12. U.S. *Congressional Record,* 65 Cong., 1 Sess., 55 (1917), 2261, 5351, 5357; RML to James Kerwin, January 5, 1917, RML MSS LC; *La Follette's* 9 (August, 1917), 3, 14.

13. RML to E. M. Wing, November 28, 1917, RML MSS LC; cf. B & F La Follette, *La Follette,* pp. 749-60.

14. U.S. *Congressional Record,* 65 Cong., 1 Sess., 55 (1917), 7878-86.

15. RML to T. P. Roe, August 1, 1917, RML MSS LC.

16. *La Follette's* 9 (May, 1917), 1-2; 9 (August, 1917), 1; B & F La Follette, *La Follette*, pp. 749-60.

17. Link, *Wilson, the Diplomatist*, pp. 66-104.

18. *La Follette's* 10 (January, 1918), 1-4. Had he been present he would have offered an amendment disassociating the U.S. from secret treaties depriving Austria of territories; U.S. *Congressional Record*, 65 Cong., 2 Sess., 56 (1917), 68.

19. RML to James Kerwin, January 5, 1917, RML MSS LC; B & F La Follette, *La Follette*, pp. 731-33. He tried to help Clarence Darrow when the post office revoked mailing privileges of Socialist magazines. He was attracted by the suggestion of one Socialist that his magazine by shipped in place of Socialist journals to foil the post office. RML to BCL, July 17, 1917, RML MSS LC. *La Follette's* 10 (March, 1918), 1-2; cf., Robert K. Murray, *Red Scare*, pp. 3-32.

20. U.S. *Congressional Record*, 65 Cong., 1 Sess., 55 (1917), 7878-86.

21. RML to Fred Holmes, November 21, 1917, RML MSS LC; *La Follette's* 9 (June, 1917), 1-3.

22. B & F La Follette, *La Follette*, pp. 761-69.

23. *Hearings Before a Subcommittee of the Committee on Privileges and Elections*, U.S. Senate, 65 Cong., 1 Sess., on Resolutions from the Minnesota Commission of Public Safety Petitioning for Proceedings Looking to the Expulsion of Senator Robert M. La Follette; B & F La Follette, *La Follette*, pp. 761-886.

24. P. F. La Follette, *Adventures in Politics*, pp. 51-53; B & F La Follette, *La Follette*, pp. 780-81, 843-47, 858-62, 887-88; Margulies, *Progressive Decline*, pp. 193-215; Edwin Gross to RML, April 17, 1919; Edwin Gross, "A Political Grab Bag," Edwin Gross MSS WSHS; Henry Huber, "War Hysteria," Henry Huber MSS WSHS; Richard Lloyd Jones to John J. Blaine, November 7, 1917, John J. Blaine MSS WSHS; William Esch to John Esch, July 2, 1918; John Esch to W. P. Welch, July 27, 1918; Frank Hanson to Esch, October 15, 1918, John S. Esch MSS WSHS.

25. *Current Opinion* 63 (1917), 289-92.

26. B & F La Follette, *La Follette*, pp. 772-831; RML to A. D. Bursch, November 6, 1917; RML to J. F. Hasskarl, November 13, 1917; RML to PFL, May 26, 1918, RML MSS LC; James Stone to Frank Winter, January 24, 1918; Stone to Henry Campbell, February 25, 1918; Stone to RML, April 3, 1917; Stone to A. W. Sanborn, March 11, 1918, James Stone MSS WSHS.

27. B & F La Follette, *La Follette*, pp. 774-89; RML to Atlee Pomerene, October 5, 10, 1917. He refused to send stenographic copies of the speech while the investigation was still in progress. RML to A.

B. Graf, November 16, 1917, RML MSS LC; *La Follette's* 9 (November, 1917), 6.

28. B & F La Follette, *La Follette*, pp. 761-886; clipping, Milwaukee *Journal*, November 26, 1917, RML MSS LC: Merle Curti, *Bryan and World Peace*, p. 200; William Jennings Bryan, *Memoirs*, pp. 398-99; Colin Simpson, *The Lusitania*, p. 97.

29. RML to James Pierce, January 12, 1918, RML MSS LC.

30. BCL to PFL, February 9, 16, 22, 25, 1918, April 5, 1918, May 9, 18, 26, 1918; RML to Alfred Rogers, tgm., February 1, 1918; RML to Fola La Follette, October 10, 1918, RML MSS LC.

31. Quoted in B & F La Follette, *La Follette*, p. 892; cf., Richard Barry, "A Radical in Power: A Study of La Follette," *Outlook* 132 (1922), 564-7.

32. B & F La Follette, *La Follette*, pp. 874-931; BCL to PFL, May 26, 1918; RML to PFL, May 16, 21, 1918; RML to family, November 5, 1918, January 16, 1919. La Follette was very concerned about the proceedings. He felt that if expelled there was doubt whether he could be reelected. Governor Philipp concurred in this evaluation and challenged him to resign and to put the issue to the electorate. Nevertheless, La Follette felt he gained more than he lost. RML to Charles Crownhart, January 4, 1918, RML MSS LC.

33. B & F La Follette, *La Follette*, pp. 807-10, 822-29, 856-57, 884-85; P. F. La Follette, *Adventures in Politics*, pp. 53-54; RML to family, October 6, 24, 1918, RML MSS LC.

34. "I . . . am suffering the tortures of an innocent crucifixion." James Thompson to George Thompson, April 11, 1918, March 26, 1918; James Thompson to Gena Thompson, March 27, 1918; RML to Dear Friend, March 13, 1918; John Hannan to RML, March 9, 10, 1918, RML MSS LC; Margulies, *Progressive Decline*, pp. 214-30.

35. Charles Rosa to James Thompson, August 2, 1918, Thompson MSS WSHS; Margulies, *Progressive Decline*, pp. 230-43. Philipp had opposed the campaign of vilification against La Follette, had resisted interference with the press, and attempted to protect citizens against the Loyalty Legion, Maxwell, *Philipp*, pp. 150-75; cf., Edwin Gross, "Why Governor Philipp was Unopposed for a Third Term," Gross MSS WSHS; Conference of Progressive Republicans of Wisconsin, June 14, 1918; John Hannan to Ed Dithmar, June 20, 22, 1918; Hannan to A. H. Hartwig, July 5, 1918; C. N. Saugen to Charles Rosa, August 14, 1918, mentions quiet support for him from Philipp's men; A. H. Hartwig to Rosa, August 17, 1918, Charles Rosa MSS WSHS.

*Chapter Eleven*

1. Cf., John Chalmers Vinson, *Referendum for Isolation*, pp. 1-35.

2. Cf., Link, *Wilson, the Diplomatist,* pp. 127-56.

3. RML to family, November 7, 1918, RML MSS LC. Progressive Republicans, having accrued seniority, had key committee posts. La Follette chaired the Committee on Manufactures, and three progressives shared the assignment with him. Progressives dominated the Committee on Agriculture, presided over by Gronna. Kenyon was the chairman of the Committee on Education and Labor. The bloc had seats on Appropriations, Banking and Currency, Commerce, Conservation, Finance, Foreign Relations, Commerce, Military Affairs, Public Lands, and Rules, among others. U.S. *Congressional Record,* 66 Cong., 1 Sess., 58 (1919), 314.

4. RML to BCL and RML, Jr., May 5, 1919, RML MSS LC.

5. *La Follette's* 13 (1921), 35-36; 11 (1919), 48-49, 117-18; U.S. *Congressional Record,* 65 Cong., 3 Sess., 57 (1919), 4984-91; 66 Cong., 1 Sess., 58 (1919), 4588-92; RML to family, December 10, 1918, March 30, 1919, RML MSS LC.

6. RML to family, January 12, 1919, February 8, 1919, RML MSS LC; *La Follette's* 11 (1919), 69.

7. *La Follette's* 11 (1919), 102, 136; 16 (1924), 1-2; U.S. *Congressional Record,* 66 Cong., 2 Sess., 59 (1919), 506-507, 4987; RML to RML, Jr., May 16, 1919, RML MSS LC.

8. RML to family, February 23, 1919; RML to RML, Jr., and PFL, June 3, 1919, RML MSS LC.

9. *La Follette's* 12 (1920), 34.

10. Robert K. Murray, *Red Scare;* George Soule, *Prosperity Decade,* pp. 64-93, 187-208; RML to family, January 21, 1919, August

11. U.S. *Congressional Record,* 65 Cong., 3 Sess., 57 (1919), 1986-89; 66 Cong., 1 Sess., 58 (1919), 521-27, 7758, 8428; 67 Cong., 2 Sess., 62 (1922), 2380-88; *La Follette's* 11 (1919), 165-67; 12 (1920), 177-78; 13 (1921), 1-2, 145-46; 14 (1922), 50-51; RML to family, April 22, 1919; RML to George Murdo, January 8, 1921, RML MSS LC.

12. U.S. *Congressional Record,* 65 Cong., 3 Sess., 57 (1919), 5852-56.

13. RML to family, October 24, 1918, November 5, 9, 10, 1918; RML to PFL, November 5, 1918, RML MSS LC; *La Follette's* 10 (November, 1918), 1-2.

14. RML to family, December 27, 1918; BCL to PFL, September 27, 1921, RML MSS LC.

15. U.S. *Congressional Record,* 65 Cong., 3 Sess., 57 (1919), 1101-104; *La Follette's* 11 (1919), 60. La Follette opposed government intervention even where he approved of the ends to be accomplished. In a form letter on the question of the Armenian massacres he said he would support executive or legislative action "to interpose the moral influence of this country as a restraint upon the Turks" but he rejected

dispatching troops or imperialistic entanglement. Form letter, June 20, 1921, RML MSS LC.

16. *La Follette's* 11 (1919, 102+; RML to family, December 27, 1918; January 19, 1919; February 7, 13, 15, 1919; April 30, 1919, RML MSS LC.

17. U.S. *Congressional Record,* 65 Cong., 3 Sess., 57 (1919), 1983-95.

18. RML to family, November 5, 13, 20, 1918; December 5, 1918, RML MSS LC. Wilson must have known of the secret treaties before taking us into the war, and before espousing the fourteen points, La Follette wrote. "If we are to have faith in the integrity of President Wilson, we are bound to believe that he had secured the consent of the Allied powers for the abrogation of the Secret Treaties." *La Follette's* 11 (1919), 1-2.

19. RML to family, November 30, 1918; December 4, 1918; January 16, 1918; March 10, 1918, RML MSS LC; *La Follette's* 10 (December, 1918), 1-2.

20. *La Follette's* 11 (1919), 33-35, 52-54, 59-60; U.S. *Congressional Record,* 65 Cong., 3 Sess., 57 (1919), 4981-91; 66 Cong., 1 Sess., 58 (1919), 8001-11.

21. B & F La Follette, *La Follette,* pp. 952-53.

22. RML to family, March 30, 1919; April 21, 1919; RML to BCL and RML, Jr., May 4, 1919; RML to RML, Jr., May 10, 1919, RML MSS LC.

23. *La Follette's* 11 (1919), 101-102.

24. U.S. *Congressional Record,* 66 Cong., 1 Sess., 58 (1919), 8428-33, 8728-29.

25. *La Follette's* 1 (August 4, 1909), 5-6; 11 (1919), 101-102; 12 (1920), 54-55; 13 (1921), 77-78; U.S. *Congressional Record,* 66 Cong., 1 Sess., 58 (1919), 7011-12; 7669-77; 8428-33, 8728-29; 67 Cong., 1 Sess., 61 (1921), 637-51.

26. U.S. *Congressional Record,* 66 Cong., 1 Sess., 58 (1919), 8728-29.

27. John A. Garraty, *Henry Cabot Lodge,* pp. 336-82; Thomas A. Bailey, *Woodrow Wilson and the Great Betrayal,* pp. 149-287; cf. Ralph Stone, "The Irreconcilables' Alternatives to the League of Nations," *Mid America* 49 (1967), 163-73. La Follette felt that opponents of the treaty had the votes to defeat it from the first and the Democrats were stalling to obtain concurrence, RML to RML, Jr., and PFL, June 21, 1919, RML MSS LC.

28. U.S. *Congressional Record,* 67 Cong., 1 Sess., 61 (1921), 1252, 6435-38; *La Follette's* 13 (1921), 99; 15 (1923), 68.

29. *La Follette's* 10 (November, 1918), 2.

30. RML to family, January 3, 7, 1919, RML MSS LC.

31. U.S. *Congressional Record,* 66 Cong., 2 Sess., 59 (1919), 522-29, 8746-61; 66 Cong., 3 Sess., 60 (1921), 4602-607; *La Follette's* 11 (1919), 181-83; 12 (1920), 1-2, 71, 147; 15 (1923), 97-98; cf. RML to Henry Ford, August 17, 1921; RML to W. G. McAdoo, August 17, 1921, RML MSS LC.

32. Mark Sullivan, "McAdoo's chances for the Democratic nomination," *Worlds' Work* 46 (1923), 193-201; Walter Lippmann, "Two leading Democratic candidates: McAdoo," *New Republic* 23 (June 2, 1920), 10-11; J. P. Tumulty to W. G. McAdoo, November 20, 1919; McAdoo to Tumulty, November 21, 1919, McAdoo MSS LC; Mary Austin," Hoover and Johnson, West is West," *Nation* 110 (1920), 642-44.

33. Margulies, *Progressive Decline,* pp. 244-59; B & F La Follette, *La Follette,* pp. 991-95; RML to Andrew Noll, April 3, 1920, RML MSS LC; cf. Edwin Gross to RML, April 17, 1919; Gross to W. T. Evjue, January 10, 1920, Gross MSS WSHS.

34. RML to RML, Jr., and PFL, June 3, 1919; June 21, 1920; RML, Jr., to RML, June 21, 1920, July 11, 1920, RML MSS LC; B & F La Follette, *La Follette,* pp. 996-1010. George Record wanted a platform of one or two simple ideas, not the eighteen points presented to the Republican convention. Record to RML, June 25, 1920, RML MSS LC.

35. George Record to RML, July 16, 1920; Basil Manly to Gilbert Roe, July 18, 1920; Roe to RML, July 22, 1920; memo by Manly of a conference, July 25-27; phone memo, RML, Jr. to James Pierce, July 28, 1920; phone memo, RML, Jr., to J. A. H. Hopkins, July 31, 1920; RML, Jr., to Roe, August 2, 1920; RML, Jr., to Manly, August 2, 1920; Manly to RML, August 6, 1920; RML to My Dear Senator, August 13, 1920, RML MSS LC.; B & F La Follette, *La Follette,* pp. 1011-13.

36. La Follette wrote to a prohibitionist supporter that he opposed the saloon and favored temperance and government regulation but could not accept prohibition. He told the Senate that a law imposed on a community against its will could not be enforced and brought reproach on law and order. He voted to submit the amendment to the country but against the Volstead Act. Once declared constitutional, he insisted that the law be impartially enforced. RML to Mabel Costigan, August 11, 1924; RML to the family, July 7, 1917, August 7, 1917; RML to Clarence Wise, April 12, 1920; RML, Jr., to Charles Crownhart, August 20, 1920; Grace Lynch to Mark Sullivan, August 27, 1920; Walter Corrigan to RML, October 20, 1920, RML MSS LC; Margulies, *Progressive Decline,* pp. 263-69.

37. RML, Jr., to BCL, January 24, 1920; RML, Jr., to family, April 26, 1920; May 8, 17, 1920; John Hannan to RML, May 8, 1920, RML

MSS LC; Margulies, *Progressive Decline,* pp. 260-71.

38. Margulies, *Progressive Decline,* pp. 272-82; RML to Ernst Kronshage, October 4, 1920; RML to David Walsh, October 9, 1920; F. E. Carswell to John Blaine, November 3, 1920; Eugene Meyer to Blaine, November 5, 1920, Blaine MSS WSHS.

39. RML speech, A. F. of L. Convention, Cincinnati, Ohio, June 14, 1922, New York Public Library. In 1912 La Follette had charged that "the courts pervert justice almost as often as they administer it." He hoped to remove "the dead hand of precedent from the judiciary" and infuse into it "the spirit of the times." Neither courts nor their decisions should remain beyond the control of the electorate. R. M. La Follette, Introduction to Gilbert Roe, *Our Judicial Oligarchy.* It did not take long for Chief Justice Taft to hand down the Coronado decision enabling the seizure of the entire resources of an organization in an anti-trust judgment, a new low endangering the existence of labor organizations and farm cooperatives. *La Follette's* 14 (1922), 81-82.

40. Cf., *Literary Digest* 74 (July 1, 1922, 21); Noel Sargent, "The La Follette Veto," *Forum* 68 (1922), 775-83; Charles Warren, "Borah and La Follette versus the Supreme Court," *Saturday Evening Post* 196 (October 13, 1923), 31, 190-94, in which Warren showed the small number of 5-4 decisions holding a law unconstitutional; Karl Frederick, "Senator La Follette and the Courts," *Outlook* 138 (1924), 200-201; B & F La Follette, *La Follette,* pp. 1055-58.

41. B & F La Follette, *La Follette,* pp. 1056-61.

42. BCL to Mary La Follette, October 6, 19, 1922; BCL to Fola and George Middleton, October 2, 1922; November 4, 1922, RML MSS LC; B & F La Follette, *La Follette,* pp. 1061-64.

43. *Labor* 4 (November 11, 1922), in John Hicks, *Republican Ascendancy, 1921-1933,* pp. 88-89; B & F La Follette, *La Follette,* pp. 1064-65; RML to RML, Jr., June 16, 1923, RML MSS LC: cf., Robert K. Murray, *The Harding Era,* pp. 294-326.

## Chapter Twelve

1. William Kent to William Hard, January 18, 1918; Kent to Irvine Lenroot, February 1, 1919; Kent to Frank Taussig, May 20, 1919; Kent to J. W. Good, May 29, 1919, William Kent MSS U Yale; U.S. *Congressional Record,* 64 Cong., 1 Sess., 53 (1916), 13869-70; 66 Cong., 1 Sess., 58 (1919), 1964-86; RML to RML, Jr., and PFL, June 27, 1919, RML MSS LC; cf., *La Follette's* 3 (January 9, 1909), 4; 3 (February 27, 1909), 3-4; 3 (March 6, 1909), 3.

2. Greenbaum, *Fighting Progressive,* pp. 88-104; *Hearings on S.R. 162, to Investigate the U.S. Tariff Commission,* 69 Cong., 1 Sess., 1926; William Culbertson's memorandum on Chairman Thomas Marvin, July 23, 1925; Costigan to Denver *Post,* September 8, 1924,

Costigan MSS U Colo; David J. Lewis and Edward Costigan to Calvin
Coolidge, July 24, 1924; Culbertson to Father Edmund Walsh,
October 20, 1924; RML to Tariff Commission, July 29, 1924,
Culbertson MSS LC.

3. RML to RML, Jr., and PFL, June 27, 1919, RML MSS LC;
George Soule, *Prosperity Decade,* pp. 135-59; George Norris, "Boring
from Within," *Nation* 21 (September 16, 1925), 297-99; U.S.
*Congressional Record,* 67 Cong., 2 Sess., 92 (1922), 2646; 68 Cong., 1
6, 1919, RML MSS LC.

4. *La Follette's* 13 (1921), 36, 81-82. For a different view of
Harding's initial program see Murray, *Harding,* pp. 125-27.

5. *La Follette's* 15 (1923), 177; for a different view see Donald R.
McCoy, *Calvin Coolidge,* pp. 155-56, 199-202.

6. After his election Harding had remarked to La Follette on
passing him in the Senate, "Now, Bob, be good." "I'll be busy making
you be good," was his response. B & F La Follette, *La Follette,* p. 1020;
U.S. *Congressional Record,* 67 Cong., 1 Sess., 61 (1921), 5415-17;
RML to R. F. Paine, October 19, 1921, RML MSS LC.

7. *La Follette's* 14 (1922), 102-103; U.S. *Congressional Record,* 67
Cong., 2 Sess., 62 (1922), 10054-63, 10074-86. La Follette tried to
persuade such influential segments of the population as the wool
growers that the new rates would cost them more than they gained
from the increased wool schedule, William Hard, "Fighting Bob —
Elder Statesman," *Collier's* 72 (September 8, 1923), 12. But just as a
decade earlier he had opposed the Payne-Aldrich Tariff and then
supported protection for agriculture, he had voted for the Emergency
Agricultural Tariff of 1921. U.S. *Congressional Record,* 67 Cong., 1
Sess., 61 (1921), 1306-308, 1578.

8. He was particularly disturbed by the meat packing oligopoly.
He opposed the merger between Armour and Morris, for in some
towns they were the only competition. He wanted to keep them from
entering other fields. They had already grown so large as to become in-
efficient. Higher meat prices and company losses were due to over-
extension. U.S. *Congressional Record,* 67 Cong., 2 Sess., 62 (1922),
1969-71, 2100-107; 67 Cong., 4 Sess., 64 (1922), 128-32; *La Follette's* 14
(1922), 12-14, 27, 100-104; 16 (1924), 20, 24, 133-35, 145-46, for a different view of Harding's farm program see Murray, *Harding,* pp. 199-226.

9. He sought information on whether British citizens and
corporations abroad paid taxes. RML to Sir Auckland Geddes,
October 6, 1921; Grace Lynch to RML, November 2, 1922; RML to
Charles Amidon, October 4, 1921, RML MSS LC; U.S. *Congressional
Record,* 67 Cong., 1 Sess., 61 (1921), 5415-19, 7364-73; *La Follette's* 13
(1921), 82-83, 97-98. For Mellon's economic rationale see Murray,
*Harding,* pp. 182-91, 381.

10. George Norris was particularly forceful in trying to use a model of the Isthmian Canal Company for a government owned shipping corporation to restore an effective merchant fleet. U.S. *Congressional Record*, 67 Cong., 1 Sess., 61 (1921), 1412-15, 1502-506, 4237-44, 4511-28; 67 Cong., 2 Sess., 62 (1922), 2430-31; 67 Cong., 4 Sess., 64 (1922), 508-18; RML to Frederick Paxson, February 2, 1915, RML MSS LC; *La Follette's* 14 (1922), 103; Murray, *Harding*, pp. 280-93.

11. RML to PFL, February 28, 1919, RML MSS LC.

12. RML to C. F. Bundy, undated [ca. November 20, 1910]; RML to A. H. Smith, November 1, 1910, RML MSS LC.

13. RML to Samuel Untermeyer, January 13, 1922, RML MSS LC; *La Follette's* 16 (1924), 67, 73; 17 (1925), 54-55.

14. U.S. *Congressional Record*, 66 Cong., 1 Sess., 58 (1919), 4733-61; RML to PFL, February 28, 1919; RML to family, March 2, 1919, RML MSS LC. Cf. David Stratton, "Splattered with Oil: William G. McAdoo and the 1924 Democratic Presidential Nomination," *Southwestern Social Science* 44 (1963), 62-75; *Literary Digest* 80 (February 23, 1924), 13. Joseph Tumulty had warned McAdoo against representing Doheny in his Mexican claims if he wanted to run for President in 1920. Tumulty to McAdoo, November 20, 1919; McAdoo to Tumulty, November 21, 1919, McAdoo MSS LC; Burl Noggle, *Teapot Dome*, pp. 17-18, 96-105, 136-41; B & F La Follette, *La Follette*, pp. 1042-43.

15. Noggle, *Teapot Dome*, pp. 4-42, 46-50, 67-8, 183-211; B & F La Follette, *La Follette*, pp. 1041, 1052-54; U.S. *Congressional Record*, 67 Cong., 2 Sess., 62 (1922), 6041-50, 6101-105; 68 Cong., 1 Sess., 65 (1924), 2230-35; RML to Josephus Daniels, April 6, 19, 22, 1922; Daniels to RML, April 18, 19, 1922; RML to Thomas Gregory, April 19, 1922; RML to Edward Britton, April 19, 1922; RML to Admiral Robert Griffin, April 19, 1922; RML to Robert Carey, tgm., April 22, 1922; RML to F. G. Bonfils, tgm., April 22, 1922; RML to G. B. Morgan, tgm., April 22, 1922; RML to W. A. Blackman, tgm., April 22, 1922; RML to Edward Finney, April 22, 1922; RML to Edward Denby, April 22, 1922; RML to W. R. Hearst, April 25, 1922, RML MSS LC; Murray, *Harding*, pp. 461-73; McCoy, *Coolidge*, pp. 204-21.

16. *La Follette's* 13 (1921), 17-18, 113-14, 161, 177-78; 15 (1923), 1-2; U.S. *Congressional Record*, 67 Cong., 1 Sess., 61 (1921), 1731-55; 67 Cong., 2 Sess., 62 (1922), 4227-35; RML to *La Follette's*, tgm., November 17, 1921, RML MSS LC.

17. U.S. *Congressional Record*, 67 Cong., 1 Sess., 61 (1921), 5869-73; *La Follette's* 13 (1921), 146, 148, 184.

18. U.S. *Congressional Record*, 67 Cong., 4 Sess., 64 (1923), 3741-47; *La Follette's* 13 (1921), 113-14; 15 (1923), 17-20; Murray, *Harding*, pp. 360-67.

19. *La Follette's* 12 (1920), 3; 16 (1924), 1-2.

20. B & F La Follette, *La Follette*, pp. 1074-87; W. T. Rawleigh to RML, Jr., October 29, 1920; Basil Manly to RML, June 14, 1923; BCL to Ralph and Mary Sucher, August 7, 1923; RML to family, August 10, 1923; BCL to family, August 14, 1923; BCL to Mary La Follette, September 2, 9, 13, 17, 19, 25, 1923; BCL to Isen La Follette, October 4, 1923; BCL to Fola La Follette, October 11, 1923, RML MSS LC.

21. *La Follette's* 15 (1923), 180-81, 187; 16 (1924), 4-6, 26-28, 41, 45; U.S. *Congressional Record*, 68 Cong., 1 Sess., 65 (1924), 10984-986; RML to family, January 18, 1919; BCL to Fola La Follette, November 11, 1923, RML MSS LC.

22. *La Follette's* 15 (1923), 161; 16 (1924), 4-6, 26-28, 41, 45.

23. John W. Owens, "La Follette," *New Republic* 33 (1922), 87-89; RML to RML, Jr., June 16, 1923, RML MSS LC.

24. RML to A. C. Holzapfel, June 16, 1921, RML MSS LC.

25. When his magazine was in danger La Follette thought of going public. Rawleigh put up $10,000 for promotion and offered to buy as much stock as La Follette wanted to sell. RML, Jr., to Alfred Rogers, March 17, 1922; RML to J. A. H. Hopkins, April 5, 1921; Basil Manly to RML, October 13, 1922; June 18, 1923; RML, Jr., to W. T. Rawleigh [ca. 1922], RML MSS LC; William Hard, "Fighting Bob — Elder Statesman," *Collier's* 72 (September 8, 1923), 12; R. M. La Follette, *Government by Private Monopoly, The Sugar Trust.*

26. Kenneth MacKay, *The Progressive Movement of 1924*, pp. 59-74; B & F La Follette, *La Follette*, pp. 1065-68; La Follette commented on the Labour victory in 1924: "It comes into control of the British Government because it is devoted to the interest of the whole mass of the people, as against the Landed Aristocracy which has dominated the lives of the people of Great Britain in much the same fashion as organized Monopoly has exploited the people of this country." *La Follette's* 16 (1924), 17. There was a general wariness on the subject of a third party for fear that progressive congressional candidates might be injured. The AFL was particularly adamant in opposing a new party. Cf., Ronald Radosh, "The Development of the Corporate Ideology of American Labor Leaders, 1914-1933," pp. 160-66.

27. Lee Allen, "The McAdoo Campaign for the Presidential Nomination in 1924," *Journal of Southern History* 29 (1963), 211-28; Basil Manly to RML, October 9, 1922; RML to dear Governor, April 11, 1923; RML, Jr., to George Norris, Edwin Ladd, Smith Brookhart, Lynn Frazier, Magnus Johnson, Hendrik Shipstead, November 30, 1923; RML, Jr., to W. T. Rawleigh, December 19, 1923; RML, Jr., to

Karl Bickel, April 22, 1924, RML MSS LC.

28. RML to Ralph Sucher, May 19, 1924; RML to W. T. Rawleigh, June 5, 1923; March 19, 1924; RML, Jr., to George Norris, November 19, 1923; RML and RML, Jr., to PFL, January 20, 1924; RML to Thomas Hall, tgm., February 28, 1924; RML to John Andrews, March 1, 1924; RML to Charles Deland, March 4, 1924; RML, Jr., to Alfred Rogers, tgm., April 4, 15, 1924; RML, Jr., to Frank Heney, May 22, 1924; RML to Herman Ekern, May 26, 1924; RML to John Blaine, June 7, 1924; RML, Jr., to Gilbert Roe, July 28, 1924; D. C. Burns to E. P. Costigan, July 30, 1924; RML, Jr., to PFL, tgm., August 5, 1924; Costigan to RML, Jr., tgm., September 11, 1924; RML to Samuel Gombers, tgm., August 4, 1924, RML MSS LC.

29. RML to RML, Jr., and PFL, January 20, 1924, RML MSS LC; B & F La Follette, *La Follette,* pp. 1108-10.

30. BCL to Mary La Follette, July 3, 1924, RML MSS LC; B & F La Follette, *La Follette,* pp. 1108-15; Benjamin Stolberg, "La Follette Crosses the Rubicon," *Independent* 113 (1924), 34, 56; Robert Litell, "La Follette for President," *New Republic* 39 (1924), 201-202; Oswald Garrison Villard, "An Honest Convention," *Nation* 119 (1924), 63-65; McAlister Coleman, "La Follette Day at Cleveland," *Outlook* 137 (1924), 425-26.

31. La Follette was not a church member. They were philosophically Unitarian and not much accustomed to going to theological churches. BCL to Mary La Follette, July 10, 1924; RML to L. Schach, December 15, 1911, RML MSS LC.

32. B & F La Follette, *La Follette,* pp. 1115-16; MacKay, 1924, pp. 134-42.

33. MacKay, *1924,* pp. 11, 143-48, *New Republic* 39 (1924), 88-90; Edward Lowry, "La Follette's Own Platform," *World's Work* 48 (1924), 513-18; *Outlook* 137 (1924), 414, 421; *Literary Digest* 82 (September 6, 1924), 10.

34. In attacking anti-semitism he wrote: "He is an enemy of American democracy who assails any man or any people because of nationality or religion." *La Follette's* 11 (1919), 118-19; 12 (1920), 179; 14 (1922), 3, 43; 16 (1924), 133-35; Edward Doan, *The La Follettes and the Wisconsin Idea;* RML to G. J. Bowens, November 16, 1911; RML to Robert Scripps, August 5, 1924, RML MSS LC; Villard, "An Honest Convention"; Lahman, *La Follette,* pp. 222-24, 236-38.

35. *Literary Digest* 82 (September 13, 1924), 8; speech in St. Louis, October 14, 1924; speech in Cincinnati, October 10, 1924, *Nation* 119 (1924), 476-80.

36. BCL to Phil and Iselen La Follette, August 25, 1924, RML MSS LC; James Shideler, "The La Follette Progressive Party Campaign of

1924," *Wisconsin Magazine of History* 33 (1950), 444-57; *La Follette's* 16 (1924), 98-100, 105; MacKay, *1924*, pp. 175-94; *Radio Broadcast* 5 (1924), 476; McCoy, *Coolidge*, p. 262.

37. Fred Greenbaum, "The Social Ideas of Samuel Gompers," *Labor History* 7 (1966), 35-61; Ronald Radosh, "Labor and the American Economy: The 1922 Railroad Shop Craft Strike and the 'B & O Plan'," in Gerald Israel, ed., *Building the Organizational Society,* pp. 73-87.

38. Polis, "The Presidency in 1924? (2) Robert M. La Follette," *Forum* 69 (1923), 1233-40; Samuel Blythe, "Let X = La Follette," *Saturday Evening Post* 197 (October 18, 1924), 3-4, 190-94; "The New Alignment," *Saturday Evening Post* 197 (November 1, 1924), 24; Washington Pezet, "The La Follette Decision," *Forum* 72 (1924), 673-89; Elizabeth Frazer, "La Follette's Pink Tea," *Saturday Evening Post* 197 (November 1, 1924), 17, 145-50; *Outlook* 137 (1924), 414, 421; 138 (1924), 12, 155, 242-44; Frederick, "La Follette and the Courts"; Warren, "Borah and La Follette versus the Supreme Court"; MacKay, *1924*, pp. 162-74; McCoy, *Coolidge*, pp. 257-63.

39. *New Republic* 40 (1924), 36-37, 63-65, 108-10, 115-16, 137-38, 168-69, 199-201; Clarence Alvord, "La Follette and the Wisconsin Idea," *Contemporary Review* 126 (1924), 425-32; William Hard, "Robert M. La Follette," *Review of Reviews* 70 (1924), 275-79; *World's Work* 49 (1924), 119-20; MacKay *1924*, pp. 219-42; McCoy, *Coolidge,* pp. 208-17. While Al Smith only carried eight major cities in 1928, two had been carried by John Davis in 1924, one by La Follette and in two La Follette had run very strongly, though Coolidge had won. By 1932 large cities had become Democratic, and in many of them La Follette had outpolled Davis — Edgar Eugene Robinson, *The Presidential Vote, 1896-1932.*

40. RML to Josephine Siebecker, December 27, 1924; RML, Jr., to W. T. Rawleigh, December 29, 1924; RML to Gilbert Roe, February 3, 1925; RML to RML, Jr., February 2, 6, 10, 1925, RML MSS LC; *La Follette's* 18 (1924), 165-66, 181-82; B & F La Follette, *La Follette,* pp. 1148-60.

41. B & F La Follette, *La Follette,* pp. 1166-74; RML to Fred Holmes, March 1, 1925; RML to W. T. Rawleigh, December 6, 1924; RML to David Robertson, May 9, 1925, RML MSS LC.

# Selected Bibliography

  Library of Congress
    William S. Culbertson Papers
    James R. Garfield Papers
    Robert Marion La Follette Papers
    William Gibbs McAdoo Papers
    National Progressive Republican League Papers
    Gifford Pinchot Papers
    Gilbert Roe Papers
    Alfred Rogers Papers

  Wisconsin State Historical Society
    John J. Blaine Papers
    James O. Davidson Papers
    Herman Ekern Papers
    John S. Esch Papers
    Lucius Fairchild Papers
    Edwin Gross Papers
    Nils P. Haugen Papers
    Henry Huber Papers
    Elisha Keyes Papers
    Robert Marion La Follette Papers
    Willet Main Diaries, 1880, 1884
    Charles Rosa Papers
    James Stone Papers
    John Strange, *Autobiography*
    James Thompson Papers
    John Whitehead Papers

  Other Collections
    Edward Prentiss Costigan Papers, University of Colorado, Boulder Colorado.
    William Kent Papers, Yale University, New Haven, Connecticut.
    Lincoln Steffens Papers, Columbia University, New York, New York.

*257*

2. Published Materials

ANDERSON, RASMUS B. with BARTON, A. O. *The Life Story of Rasmus B. Anderson*. Madison: Privately Printed, 1915.

HAUGEN, NILS P. *Pioneer and Political Reminiscensces*. Madison: State Historical Society of Wisconsin, [ca. 1929.]

*Hearings Before a Subcommittee of the Committee on Privileges and Elections*. U.S. Senate, 65 Cong., 1 Sess., on Resolutions from the Minnesota Commission of Public Safety Petitioning for Proceedings Looking to the Expulsion of Senator Robert M. La Follette.

*Hearings of S.R. 162, to Investigate the U.S. Tariff Commission*. 69 Cong., 1 Sess., 1926.

LA FOLLETTE, PHILIP FOX. *Adventures in Politics*, ed. Donald Young. New York: Holt, Rinehart and Winston, 1970.

LA FOLLETTE, ROBERT M. *Government by Private Monopoly, The Sugar Trust*. Washington: People's Legislative Service, 1923.

———. Introduction to Roe, Gilbert. *Our Judicial Oligarchy*. New York: W. B. Huebsch, 1912.

———. *La Follette's Autobiography*. Madison: University of Wisconsin Press, 1963.

———. Ed., *Making of America*, Vol. I, Introduction. Chicago: The Making of America Co., 1906.

———. Speech before the American Federation of Labor, Cincinnati, June 14, 1922.

———. Speech in St. Louis, October 14, 1924. Speech in Cincinnati, October 10, 1924, *Nation* 119 (1924), 476-80.

———. *La Follette's Magazine*.

MORISON, ELTING. *Letters of Theodore Roosevelt*. Cambridge: Harvard University Press, 1951.

NORRIS, GEORGE W. *Fighting Liberal*. New York: Collier Books, 1961.

———. "Boring from Within," *Nation* 21 (1925), 297-99.

———. "The Insurgents and the Party," *Metropolitan Magazine* 32 (1910), 656-62.

PHILIPP, EMANUEL, assisted by Wheelock, Edgar. *Political Reform in Wisconsin*. Milwaukee: E. L. Philipp, [ca. 1910.]

———. *The Truth about Wisconsin Freight Rates*. Milwaukee: Pamphlet, 1904.

STEPHENSON, ISAAC. *Recollections of a Long Life, 1829-1915*. Chicago: Privately Printed, R. R. Donnelly, 1915.

TORELLE, ELLEN, Ed., *The Political Philosophy of Robert M. La Follette*. Madison: Robert M. La Follette Co., 1920.

U.S *Congressional Record*, 1880-1925.

## Secondary Sources

### 1. Dissertations and Theses

ACREA, KENNETH. "Wisconsin Progressivism: Legislative Response to Social Change, 1891-1909." Ph. D. dissertation, University of Wisconsin, 1968.

BAIRD, RUSSELL N. "Robert M. La Follette and the Press, 1880-1905." M.A. thesis, University of Wisconsin, 1947.

BRANDES, STUART. "Nils P. Haugen and the Wisconsin Progressive Movement." M. S. thesis, University of Wisconsin, 1965.

LAHMAN, CARROLL POLLOCK, "Robert Marion La Follette as Public Speaker and Political Leader, 1885-1905." Ph. D. dissertation, University of Wisconsin, 1939.

MANNING, EUGENE. "Old Bob La Follette: Champion of the People." Ph. D. dissertation, University of Wisconsin, 1966.

MEYER, KARL ERNEST. "The Politics of Loyalty from La Follette to McCarthy in Wisconsin: 1918-1952." Ph. D. dissertation, Princeton University, 1956.

RADOSH, RONALD. "The Development of the Corporate Ideology of American Labor Leaders, 1924-1933." Ph. D. dissertation, University of Wisconsin, 1967.

TWOMBLY, ROBERT C. "The Reformer as Politician, Robert M. La Follette in the Election of 1900." M.A. thesis, University of Wisconsin, 1964.

WYMAN, ROGER. "Voting Behavior in the Progressive Era: Wisconsin as a Case Study." Ph. D. dissertation, University of Wisconsin, 1970.


### 2. Published Materials

ACREA, KENNETH. "The Wisconsin Reform Coalition, 1892 to 1900: La Follette's Rise to Power," *Wisconsin Magazine of History* 52 (1968), 132-58.

ADAMS, T. S. "The Drama of Wisconsin Politics," *Independent* 54 (1902), 1824-26.

ADDAMS, JANE. "Why I Shall Vote for La Follette," *New Republic* 4 (1924), 36-37.

ALEXANDER, HOLMES. *The Famous Five.* New York: The Bookmailer, 1958.

ALLEN, HOWARD W. "Geography and Politics: Voting on Reform Issues in the U.S. Senate, 1911-1916," *Journal of Southern History* 27 (1961), 216-28.

ALLEN, HOWARD W. and JEROME CLUBB. "Party Loyalty in the Progressive Years: The Senate, 1909-1915," *The Journal of Politics* 29 (1967), 567-84.

ALLEN, LEE N. "The McAdoo Campaign for the Presidential Nomination in 1924," *Journal of Southern History* 29 (1963), 211-28.

ALVORD, CLARENCE WALWORTH. "La Follette and the Wisconsin Idea," *Contemporary Review* 126 (1924), 425-32.

AUSTIN, MARY. "Hoover and Johnson, West is West," *Nation* 110 (1920), 642-44.

BAILEY, THOMAS A. *Woodrow Wilson and the Great Betrayal.* Chicago: Quadrangle, 1963.

BARRY, RICHARD. "A Radical in Power: A Study of La Follette," *Outlook* 132 (1922), 564-67.

BARTON, ALBERT O. *La Follette's Winning of Wisconsin.* Madison: Homestead Co., 1922.

BEMIS, SAMUEL FLAGG. *A Diplomatic History of the United States.* New York: Henry Holt, 1950.

BLIVEN, BRUCE. "Robert M. La Follette's Place in Our History," *Current History* 22 (1925), 716-22.

BLUM, JOHN MORTON. *The Republican Roosevelt.* New York: Atheneum, 1966.

— — —. *Woodrow Wilson and the Politics of Morality.* Boston: Little, Brown, 1956.

BLYTHE, SAMUEL G. "Let X = La Follette," *Saturday Evening Post* 197 (October 18, 1924), 190-94.

— — —. "The New Alignment," *Saturday Evening Post* 197 (November 1, 1924), 24.

BOLLES, BLAIR. *Tyrant from Illinois.* New York: W. W. Norton, 1951.

CAMPBELL, BALLARD. *"The Good Roads Movement in Wisconsin, 1890-1911." Wisconsin Magazine of History* 49 (1966), 273-93.

COLEMAN, MCALLISTER. "La Follette Day at Cleveland," *Outlook* 137 (1924), 425-26.

COMMONS, JOHN R. "La Follette and Wisconsin," *New Republic* 40 (1924), 63-65, 108-10.

— — —. "Robert M. La Follette," *North American Review* 187 (1908), 672-77.

— — —. "The La Follette Railroad Law in Wisconsin," *Review of Reviews* 32 (1905), 76-79.

CRABTREE, L. I. *The Wayback Club. A Textbook of Progressivism in Wisconsin.* Crandon, Wisconsin: Crandon Publishing Co., 1912.

CROLY, HERBERT. "La Follette," *New Republic* 40 (1924), 221-24.

CURRENT, RICHARD. *Pine Logs and Politics. A Life of Philetus Sawyer.* Madison: State Historical Society of Wisconsin, 1950.

DAGGY, MAYNARD L. "Robert M. La Follette," in Webb, Edna. *Famous Living Americans,* 287-99. Greencastle, Indiana: Charles Webb and Co., 1915.

DAVIS, ALLEN F. *Spearheads for Reform.* New York: Oxford University Press, 1967.

DAVIS, O. K. "La Follette, Political Evangelist," *Hamptons* 20 (1909), 381-86.

DEVINE, EDWARD T. "Why I Shall Vote for La Follette," *New Republic* 40 (1924), 36-37.

DOAN, EDWARD. *The La Follettes and the Wisconsin Idea.* New York: Rinehart and Co., 1947.

EATON, EARLE HOOKER. "A Personal Sketch of Governor La Follette," *Harper's Weekly* 48 (1904), 2025-26.

EPSTEIN, LEON D. *Politics in Wisconsin.* Madison: University of Wisconsin Press, 1958.

FINLEY, JOHN H. "The Rise of Robert La Follette, the Governor of Wisconsin," *Harper's Weekly* 46 (1902), 1508.

FITZPATRICK, EDWARD. *McCarthy of Wisconsin.* New York: Columbia University Press, 1944.

FOWLER, DOROTHY. *John Coit Spooner, Defender of Presidents.* New York: University Publishers, 1961.

FRANKFURTER, FELIX. "Why I Shall Vote for La Follette," *New Republic* 40 (1924), 199-201.

FRAZER, ELIZABETH. "La Follette's Pink Tea." *Saturday Evening Post* 197 (November 1, 1924), 17, 145-50.

FREDERICK, KARL T. "Senator La Follette and the Courts," *Outlook* 138 (1924), 200-201.

FROST, STANLEY. "La Follette's Private Preserves," *Outlook* 138 (1924), 281-83.

GALE, ZONA. "La Follette's Vindication," *Forum* 72 (1924), 673-89.

―――. "Why I Shall Vote for La Follette," *New Republic* 40 (1924), 115-16.

GARRATY, JOHN. "La Follette: The Promise, Unfulfilled," *American Heritage* 13 (April, 1962), 76-79, 84-88.

―――. *Henry Cabot Lodge.* New York: Alfred Knopf, 1965.

GRAHAME, PAULINE. "La Follette Wins," *Palimpsest* 12 (1931), 179-89.

GREENBAUM, FRED. *Fighting Progressive, A Biography of Edward Prentiss Costigan.* Washington: Public Affairs Press, 1971.

―――. "Progressivism: A Complex Phenomenon," *New Politics* 6 (1968), 85-90.

―――. "The Progressive World of Gabriel Kolko," *Social Studies* 55 (1969), 224-28.

―――. "The Social Ideas of Samuel Gompers," *Labor History* 7 (1966), 35-61.

―――. "The Social Origins of Wisconsin Progressives," *QCC Scholar* 2 (1968), 35-43.

GRIFFITH, ROBERT. "Prelude to Insurgency: Irvine Lenroot and the Republican Primary of 1908," *Wisconsin Magazine of History* 49 (1965), 16-28.

HALE, WILLIAM BAYARD. "La Follette, Pioneer Progressive," *World's Work* 22 (1911), 14591-600.

HANTKE, RICHARD W. "Elisha W. Keyes, The Bismarck of Western Politics," *Wisconsin Magazine of History* 31 (1947), 29-41.

HAPGOOD, NORMAN. "Why I Shall Vote for La Follette," *New Republic* 40 (1924), 168-69.

HARBESON, ROBERT W. "Railroads and Regulation, 1877-1916," *Journal of Economic History* 27 (1967), 29-41.

HARD, WILLIAM. "Fighting Bob — Elder Statesman," *Colliers* 72 (September 8, 1923), 12.

———. "La Follette and Standard Oil," *Nation* 119 (1924), 286-87.

———. "La Follette's Party — Will It Last?" *Nation* 119 (1924), 142-43.

———. "Robert M. La Follette," *Review of Reviews* 70 (1924), 275-79.

HARVEY, ALEXANDER. "The Advantage of Senator La Follette," *American Mercury* 3 (1924), 208-10.

HAYS, SAMUEL P. "The Politics of Reform in Municipal Government in the Progressive Era," *Pacific Northwest Quarterly* 55 (1964), 157-69.

HAYNES, F. E. "La Follette and La Follettism," *Atlantic Monthly* 134 (1924), 536-44.

HECHLER, KENNETH. *Insurgency.* New York: Columbia University Press, 1940.

HESSELTINE, WILLIAM B. "Robert Marion La Follette and the Principles of Americanism," *Wisconsin Magazine of History* 31 (1948), 261-67.

HICKS, JOHN. *Republican Ascendancy.* New York: Harper Torchbooks, 1963.

HIGH, STANLEY. "A Soldier in Politics," *New Republic* 40 (1924), 247-48.

HOLMES, FRED L. *Regulation of Railroads and Public Utilities in Wisconsin.* New York: D. Appleton and Co., 1915.

———. "Triumph of the Progressive Movement," in Quaife, Milo. *Wisconsin, Its History and Its People.* II, 3-39. Chicago: S. J. Clarke Publishing Co., 1924.

HOSTETTLER, GORDON "The Public Speaking of Robert M. La Follette," in Reid, Loren, ed. *American Public Address.* Columbia, Missouri: University of Missouri Press, 1961.

JOHNSTON, CHARLES. "A Talk with La Follette," *Harper's Weekly* 55 (June 24, 1911), 9.

JONES, RICHARD LLOYD. "Among La Follette's People," *Colliers* 45 (September 3, 1910), 17-18.

KALLEN, H. M. "Politics, Profit, and Patriotism in Wisconsin," *Nation*

106 (1918), 257-59.

KENNEDY, PADRAIC. "La Follette's Imperialist Flirtation," *Pacific Historical Review* 29 (1960), 131-44.

———. "Lenroot, La Follette and the Campaign of 1906," *Wisconsin Magazine of History* 42 (1959), 163-74.

KITTLE, WILLIAM, "Robert M. La Follette, A Statesman after the Order of Lincoln," *Arena* 38 (1907), 571-76.

———. "Senator Robert M. La Follette for President," *Arena* 38 (1907), 237-58.

KOLKO, GABRIEL. *Railroads and Regulation, 1877-1916.* Princeton: Princeton University Press, 1965.

———. *The Triumph of Conservatism, a Reinterpretation of American History, 1900-1916.* London: The Free Press of Glencoe, 1963.

KORMAN, GERD. "Political Loyalties, Immigrant Traditions and Reform: The Wisconsin German American Press and Progressivism," *Wisconsin Magazine of History* 40 (1957), 161-68.

LA FOLLETTE, BELLE CASE and LA FOLLETTE, FOLA. *Robert M. La Follette.* New York: MacMillan Co., 2 vols., 1953.

LA FOLLETTE, FOLA. "Robert M. La Follette, My Father," *Twentieth Century Magazine* 5 (1912), 515-19.

LEVINE, DANIEL. *Varieties of Reform Thought.* Madison: State Historical Society of Wisconsin, 1964.

LIEBERMAN, MARK. "Progressivism, Wisconsin and the Status Revolution," *Explorations in Entrepreneurial History* 6 (1969), 297-307.

LINK, ARTHUR S. *Wilson the Diplomatist.* Chicago: Quadrangle, 1965.

———. *Woodrow Wilson and the Progressive Era.* New York: Harper Torchbooks, 1963.

LIPPMAN, WALTER. "Two leading Democratic candidates: McAdoo," *New Republic* 23 (June 2, 1920), 10-11.

LITELL, ROBERT. "La Follette for President!" *New Republic* 39 (1924), 201-202.

LOVEJOY, ALLAN O. *La Follette and the Direct Primary in Wisconsin.* New Haven: Yale University Press, 1941.

LOWRY, EDWARD G. "La Follette's Own Platform," *World's Work* 48 (1924), 513-18.

McADOO, WILLIAM G. *Public Service Corporations and the Public.* New York: Alexander Hamilton Institute, 1910.

McCOY, DONALD. *Calvin Coolidge.* New York: MacMillan, 1967.

MACKAY, KENNETH C. *The Progressive Movement of 1924.* New York: Columbia University Press, 1947.

MADISON, CHARLES. "Robert M. La Follette: Prophet of the New Deal," *Chicago Jewish Forum* 10 (1952), 116-22.

MANNERS, WILLIAM. *TR and Will.* New York: Harcourt, Bruce and World, 1969.

MARGULIES, HERBERT F. "Political Weakness in Wisconsin Progressivism, 1905-1908," *Mid America* 41 (1959), 154-72.

———. "Recent Opinion of the Decline of the Progressive Movement." *Mid America* 45 (1963), 249-68.

———. "The Background of the La Follette-McGovern Schism," *Wisconsin Magazine of History* 40 (1956), 21-29.

———. *The Decline of the Progressive Movement in Wisconsin, 1890-1920.* Madison: State Historical Society of Wisconsin, 1968.

MAXWELL, ROBERT S. "A Document on the Progressive Campaign of 1912," *Mississippi Valley Historical Review* 36 (1949), 113-15.

———. *La Follette and the Rise of Progressives in Wisconsin.* Madison: State Historical Society of Wisconsin, 1956.

———. "La Follette and the Election of 1900," *Wisconsin Magazine of History* 35 (1951), 23-29.

———. *Emanuel L. Philipp: Wisconsin Stalwart:* Madison: State Historical Society of Wisconsin, 1959.

MERZ, CHARLES. "The Senator from Wisconsin," *New Republic* 43 (1925), 174-76.

MOWRY, GEORGE E. *Theodore Roosevelt and the Progressive Movement.* New York: Hill and Wang, 1960.

MURRAY, ROBERT K. *Red Scare.* New York: McGraw Hill, 1964.

———. *The Harding Era.* Minneapolis: University of Minnesota Press, 1969.

NOGGLE, BURL. *Teapot Dome.* New York: W. W. Norton, 1965.

OGG, FREDERICK A. "Robert M. La Follette in Retrospect," *Current History* 33 (1931), 685-91.

OLDS, FRANK. "Wisconsin in the Balance," *Outlook* 117 (1917), 411-12.

OTTO, MAX. "Two Views of the La Follettes, Washington, 1920s," *Wisconsin Magazine of History* 42 (1958), 102-108.

OWENS, JOHN W. "La Follette," *New Republic* 33 (1922), 87-89.

PENICK, JAMES, JR. *Progressive Politics and Conservation, the Ballinger-Pinchot Affair.* Chicago: University of Chicago, 1968.

PEZET, WASHINGTON. "The La Follette Delusion," *Forum* 72 (1924), 673-89.

PINCHOT, AMOS. *History of the Progressive Party, 1912-1916.* Ed., Hooker, Helene Maxwell. New York: New York University Press, 1958.

PLATT, CHESTER. *What La Follette's State Is Doing.* Batavia, New York: Batavia Times Press, 1924.

PLUMB, RALPH. *Badger Politics, 1836-1930.* Manitowoc, Wisconsin: Brandt Printing and Binding Co., 1930.

POLIS. "The Presidency in 1924? (2) Robert M. La Follette," *Forum* 69 (1923), 1233-40.

PRINGLE, HENRY. *William Howard Taft.* New York: Farrar and Rinehart, 2 vols., 1939.

QUIRK, ROBERT E. *An Affair of Honor.* Lexington, Kentucky: University of Kentucky Press, 1962.

RADOSH, RONALD. "Labor and the American Economy: the 1922 Shop Craft Strike and the B & O Plan," in Israel, Gerald, ed. *Building the Organizational Society.* New York: Free Press, 1973.

RANKIN, GEORGE. *William Dempster Hoard.* Ft. Atkinson, Wisconsin: W. D. Hoard and Sons, 1925.

ROE, GILBERT. "Senator La Follette and Representative Government," *Independent* 64 (1908), 717-25.

ROE, GWYNETH KING. "Two views of the La Follettes, Madison, 1890s," *Wisconsin Magazine of History* 42 (1958), 102-108.

ROSS, SAM. *The Empty Sleeve, A Biography of Lucius Fairchild.* Madison: State Historical Society of Wisconsin, 1964.

ROWELL, CHESTER. "La Follette, Shipstead and the Embattled Farmers," *World's Work* 46 (1923), 408-20.

SARGENT, NOEL. "The La Follette Veto," *Forum* 68 (1922), 775-83.

SHANNON, DAVID. "Was McCarthy a Political Heir of La Follette," *Wisconsin Magazine of History* 45 (1961), 3-9.

SHIDELER, JAMES H. "The La Follette Progressive Party Campaign of 1924," *Wisconsin Magazine of History* 33 (1950), 444-57.

SOULE, GEORGE. *Prosperity Decade.* New York: Holt, Rinehart and Winston, 1947.

STEFFENS, LINCOLN. "Enemies of the Republic. Wisconsin: A State where the People have restored Representative Government. The Story of Governor La Follette," *McClure's* 23 (1904), 563-79.

STEVENS, E. RAY. "The La Follette-Spooner Campaign," *World's Work* 4 (1902), 2677-80.

STONE, RALPH A. "The Irreconcilables' Alternatives to the League of Nations," *Mid America* 49 (1967), 163-73.

STOLBERG, BENJAMIN. "La Follette Crosses the Rubicon," *Independent* 113 (1924), 33, 56.

STRATTON, DAVID. "Splattered with Oil: William G. McAdoo and the 1924 Democratic Presidential Nomination," *Southwestern Social Science* 44 (1963), 62-75.

STROTHER, FRENCH. "The Death of the Wisconsin Idea," *World's Work* 50 (1925), 620-24.

SULLIVAN, MARK. "Looking Back on La Follette," *World's Work* 49 (1925), 324-31.

———. "McAdoo's chances for the Democratic nomination," *World's Work* 46 (1923), 193-201.

———. "The La Follette Mantle," *The Economist* 174 (1955), 996-97.

SUTTON, WALTER A. "Progressive Republican Senators and the Submarine Crisis, 1915-1916," *Mid America* 47 (1965), 75-88.

THELEN, DAVID. "Robert M. La Follette, Public Prosecutor," and "La Follette and the Temperance Crusade," *Wisconsin Magazine of History* 47 (1964), 214-23, 291-300.

———. *The Early Life of Robert M. La Follette, 1855-1884.* Chicago: Loyola University Press, 1966.

———. *The New Citizenship.* Columbia, Missouri: University of Missouri Press, 1972.

THOMPSON, E. BRUCE. *Matthew Hale Carpenter.* Madison: State Historical Society of Wisconsin, 1954.

TORELLE, ELLEN Ed., *The Political Philosophy of Robert M. La Follette.* Madison: Robert M. La Follette Co., 1920.

VILLARD, OSWALD GARRISON. "An Honest Convention," *Nation* 119 (1924), 63-65.

VINSON, JOHN CHALMERS. *Referendum for Isolation.* Athens, Georgia: University of Georgia Press, 1961.

WARREN, CHARLES. "Borah and La Follette versus the Supreme Court," *Saturday Evening Post* 196 (October 13, 1923), 31, 190-94.

WARREN, EARL. "Robert M. La Follette, Sr.," *Wisconsin Magazine of History* 38 (1955), 195-98.

WARREN, LOUIS. "The Lincoln and La Follette Families in Pioneer Drama," *Wisconsin Magazine of History* 12 (1929), 359-75.

WEIBULL, JORGEN. "The Wisconsin Progressives, 1900-1914," *Mid America* 47 (1965), 191-221.

WEINSTEIN, JAMES. *The Corporate Ideal in the Liberal State.* Boston: Beacon Press, 1968.

WELLMAN, WALTER. "The Rise of La Follette," *Review of Reviews* 31 (1905), 299-305.

WHEELER, BURTON K. "The Need for a Third Party," *Forum* 72 (1924), 673-89.

WIEBE, ROBERT. "Business Disunity and the Progressive Movement, 1901-14," *Mississippi Valley Historical Review* 44 (1958), 664-85.

———. *Businessmen and Reform.* Cambridge: Harvard University Press, 1962.

WILBUR, HENRY. "A Coming Man," *Gunton's Magaine* 23 (1902), 250-53.

WILDER, AMOS. "Governor La Follette What He Stands For," *Outlook* 70 (1902), 631-34.

# Index

75-2085

921
L13G

Greenbaum, Fred.
Robert Marion LaFollette.

| DATE | ISSUED TO |
|---|---|
| MAY 3 '76 | 75 - 31 RETURNED |
| MAR 28 '77 | 76 - 649 RETURNED |
| FEB 28 1979 | 78 - 741 MAG RETURNED |
| MAR 2 6 1979 | 78 - 741 RETURNED |
| APR 2 3 1979 | |

75-2085

921
L13G

Greenbaum, Fred.
Robert Marion LaFollette.

**Mount Mary College**

**Library**

**Milwaukee, Wisconsin 53222**

DEMCO